Advanced Rails Recipes

Advanced Rails Recipes

Mike Clark and the Rails Community

The Pragmatic Bookshelf
Raleigh, North Carolina   Dallas, Texas

Many of the designations used by manufacturers and sellers to distinguish their products are claimed as trademarks. Where those designations appear in this book, and The Pragmatic Programmers, LLC was aware of a trademark claim, the designations have been printed in initial capital letters or in all capitals. The Pragmatic Starter Kit, The Pragmatic Programmer, Pragmatic Programming, Pragmatic Bookshelf and the linking *g* device are trademarks of The Pragmatic Programmers, LLC.

Every precaution was taken in the preparation of this book. However, the publisher assumes no responsibility for errors or omissions, or for damages that may result from the use of information (including program listings) contained herein.

Our Pragmatic courses, workshops, and other products can help you and your team create better software and have more fun. For more information, as well as the latest Pragmatic titles, please visit us at

> http://www.pragprog.com

ISBN-10: 0-9787392-2-1

ISBN-13: 978-0-9787392-2-5

Printed on acid-free paper with 50% recycled, 15% post-consumer content.

P1.0 printing, April 2008

Version: 2008-4-14

Contents

Chapter 1

Introduction

1.1 What Makes a Good Recipe Book?

If you and I were building a Rails application together and you leaned over and asked me, "Hey, how do I upload a file to S3 in the background without tying up the web request?" the last thing you want to hear is the theory of networking and messaging systems. Instead, I'd just say, "Push the filename on a message queue, write a Rake task that pops messages off the queue in a loop, and use the S3 library to upload the file." And then we'd sit together and code it up.

That's what this recipe book is all about, except you're sitting next to more than fifty "great chefs" in the Rails community. These folks know how to make (and teach *you* how to make) things to help your Rails application really shine. All these recipes are extracted directly from their work on real-world projects. It's all about skipping the trial and error and jumping straight to a good solution that works on your first try. Sometimes it's even about making things you never imagined you *could* make.

Good recipe books also teach you techniques and describe *why* certain things work and others don't. Sometimes they even teach you about new tools. But they teach these skills within the context and with the end goal of *making something*—not just to teach them.

After working through these recipes, you should walk away with a new level of Rails understanding along with an impressive list of successfully implemented new features.

1.2 What Makes This an Advanced Recipe Book?

Sushi is a treat for the eyes, as much as it's a treat for my taste buds. The sushi chefs behind the bar of my favorite local spot take great pride in making not only delicious dishes but exquisite-looking ones as well. And they seem to derive a great deal of satisfaction when their creations are enjoyed by me—a hungry programmer. Their goal isn't to have me stumble away from the table stuffed to the gills but instead to have me leave pleasantly satisfied by the entire experience.

My goal for this book is similar. I don't want to load you up with heaps of cryptic, overly clever code that sits heavy in your application. That's not what being advanced is about. It's actually the other way around: the programmers I admire strive to find elegant, practical solutions to complex problems. Indeed, making the code work is the easy part. Like the sushi chef, it's the presentation that takes a lifetime to master.

At the same time, I trust that as advanced Rails developers with experience under your belts, you'll use your intuition when applying these recipes. Some recipes have a similar goal but go about solving the problem in different ways. Rather than telling you which one is "best," I leave it to you to choose the one that works best in your situation.

When the first *Rails Recipes* [Fow06] book was written, most of the Rails knowledge was concentrated in a small group of experts. These days, with new Rails applications being launched almost weekly and so many different problems being solved, the state of the art is spread across the community.

So, to accurately capture what specific problems advanced Rails developers are tackling (and how), we asked the Rails community to contribute their own secret recipes. The result is a community recipe book that reflects what some of the best developers in the Rails community think is *advanced* and *important*.

1.3 Who's It For?

Advanced Rails Recipes is for people who understand Rails and now want to see how experienced Rails developers attack specific problems. Like with a real recipe book, you should be able to flip through the table of contents, find something you need to make, and get from idea to finished feature in short order.

When you're busy trying to *make* something, you don't have spare time to read through introductory material. I'm going to assume you know the basics and that you can look up API details in a tutorial or an online reference. So if you're still in the beginning stages of learning Rails, be sure to have a copy of *Agile Web Development with Rails* [TH05] and a bookmark to the Rails API documentation handy.[1]

1.4 Who's Talking?

This book is a collection of tasty and unique recipes from the community of Rails developers. As such, I've adopted a few conventions to keep the voice of the book consistent.

When a problem is being solved, *we're* doing it together: you, the reader, and the contributor of the recipe ("Let's build an ark, shall we?"). Then, when the contributor of the recipe needs to relay something about their experience, look for *I* and *my* ("I have a yellow rubber ducky on top of my monitor.").

1.5 What Version Do You Need?

All the recipes, except where noted, were prepared with Rails 2.0.2 and the latest versions of gems and plug-ins as of this writing. To bring you dishes with the freshest ingredients, I made no attempt to try them with older versions.

1.6 Resources

The Pragmatic Programmers have set up a forum for *Advanced Rails Recipes* readers to discuss the recipes, help each other with problems, expand on the solutions, and even write new recipes. You can find the forum by following the Discussions link from the book's home page at http://pragprog.com/titles/fr_arr.

The book's errata list is located at http://pragprog.com/titles/fr_arr/errata. If you submit any problems you find, we'll list them there.

You'll find links to the source code for almost all the book's examples at http://pragprog.com/titles/fr_arr/code.

---

1. http://api.rubyonrails.org

If you're reading the PDF version of this book, you can report an error on a page by clicking the "erratum" link at the bottom of the page, and you can get to the source code of an example by clicking the gray lozenge containing the code's filename that appears before the listing.

1.7 Acknowledgments

Although only one name appears on the cover of this book, this book wouldn't have been possible without all the contributions from talented Rails developers in the community. Working with them has truly been an honor and privilege that I don't take lightly. Thank you all for taking the time to share your tips and tricks! It has been a lot of fun working on this project with you.

Thanks to my friend Chad Fowler for setting the bar high with his original *Rails Recipes* [Fow06] book. This book tries to follow the same style and format as the original. I can only hope it's as valuable.

The Rails core team was very helpful in reviewing recipes and even contributed a few recipes of their own. Thanks, guys, for patiently answering questions and suggesting ideas.

I owe a debt of gratitude to all the fine folks who participated in the beta process. Thanks for supporting the book from the very beginning and making it better through your feedback.

Nicole makes everything possible. She encouraged me to compile and edit this book, knowing full well what that actually meant. Or so she thought....

Most important, thank *you* for reading this book. It means a great deal to me that you would take the time. I hope we get to meet someday soon.

Mike Clark
March 2008
mike@clarkware.com

1.8 Tags and Thumb Tabs

I've tried to assign tags to each recipe. If you want to find recipes that have something to do with deployment, for example, find the Deployment tab at the edge of this page. Then look down the side of the book: you'll find a thumb tab that lines up with the tab on this page for each appropriate recipe.

Ajax

Asynchronous

Automation

Capistrano

Configuration

Console

Database

Deployment

Design

E-mail

Integration

Performance

REST

Routing

Search

Security

Testing

User Interface

Part I

REST and Routes Recipes

Create a RESTful Resource

You've heard all the buzz about creating RESTful this and that. There's little doubt that Rails 2.0 heavily favors the REST architectural style[1] and that it will continue to do so.

You're feeling a little out of the loop, and what you've heard so far is a tad too academic. As a practical matter, you'd like to create a web-accessible API for one of your models and write a client program to administer that model remotely. What can resources do for *you*?

Solution

Let's forget about REST for a moment and try to solve a problem. Suppose we organize events and we want a web-based interface for creating, reading, updating, and deleting events (affectionately known as CRUD).

The first part of the solution comes in a single command, but what it does can be confusing. The *scaffold* generator churns out all the CRUD support code for administering events in a RESTful way.[2] We'll put up event scaffolding in one fell swoop:

```
$ script/generate scaffold event name:string description:text ←
    capacity:integer price:decimal starts_at:datetime
```

That single command generates a bunch of code: a model, a controller with no fewer than seven actions, view template files for actions that need them, tests, and even a migration file with the database columns we listed on the command line.

Next, we just need to create the database and apply the migration:

```
$ rake db:create
$ rake db:migrate
```

That's all there is to it! Fire up the application, and, lo and behold, we now have a full HTML interface to CRUD (the verb form) events.

---

1. http://www.ics.uci.edu/~fielding/pubs/dissertation/rest_arch_style.htm
2. There's also a *resource* generator that generates a model, migration, empty controller, but no view templates.

Before we move on to the second part of the solution, let's dive a bit deeper to see what just happened. In some ways, it's just like the old Rails scaffolding, but there's a significant twist. You may have noticed that the following line was added to our config/routes.rb file:

```
map.resources :events
```

That line is the key ingredient to our RESTful application. It dynamically creates a set of named RESTful routes for accessing our events (called *resources*) via URLs. The routes map to the seven actions in our controller: index, show, new, create, edit, update, and destroy.

The best way to see what's going on behind the scenes is to print out all the defined routes by typing this:

```
$ rake routes
```

Let's look at a few just to get a taste of how this works (you'll see more in your output). First, we have routes for dealing with the events *collection*:

```
events GET  /events     {:controller=>"events", :action=>"index"}
       POST /events     {:controller=>"events", :action=>"create"}
```

The leftmost column gives the name of the route (events), followed by the matching HTTP verb and URL path, and then the action/controller pair that the route ends up invoking. So, to list all our events—the index action—we would issue an HTTP GET request to the URI /events. Then, inside our application, we use the events_url route helper to generate the full URL for listing events. (Alternatively, you can use the events_path method to just get the path part of the URL, often referred to as the URI.)

Notice that the same incoming URL path is mapped to our create action. The only difference is the HTTP verb that's used: GET is a read-only operation that lists the events, and POST is a write operation that creates a new event.

We also have RESTful routes for dealing with a specific *member* of the events collection:

```
event GET /events/:id {:controller=>"events", :action=>"show"}
      PUT /events/:id {:controller=>"events", :action=>"update"}
```

In these cases, the name of the route is singular (event) because it's dealing with one particular event. Again, the URL path is the same for both actions. The HTTP verb is used to disambiguate whether we want to read or update a single event by its primary key (the :id route parameter). Inside our application, we use the event_url(@event) route helper, for example, to generate a URL to show our event. Passing @event to the route helper will automatically fill in the :id route parameter with the ID of the event.

So, in a nutshell, the map.resources line generates RESTful routes into our application based on both the incoming URL path *and* an HTTP verb. Now, browsers generally issue GET and POST requests, leaving the other HTTP verbs to the academics. So, how do we tell our application that we want to update an existing event (the PUT verb) or to delete an event (the DELETE verb)? Well, that involves a few more new conventions.

If we have an @event model object (and it's declared to be a resource), then in our new.html.erb and edit.html.erb forms, we can simply use this:

Rest/app/views/events/new.html.erb
```
<% form_for @event do |f| -%>
```

The form_for will generate the appropriate form tag depending on the state of the @event object. If it's a new record that hasn't yet been saved, Rails knows that it needs to be created. So, the form_for generates a form tag that looks like this:

```
<form action="/events" method="post">
```

This form will post to our create action because, according to the RESTful routing conventions, the HTTP verb and URL path map to that action.

However, if the event is an existing record that has previously been saved, then Rails knows we're trying to update it. In this case, the form should post to the update action. To do that, the form_for method slaps in a hidden field to simulate a PUT operation. This in turn triggers the proper RESTful route when Rails intercepts the request. It looks something like this in the generated form:

```
<form action="/events/1" method="post">
  <input name="_method" type="hidden" value="put" />
```

OK, so at the end of all this, we're still administering events in the browser, just with special URLs. The immediate upshot is we can turn any of our models into resources—events, registrations, users, and so on—and then administer them through a consistent URL scheme. It's just one more example of Rails conventions removing guesswork.

Now let's move on to the second part of the solution. Let's say we'd like to write a client program to administer events remotely. We'll have our client program speak XML back and forth with our Rails application (imagine what that must sound like!). To do that, let's turn our attention to the scaffold-generated index action in our EventsController. It has all the familiar stuff, plus a respond_to block:

> Rest/app/controllers/events_controller.rb

```
def index
  @events = Event.find(:all)

  respond_to do |format|
    format.html # index.html.erb
    format.xml  { render :xml => @events }
  end
end
```

The action starts by setting up a collection of events. The respond_to block determines how those events are rendered based on which format the client requests. By default, browsers prefer the HTML format. In that case, the index action renders the index.html.erb template to generate an HTML response.

However, the index action also responds to requests for events in an XML format. To get the collection of events as XML, we just need our client program to issue a GET request with .xml tacked to the end of the URL, like this:

http://localhost:3000/events.xml

Here's where things get interesting. We already have a consistent way to administer our events using the RESTful URL conventions. And we already have a way to vary how the events are represented using the respond_to block in actions.

Therefore, we already have a web-accessible API to our event resources. All we need to do is write a client program to administer our events remotely. Active Resource makes that really easy.

First, we write a stand-alone Ruby program: the Active Resource client. (I typically put these in a services directory, but they could live anywhere.) It doesn't need to load Rails per se, but we do need to require the activeresource gem:

> Rest/services/event_client.rb

```
require 'rubygems'
require 'activeresource'
```

Then we create an Event proxy class that points to the server where the event resources live:

`Rest/services/event_client.rb`

```ruby
class Event < ActiveResource::Base
  self.site = "http://localhost:3000"
end
```

Active Resource now knows how to build URLs for accessing our event resources, and it'll push XML over HTTP until the cows come home. Indeed, here's where having an application that responds to XML really shines. All the standard CRUD-level operations are available, as if our proxy class were a real Active Record model.

Next, we'll find all the events and print their names:

`Rest/services/event_client.rb`

```ruby
events = Event.find(:all)
puts events.map(&:name)
```

Then we'll find a specific event and update its attributes:

`Rest/services/event_client.rb`

```ruby
e = Event.find(1)
e.price = 20.00
e.save
```

Finally, we'll create and delete an event:

`Rest/services/event_client.rb`

```ruby
e = Event.create(:name      => "Shortest event evar!",
                 :starts_at => 1.second.ago,
                 :capacity  => 25,
                 :price     => 10.00)
e.destroy
```

Before we run the client, we'll configure a logger to see what happened behind the scenes by adding this line before the Event class definition:

`Rest/services/event_client.rb`

```ruby
ActiveResource::Base.logger = Logger.new("#{File.dirname(__FILE__)}/events.log")
```

Then, to run the client, we just use this:

```
$ ruby event_client.rb
```

Here's the output in the events.log file, which can be quite handy for debugging an ornery client:

```
GET http://localhost:3000/events.xml
--> 200 OK (<?xml version="1.0" encoding="UTF-8"?> ...
```

```
GET http://localhost:3000/events/1.xml
--> 200 OK (<?xml version="1.0" encoding="UTF-8"?> ...
PUT http://localhost:3000/events/1.xml
--> 200 OK ( b 0.11s)
POST http://localhost:3000/events.xml
--> 201 Created (<?xml version="1.0" encoding="UTF-8"?> ...
DELETE http://localhost:3000/events/12.xml
--> 200 OK ( b 0.11s)
```

Now we have a full API for creating, reading, updating, and deleting events via the browser or a remote client program. And we have conventions: a consistent set of URLs that map to a consistent set of actions. This generally makes deciding where things go a lot easier. In particular, we no longer have controllers that are dumping grounds for spurious actions.

Discussion

It is important to note here that REST (map.resources in particular) and respond_to blocks are orthogonal. You can use respond_to without resources, and vice versa.

Although Active Resource ships with Rails and uses some of its support classes, it's not necessarily Rails-specific. You can use it to reach out to any server supporting the RESTful conventions of Rails.

Also See

The map.resources method generates routes only for the seven CRUD actions. This begs the question, how do I call actions outside of this set? Recipe 2, *Add Your Own RESTful Actions*, on the facing page shows how to customize the routes for application-specific concerns.

Add Your Own RESTful Actions

The RESTful conventions baked into Rails are working well for some things, but you just can't get your head wrapped around the special cases. The devil is in the details, as they say. When the seven CRUD actions of a resource seem to fall short, how—and more important, *where*—do you deal with the special cases?

Let's walk through a few examples where REST commonly trips us up, and then we'll step back to see whether we can tease out some guidelines. Before we do that, though, I'll give you the bad news: there are no hard and fast rules we can apply in this recipe. This is largely a matter of software design, and design is all about trade-offs. The real world is a wonderfully messy place, and modeling it with straight-line boxes and arrows is anything but exact. REST, on the other hand, is an idyllic world. Our job is to find the common ground for the good of our application and its users.

First, imagine we have a collection of event resources that we'd like to display in a sorted order. Now, we *could* define a new sort action, for example, and punch a hole in the RESTful routes for it. But the only difference between that action and our existing index action is that the events would need to be fetched in the proper order in the sort action.

Adding a new action in this case is overkill. All we need to do to display events in sorted order is update our index action to handle sorting via a parameter and use a default sort order if one isn't provided:

`Rest/app/controllers/events_controller.rb`

```ruby
def index
  sort_by = (params[:order] == 'starts_at' ? 'starts_at desc' : 'name')
  @events = Event.find(:all, :order => sort_by)

  respond_to do |format|
    format.html # index.html.erb
    format.xml  { render :xml => @events }
  end
end
```

Then, to sort events, we send in this URL, for example:

http://localhost:3000/events?order=starts_at

That URL is a resource in its own right: it uniquely identifies a collection of events.

Next, we'd like to search for events given a search term, such as the event name. Similar to sorting, we could send a q parameter to the index method. However, our search implementation has slightly different concerns than the index action. For example, we might want to render search results with rankings, a reminder of the search term we used, and a "Did you really mean..." tip.

In this case, search doesn't fit as neatly into the index box. Instead, we'll go ahead and create a new search action in our EventsController:[1]

```
Rest/app/controllers/events_controller.rb
def search
  @events = Event.search(params[:q])

  respond_to do |format|
    format.html # search.html.erb
    format.xml  { render :xml => @events }
  end
end
```

The routes generated by map.resources :events don't know about this new action. So, we also need to add an extension to the map.resources call in config/routes.rb, like so:

```
map.resources :events, :collection => { :search => :get }
```

This gives us a route to the search action, accessible via a GET request. It applies to all the events—the collection of event resources. To get there, we can use the following URL, for example:

http://localhost:3000/events/search?q=rubyconf

Again, this is a totally RESTful URL. You can think of search as a sub-resource of the events resource.

---

1. See Recipe 24, *Find Stuff (Quick and Dirty)*, on page 133 for an example Event.search implementation.

Next, we'll add a search form and use the search_events_path route
helper to generate a URL routing back to our new search action:

Rest/app/views/events/index.html.erb

```erb
<% form_tag search_events_path, :method => :get do -%>
  <%= text_field_tag :q, params[:q] %>
  <%= submit_tag 'Search Events' %>
<% end -%>
```

Notice that we've used the :method option here to force the form to post
to the search action using a GET request. That way, the search results
can be easily bookmarked.

Next, we'd like to be able to copy an existing event to make event admin-
istration a little easier. This changes our perspective slightly. Up until
now we've been dealing with the entire collection of events. Now we
want to deal with specific members of the events collection. Copying an
event doesn't fit neatly into any of the other standard CRUD actions, so
we'll just create another new action and a RESTful route extension.

We'll start with the copy action, which requires an id parameter for the
event we want to copy:

Rest/app/controllers/events_controller.rb

```ruby
def copy
  event = Event.find(params[:id])
  @event = Event.copy(event)

  # render
end
```

Then, back in the config/routes.rb file, we'll add a :member extension for
posting to the copy action. Here's the final map.resources call:

```ruby
map.resources :events,
  :collection => { :search => :get },
  :member     => { :copy   => :post }
```

Next, we'll create a Copy button using the copy_event_path route helper
and hand it the event we want to copy:

```erb
<%= button_to "Copy", copy_event_path(@event) %>
```

The button_to helper generates a form that posts back to our copy action
and includes the ID of the event we're copying. Here's what the form tag
looks like:

```html
<form method="post" action="/events/7/copy" ...>
```

Finally, we'd like people to be able to register for events. Having come this far, our first instinct may be to add a register action to the Events-Controller. Not so fast!

What this really tells us is we're missing a key resource: registrations. Rather than polluting the EventsController, we're wise to create a new registrations resource. In this case, the best way to do that is with a nested resource. We tackle nested resources in Recipe 3, *Nest Resources to Scope Access*, on the facing page.

What have we learned? In the first example, we reused an existing action because sorting had similar concerns. In the second example, we extended the :collection routes and added a new action for searching, because it had unique concerns. And in the third example we extended the :member routes and added a new action for copying, because none of the existing actions was a good fit. Finally, looking at our application through the REST lens unveiled a missing resource. So if there is a lesson here, it's that resources serve as expert guides, if only we listen to them.

Discussion

Should searching always be a new action? Well, it depends. If the search templates and everything else are similar enough to index, then it's perfectly acceptable (in the eyes of REST) to implement searching as a variant of the index action. If searching is fundamentally different, then it may well deserve its own action.

Remember that Rails action and page caching is strictly URL based and doesn't take into account the URL parameters. Therefore, if caching is important, you may not want to overload existing URLs.

Nest Resources to Scope Access

By Adam Wiggins (http://adam.blog.heroku.com/)
Adam is an entrepreneur, open source enthusiast, and programmer in San Francisco, California. His current venture is Heroku, a turnkey Rails development environment and hosting solution.

Problem

You have RESTful resources that must be accessed in a hierarchical fashion to ensure proper scoping: registrations can be made only in the context of an event, tasks are always accessed through their project, and so on. How do you nest resources in this way?

Solution

Let's imagine we're building an event registration application and we've already created event and registration resources using scaffolding. We've also arranged events and registrations in a classic has_many relationship: each registration is associated with a particular event, and an event has many registrations.

Now we want to set up routing to make sure that registrations are always accessed in the context of their event. In other words, we want a URL that has a registration *nested* inside its event, like this:

/events/7/registrations/3

First we'll revise the config/routes.rb file to create the RESTful routes for nesting the registration resources inside their event resource. The has_many syntax takes care of that:

`NestedResource/config/routes.rb`

```
map.resources :events, :has_many => :registrations
```

This line of code adds a slew of named RESTful routes for managing events and registrations. The best way to see (and remember) what happened is to run the rake routes command to print out all the defined routes.

In particular, here are a few nested routes we'll be using (you'll see more in your output):

```
event_registrations      GET   /events/:event_id/registrations
                               {:controller=>"registrations", :action=>"index"}
                         POST  /events/:event_id/registrations
                               {:controller=>"registrations", :action=>"create"}
new_event_registration   GET   /events/:event_id/registrations/new
                               {:controller=>"registrations", :action=>"new"}
edit_event_registration  GET   /events/:event_id/registrations/:id/edit
                               {:controller=>"registrations", :action=>"edit"}
event_registration       GET   /events/:event_id/registrations/:id
                               {:controller=>"registrations", :action=>"show"}
```

The nested route syntax takes a little getting used to. Notice that the naming scheme for nested routes always includes the parent resource (event, singular), then the child resource (registration, either singular or plural). So, without nesting you might have simply used registrations_path; with nesting you now use event_registrations_path. Likewise, new_registration_path becomes new_event_registration_path, and so on.

These nested routes also impose some important constraints. Notice that in every case, we must provide the event resource (the :event_id route parameter) in which the registration is nested.

To see how all this plays out in our application, let's start using some of our new nested routes. When we're viewing a particular event, we want a link to show all its registrations. To do that, we will use the event_registrations_path route helper:

NestedResource/app/views/events/show.html.erb

```
<p>
  <%= link_to 'Registrations',
              event_registrations_path(@event) %>
</p>
```

We've satisfied the nesting constraint by providing an event resource to fill in the :event_id routing parameter.[1]

According to the RESTful routing conventions, clicking this link invokes the index action of the RegistrationsController.

Now, we want to list the registrations only for a particular event. So over in our RegistrationsController, we'll use a before_filter to make sure we load up the event in which the registrations are nested.

---

1. You can also use event_registrations_path(:event_id => @event) if you prefer.

Then, in the index action, we'll use the @event variable as the context for finding registrations.

NestedResource/app/controllers/registrations_controller.rb

```ruby
class RegistrationsController < ApplicationController

  before_filter :find_event

  def index
    @registrations = @event.registrations.find(:all)

    respond_to do |format|
      format.html # index.html.erb
      format.xml  { render :xml => @registrations }
    end
  end

  # other CRUD actions

private

  def find_event
    @event = Event.find(params[:event_id])
  end
end
```

The Active Record find operation is scoped to fetch only those registrations that are associated with the @event object. That's the event we used in the link created by the event_registrations_path route helper.

Next, we'll change the index.html.erb template to list all the registrations and use a few more route helpers for the standard admin links:

NestedResource/app/views/registrations/index.html.erb

```erb
<% for registration in @registrations -%>
  <!-- render registration attributes -->
  <%= link_to 'Show',
      event_registration_path(@event, registration) %> |

  <%= link_to 'Edit',
      edit_event_registration_path(@event, registration) %> |

  <%= link_to 'Destroy',
      event_registration_path(@event, registration),
      :confirm => 'Are you sure?',
      :method => :delete %>
<% end -%>
```

Again, in every case we must provide the event to fill in the :event_id route parameter. In these particular links, we also must provide the registration to fill in the :id route parameter because we're dealing with a registration that has already been saved.

Then we need to make sure the show, edit, and destroy actions in the RegistrationsController are properly scoped, as well. The find_event before filter applies to them, so we already have an @event variable handy. Here's what those actions look like:

NestedResource/app/controllers/registrations_controller.rb

```ruby
def show
  @registration = @event.registrations.find(params[:id])

  respond_to do |format|
    format.html # show.html.erb
    format.xml  { render :xml => @registration }
  end
end

def edit
  @registration = @event.registrations.find(params[:id])
end

def destroy
  @registration = @event.registrations.find(params[:id])
  @registration.destroy

  respond_to do |format|
    format.html { redirect_to(event_registrations_url(@event)) }
    format.xml  { head :ok }
  end
end
```

That leaves us with one final step: letting users register for an event. We'll start by adding a Register link to an event's show template:

NestedResource/app/views/events/show.html.erb

```erb
<%= link_to 'Register', new_event_registration_path(@event) %>
```

Clicking this link invokes the new action in our RegistrationsController, which isn't all that interesting:

NestedResource/app/controllers/registrations_controller.rb

```ruby
def new
  @registration = @event.registrations.new

  respond_to do |format|
    format.html # new.html.erb
    format.xml  { render :xml => @registration }
  end
end
```

However, things do get interesting when we create the form that the new action renders. We need to hand it both the event resource *and* the registration resource, like so:

NestedResource/app/views/registrations/new.html.erb

```erb
<% form_for([@event, @registration]) do |f| -%>
  <p>
    <b>Name</b><br />
    <%= f.text_field :name %>
  </p>
  <p>
    <b>Email</b><br />
    <%= f.text_field :email %>
  </p>
  <p>
    <%= f.submit "Create" %>
  </p>
<% end -%>
```

Given these two resources, the form_for generates the following form tag:

```erb
<form action="/events/1/registrations" method="post" ...>
```

Looking back at the RESTful routes that we created, you'll notice there's a route for that URL path with an HTTP POST method. It posts to the create action in our RegistrationsController. In that action, we need to scope the Active Record new method to make sure the registration is associated with its event before the registration is saved:

NestedResource/app/controllers/registrations_controller.rb

```ruby
def create
  @registration = @event.registrations.new(params[:registration])

  respond_to do |format|
    if @registration.save
      flash[:notice] = 'Registration was successfully created.'
      format.html { redirect_to([@event, @registration]) }
      format.xml  { render :xml => @registration,
                           :status => :created,
                           :location => [ @event, @registration ] }
    else
      format.html { render :action => "new" }
      format.xml  { render :xml => @registration.errors,
                           :status => :unprocessable_entity }
    end
  end
end
```

Notice that the redirect_to also takes both resources. For example, if the registration saves successfully, we redirect to events/1/registrations/2.

The form_for in the edit.html.erb template is no different from the one in the new.html.erb template. However, because the registration has already been saved, the URL path in the generated form tag will include the registration ID:

```
<form action="/events/1/registrations/1" method="post" ...>
```

Finally, we need to make sure our update action is properly scoped:

NestedResource/app/controllers/registrations_controller.rb

```
def update
  @registration = @event.registrations.find(params[:id])

  respond_to do |format|
    if @registration.update_attributes(params[:registration])
      flash[:notice] = 'Registration was successfully updated.'
      format.html { redirect_to([@event, @registration]) }
      format.xml  { head :ok }
    else
      format.html { render :action => "edit" }
      format.xml  { render :xml => @registration.errors,
                           :status => :unprocessable_entity }
    end
  end
end
```

Nested routes can be confusing the first couple times you use them. I find it really helpful to start with standard RESTful routes and then incrementally change (and test!) them to use nested routes.

Discussion

Keep in mind that nested routes are best used to enforce situations where one resource is always accessed in the context of another. It's a design decision, and not all resources or has_many relationships benefit from nesting.

Toggle Attributes with Ajax

By David Heinemeier Hansson (http://loudthinking.com)
Thanks to David for the idea for this recipe.

Problem

You want to allow users to toggle certain model attributes on a form with Ajax. How do you handle it in a RESTful way?

Solution

Our dear readers often find mistakes or have suggestions. We live for that kind of online feedback (OK, we grimace in pain when it's a mistake). Being agile authors, let's imagine we have the following interface for submitting book errata:

Errata

Page	Created by	Description		
<u>9</u>	Chad	The first paragraph is complete ...	**Fixed?**	☑
<u>105</u>	Dave	I suggest you show Ajax toggling...	**Fixed?**	☑
<u>218</u>	Nicole	"He am also.."?! Try again.	**Fixed?**	☐

<u>Create a New Erratum</u>

If an author is logged in, he sees a checkbox for marking each erratum as being fixed. (It's good fun and a great relief from writer's block.) When he checks off an erratum, we want to update the Errata resource's fixed attribute. Rather than creating a new controller action just for this case, instead we can piggyback on the standard update action in our ErrataController.

First, we need to modify the checkbox part of each row in the list of errata to call a toggle_value helper via an onclick handler. We'll also include a spinner image, which is initially hidden.

AjaxRestToggle/app/views/errata/index.html.erb

```
<%= check_box_tag 'erratum[fixed]', "1", erratum.fixed,
                  :onclick => toggle_value(erratum) %>
<%= image_tag 'spinner.gif', :id => "spinner-#{erratum.id}",
                  :style => 'display: none' %>
```

Next, we need to write the toggle_value helper. When the checkbox is clicked, it calls the helper, passing in the Erratum resource. In this example, the resource is an Erratum object, but the helper is generic— it will take any resource and use the checkbox name in the enclosing template.

AjaxRestToggle/app/helpers/application_helper.rb

```
def toggle_value(object)
  remote_function(:url      => url_for(object),
                  :method   => :put,
                  :before   => "Element.show('spinner-#{object.id}')",
                  :complete => "Element.hide('spinner-#{object.id}')",
                  :with     => "this.name + '=' + this.checked")
end
```

This code uses remote_function to fire off an asynchronous request to the update action of our ErrataController. While that's happening, we light up the spinner image to let our tireless authors know that something is going on in the background.

The URL that the url_for method creates is purely RESTful. Here's an example HTTP verb and URL path used to toggle the fixed attribute:

```
PUT /errata/4?erratum[fixed]=1
```

The map.resources :errata line in our routes file recognizes this HTTP verb and URL path without any changes. Indeed, the advantage of using this technique is that updating a single attribute just piggybacks onto the update action.

Our final step to support the single-attribute update is to add a new format.js stanza to the respond_to block in the update action. Here's the full version:

AjaxRestToggle/app/controllers/errata_controller.rb

```
def update
  @erratum = Erratum.find(params[:id])

  respond_to do |format|
    if @erratum.update_attributes(params[:erratum])
      flash[:notice] = 'Erratum was successfully updated.'
      format.html { redirect_to(@erratum) }
      format.xml  { head :ok }
      format.js   { head :ok }
```

```
    else
      format.html { render :action => "edit" }
      format.xml  { render :xml     => @erratum.errors,
                           :status => :unprocessable_entity }
      format.js   { head :unprocessable_entity }
    end
  end
end
```

With a JavaScript request, all the browser needs to know is that the request was successful so it can turn off the spinning image. If the update succeeds, we use head :ok to return an HTTP 200 response. If the update fails, we use head :unprocessable_entity to return an HTTP 422 response.

This works well when you're toggling attributes with Ajax, because you don't care about the response. The fixed attribute in this case isn't bound by any validation rules, so updating it isn't likely to fail. If the update is dependent on validation, then your best bet is to use a full form and a synchronous request.

Authenticate REST Clients

You're developing a RESTful application such as an event management system with user accounts. Naturally, you need to protect access to resources of the site with a login and password. You've done this before, you know, back in the old days. But this is a new day. How do you authenticate users in a RESTful way via the browser and an Active Resource client?

Let's assume we already have a User model. To check whether a user exists for a given login and password, we can call this:

```
User.authenticate(login, password)
```

Given that, we need a form to accept the login and password. We'll also need a couple controller actions to pop the form and authenticate the user. Now, we could slap those actions into any controller, but REST is always asking the question, what's the resource?

The thing we're really trying to manage when dealing with web-based authentication is an HTTP session. It's the resource that knows whether a user is currently logged in.

So, let us start by adding the RESTful routes for a session to our config/routes.rb file:

```
map.resource :session
```

Notice that we're using map.resource (singular) here, not plural as is usually the case. For a given user, we need only one session. The singular form generates routes and helpers using the singular name (session), as we'll see in minute.

Next, we'll create a SessionsController for the session. (Resource controllers are always plural.) The new action pops the empty login form, and the create action stashes the user's ID in the session if the user logs in successfully.

Rest/app/controllers/sessions_controller.rb

```ruby
def new
end

def create
  user = User.authenticate(params[:login], params[:password])
  if user
    session[:user_id] = user.id
    flash[:notice] = "Welcome back, #{user.login}!"
    redirect_to events_url
  else
    flash[:error] = "Invalid email/password combination!"
    render :action => :new
  end
end
```

Then we'll add a destroy action to delete the user's session when she logs out:

Rest/app/controllers/sessions_controller.rb

```ruby
def destroy
  reset_session
  flash[:notice] = "You've been logged out."
  redirect_to new_session_url
end
```

This is all pretty standard authentication stuff, with the exception of being able to call the new_session_url route helper to generate the URL back to the new action.

Next, we'll create the login form for the new action:

Rest/app/views/sessions/new.html.erb

```erb
<% form_tag session_path do -%>
<fieldset>
  <p>
    <label for="login" class="required">Login</label>
    <%= text_field_tag :login, params[:login] %>
  </p>
  <p>
    <label for="password" class="required">Password</label>
    <%= password_field_tag :password, params[:password] %>
  </p>
  <p>
    <%= submit_tag 'Log in' %>
  </p>
</fieldset>
<% end -%>
```

This is a standard form, but notice that it uses the session_path helper in the form_tag. In this case, the form will issue an HTTP POST to /session. According to the RESTful routing conventions, that HTTP verb and URL path pair will map to the create action of our SessionsController.[1]

We'll also need some links to let folks log in and out. We'll add those to the header in our layout file:

`Rest/app/views/layouts/application.html.erb`

```
<% if logged_in? -%>
  <%= link_to 'Logout', session_path, :method => :delete %>
<% else -%>
  <%= link_to 'Login', new_session_path %>
<% end -%>
```

At this point we have the session resource all ready to go and a way for users to log in and out. But we make the rules around here, and we say you have to be logged in to use the site. Easy enough. We'll just add a before_filter in the ApplicationController:

`Rest/app/controllers/application.rb`

```
before_filter :login_required
```

However, we don't want to force a login when indeed the user is trying to log in (makes for angry users), so we'll skip the before filter in the SessionsController:

`Rest/app/controllers/sessions_controller.rb`

```
skip_before_filter :login_required
```

Then we need to write the login_required method called by the before_filter:

`Rest/app/controllers/application.rb`

```
def login_required
  unless session[:user_id]
    flash[:notice] = "Please log in"
    redirect_to new_session_url
  end
end
```

If there's a user ID in the session, we know the user is logged in. If she isn't logged in, we redirect her to the login form.

OK, now we can log in via a browser in a RESTful way. So far, so good. But that's just one side of the coin. Remember that our resources can also represent themselves as XML, for example. (That's what the respond_to blocks in our controllers are all about.) And let's say we have

---

1. Run rake routes for a peek at the RESTful routes.

an Active Resource client that uses XML to chat with the resources exposed by our application. In this case, there is no browser. So, how do we authenticate this client program? The Web already has the answer: HTTP basic authentication.

First, in our Active Resource client, we include the login and password as part of the URL pointing to where the resource lives:

```
class Event < ActiveResource::Base
  self.site = "http://mike:secret@localhost:3000"
end
```

This slips the encoded login and password into the HTTP headers sent by the client to our Rails application. Note that because we're using the HTTP protocol, the encoded login and password will be sent in plain text. This isn't a big deal when we're talking to a local app in development mode. However, it's a *huge deal* if we're talking to our production app. The login and password will travel across the 'net in plain-text form, and any hacker worth his salt can decode this over lunch. So, don't forget to use the HTTPS protocol in production!

While we're talking about security, let's go ahead and use the HighLine[2] library to prompt for a login and password, rather than hard-coding them in our client. Here's the full version of the Active Resource client:

```
Rest/services/event_client_with_auth.rb
```
```
require 'rubygems'
require 'activeresource'
require 'highline/import'

def prompt(prompt, mask=true)
  ask(prompt) { |q| q.echo = mask}
end

def login
  prompt('Login: ')
end

def password
  prompt('Password: ', '*')
end

class Event < ActiveResource::Base
  self.site = "https://#{login}:#{password}@localhost:3000"
end

events = Event.find(:all)
puts events.map(&:name)
```

---

2. http://rubyforge.org/projects/highline/

Neat and tidy. We almost have all the ingredients mixed, I promise. We just need to fix up our Rails app to handle HTTP basic authentication. Remember, our login_required filter just checks for a user ID in the session. That won't work for our Active Resource client because it's sending credentials in HTTP headers (and the client doesn't have cookies to store session data in).

As the final step, we'll spiff up the login_required method to handle both types of clients:

```
Rest/app/controllers/application.rb
def login_required
  respond_to do |format|
    format.html do
      if session[:user_id]
        @current_user = User.find(session[:user_id])
      else
        flash[:notice] = "Please log in"
        redirect_to new_session_url
      end
    end
    format.xml do
      user = authenticate_with_http_basic do |login, password|
        User.authenticate(login, password)
      end
      if user
        @current_user = user
      else
        request_http_basic_authentication
      end
    end
  end
end
```

There's our old friend respond_to again. If the client wants HTML (it's the browser knocking), then we check the session.

If, on the other hand, the client wants XML (Hello, Active Resource client!), then we call the built-in authenticate_with_http_basic method. It decodes the HTTP headers for us and passes the login and password as block parameters. Then we just try to authenticate the user. If we find a matching user, we're good to go. Otherwise, we send a request back to the client to retry using the request_http_basic_authentication method.

Whew! That involved quite a few steps, but we worked through it incrementally. In the end, it's probably similar to the authentication you may already be doing in your app. The key to supporting RESTful clients is the concise login_required method with a respond_to block, which is fairly straightforward and reusable across applications.

Although several authentication libraries are available as plug-ins and generators, simple authentication is so easy to roll by hand that it's often not worth carrying around the extra baggage of a third-party plug-in. Most important, by writing your own, you will *understand* how it works. That way, when it comes time to debug what's going on, you'll be in good shape to get it done quickly.

Having said that, if you want an example of a slightly more complex authentication approach, check out Rick Olson's restful_authentication plug-in.[3] In addition to creating a RESTful session environment, it can also generate everything you need to get started with users, including an account activation step.

---

3.   http://svn.techno-weenie.net/projects/plugins/restful_authentication/

Respond to Custom Formats

By Patrick Reagan (http://www.viget.com)
Patrick is a recovering PHP user who finally realized the immense power that Rails brings to the web development space. As the development director for Viget Labs, he's been helping lead the charge in adopting Rails as the framework of choice when building applications for their start-up clients.

Problem

Rails knows about a number of predefined formats for responding to requests: HTML, JavaScript, XML, RSS, and so on. But how do you create your own formats?

Solution

Say we want to build an app to download or stream MP3 files we find online. Let's start by making it a RESTful application using scaffolding:

```
$ script/generate scaffold mp3 title:string url:string length:string
$ rake db:create
$ rake db:migrate
```

Now that we can manage MP3 resources, let's create a few MP3 files via the console:

```
$ ruby script/console
>> Mp3.create(:title => 'RoR Podcast: Chad Fowler',
   :url => 'http://paranode.com/~topfunky/audio/2005/Chad-Fowler.mp3',
   :length => "2747625")
=> #<Mp3 id: 1, ...>
>> Mp3.create(:title => 'RoR Podcast: Dave Thomas and Mike Clark',
   :url =>
'http://paranode.com/~topfunky/audio/2006/rails-032-thomas-and-clark.mp3',
   :length => "26664043")
=> #<Mp3 id: 2, ...>
```

Now let's turn our attention to the Mp3sController. Currently the show action knows only how to render our MP3 information as HTML or XML:

```
def show
  @mp3 = Mp3.find(params[:id])

  respond_to do |format|
    format.html # show.html.erb
    format.xml  { render :xml => @mp3 }
  end
end
```

In addition, we want to serve up playable audio when the show action is invoked. To do that, we'll register our MIME types in the mime_types.rb initializer file that's included by default in all new Rails applications:

RespondToFormats/config/initializers/mime_types.rb

```
Mime::Type.register 'audio/mpeg',    :mp3
Mime::Type.register 'audio/mpegurl', :m3u
```

When the browser requests the .mp3 or .m3u formats, our application will set the Content-Type header to the corresponding MIME type when it sends the response. We'll rely on the browser to handle the MIME type in the response properly.

Next, back in our Mp3sController, we'll add our formats to the show action's respond_to block:

RespondToFormats/app/controllers/mp3s_controller.rb

```
def show
  @mp3 = Mp3.find(params[:id])

  respond_to do |format|
    format.html # show.html.erb
    format.xml { render :xml => @mp3 }
    format.mp3 { redirect_to @mp3.url }
    format.m3u { render :text => @mp3.url }
  end
end
```

When a user requests the .mp3 format for download, we redirect to the MP3 file's URL. If the user requests the .m3u format to stream the MP3, we respond with a text file that includes a pointer to an actual MP3 resource. Most modern audio applications respect the M3U format and will "stream" the referenced resource by both downloading and playing the MP3 simultaneously.[1]

Let's give this a shot. To request an MP3 in the new format, we just tack on .mp3 to the end of the URL, like so:

http://localhost:3000/mp3s/1.mp3

And to stream the first MP3 into our audio player, we use this:

http://localhost:3000/mp3s/1.m3u

---

1. For me, this starts up iTunes and begins streaming the file. For Windows users, this action will typically open Windows Media Player, Winamp, or another configured application.

Next, we'll add the appropriate links to our views using named routes:

RespondToFormats/app/views/mp3s/show.html.erb

```
<p>
  <%= h @mp3.title %>
  (<%= link_to 'Download', formatted_mp3_url(@mp3, :mp3) %> |
   <%= link_to 'Stream',   formatted_mp3_url(@mp3, :m3u) %>)
</p>
```

The formatted_mp3_url route helper takes the MP3 resource and the name of the format. These are the names we used in the mime_types.rb file when we registered our MIME types. The route helpers take care of setting the appropriate format, which gets picked up by our respond_to block in the show action.

This is a good start, but let's take it a step further. Right now we're streaming files one by one. That's not always convenient. So, let's also allow a user to queue multiple MP3 streams using the playlist (PLS) file format.[2]

First, we'll register the new MIME type:

RespondToFormats/config/initializers/mime_types.rb

```
Mime::Type.register 'audio/x-scpls', :pls
```

Because an audio playlist is essentially a listing of audio files, we'll serve up the playlist through the index action:

RespondToFormats/app/controllers/mp3s_controller.rb

```
def index
  @mp3s = Mp3.find(:all)

  respond_to do |format|
    format.html # index.html.erb
    format.xml  { render :xml => @mp3s }
    format.pls  { render :layout => false } # index.pls.erb
  end
end
```

All we need to do now is add the corresponding template to render the playlist in the proper PLS format (and it's picky).

---

2. http://en.wikipedia.org/wiki/PLS_(file_format)

The template goes in the index.pls.erb file:

```
RespondToFormats/app/views/mp3s/index.pls.erb
[playlist]
NumberOfEntries=<%= @mp3s.length %>

<% @mp3s.each_with_index do |mp3, index| -%>
File<%= index + 1 %>=<%= h mp3.url %>
Title<%= index + 1 %>=<%= h mp3.title %>
Length<%= index + 1 %>=<%= h mp3.length %>

<% end -%>
Version=2
```

The naming here is important. The format we're sending back is PLS, and we're using the ERb templating system to render the format. So, the template file is called index.pls.erb. It's rendered only if the PLS format is requested.

Now a user can queue up both files we've added to our application in a playlist. Restart the server, and use this URL to access our playlist:

http://localhost:3000/mp3s.pls

Adding custom formats like this lets you easily reuse controller actions (and in turn business logic) to render results in a variety of ways. It also cleans up URLs and provides user-friendly pathways into your application.

Discussion

These custom formats aren't limited to audio—you can add your own formats to serve up calendar files, an iPhone version of your application (see Recipe 21, *Support an iPhone Interface*, on page 115), or anything that has a Content-Type recognized by a client application.

Catch All 404s

Problem

You want a permanent record of all URLs that trigger 404s in your application, perhaps to plug holes in your routing scheme or identify legacy URLs you forgot to handle. (Hey, it happens.)

Solution

Let's jump right in and follow a stray request through our application, writing code as we go. It all starts with an incoming URL that doesn't map to any action in our application:

http://railsrecipes.com/please/catch/me

Ah, poor thing. Thankfully, catching it is as easy as adding the following route to the bottom of our config/routes.rb file:

`CatchAll404s/config/routes.rb`

```
map.connect '*path', :controller => 'four_oh_fours'
```

Two things make this a catchall route: it's the last route in the config/routes.rb file, and it uses an asterisk to sponge up the incoming URL path parts. For the previous example URL, the path parameter would end up containing the array:

```
["please", "catch", "me"]
```

Next, we'll just create a FourOhFoursController to handle all the errant requests:

`CatchAll404s/app/controllers/four_oh_fours_controller.rb`

```ruby
class FourOhFoursController < ApplicationController

  def index
    FourOhFour.add_request(request.host,
                           request.path,
                           request.env['HTTP_REFERER'] || '')

    respond_to do |format|
      format.html { render :file => "#{RAILS_ROOT}/public/404.html",
                           :status => "404 Not Found" }
      format.all  { render :nothing => true,
                           :status => "404 Not Found" }
    end
  end
end
```

There's not much to this controller. We just strip out a few interesting bits of the incoming request: the hostname (railsrecipes.com), the path (/please/catch/me), and the URL of the page that triggered this request if it exists. Then, before rendering an appropriate 404 response to the client, the FourOhFour model squirrels the request information away in the database:

CatchAll404s/app/models/four_oh_four.rb

```
class FourOhFour < ActiveRecord::Base

  def self.add_request(host, path, referer)
    request = find_or_initialize_by_host_and_path_and_referer(host,
                                                              path,
                                                              referer)
    request.count += 1
    request.save
  end
end
```

Using find_and_initialize_by lets us fetch the FourOhFour record if it already exists or initialize a new object (but not save it) if this is a unique 404. Incrementing the count gives us some indication of the 404 URL's popularity.

That just leaves us with creating the migration file, with some indexes:

CatchAll404s/db/migrate/001_create_four_oh_fours.rb

```
class CreateFourOhFours < ActiveRecord::Migration

  def self.up
    create_table :four_oh_fours do |t|
      t.string  :host, :path, :referer
      t.integer :count, :default => 0

      t.timestamps
    end
    add_index :four_oh_fours, [:host, :path, :referer], :unique => true
    add_index :four_oh_fours, [:path]
  end

  def self.down
    drop_table :four_oh_fours
  end
end
```

Now when requests fall through to the bottom of our routes.rb file, we'll end up with a permanent record. List all the FourOhFour records somewhere on the admin side of your app, and you have yourself a convenient 404 report.

You could also use the catchall route to actually handle requests that don't map to a specific action. Say, for example, you have a database table that stores "pages": a URL path and the content to display when that URL is accessed. You might even be calling this a *content management system* (CMS).

By modifying the controller slightly, you can attempt to find a CMS page using the catchall route's URL path before bailing out with a 404:

```ruby
def index
  @page = CmsPage.find_by_path(params[:path])
  if @page
    render :inline => @page.body
  else
    # treat it as a 404
  end
end
```

Part II

Database Recipes

Add Foreign Key Constraints

Problem

You want to add foreign key constraints to your database to, you know, ensure referential integrity. That way you cannot accidentally delete records that are referred to by other records, be it through your Rails application or another application that shares your database.

Solution

Let's say we have a classic order, line item, and product model arrangement. A line item points to both a product and an order:

FKConstraints/app/models/line_item.rb

```ruby
class LineItem < ActiveRecord::Base
  belongs_to :order
  belongs_to :product
end
```

FKConstraints/app/models/order.rb

```ruby
class Order < ActiveRecord::Base
  has_many :line_items
end
```

FKConstraints/app/models/product.rb

```ruby
class Product < ActiveRecord::Base
  has_many :line_items
end
```

Nothing new to see here. However, the migration for the line_items table is interesting:

FKConstraints/db/migrate/003_create_line_items.rb

```ruby
class CreateLineItems < ActiveRecord::Migration
  def self.up
    create_table :line_items do |t|
      t.integer :product_id, :null => false
      t.integer :order_id,   :null => false
    end
  end
  def self.down
    drop_table :line_items
  end
```

In particular, the foreign keys can't be null. To create a line item, we must have both an order and a product:

```
item = LineItem.create(:order => an_order, :product => a_tshirt)
```

In other words, it makes no sense in our application to have a line item that doesn't reference both an order and a product. However, we can turn around and delete the a_tshirt record from the database, leaving the line item holding a nil product. That's no good—let's fix it!

Databases are smart about keeping invariants like this in check. Unfortunately, Rails migrations don't support adding foreign key constraints out of the box, but we can make it look as though they do.

Let's start by writing a MigrationHelpers module with a couple convenience methods:

FKConstraints/lib/migration_helpers.rb

```ruby
module MigrationHelpers

  def fk(from_table, from_column, to_table)
    execute %(alter table #{from_table}
              add constraint #{constraint_name(from_table, from_column)}
              foreign key (#{from_column})
              references #{to_table}(id))
  end

  def drop_fk(from_table, from_column)
    execute %(alter table #{from_table}
              drop foreign key #{constraint_name(from_table, from_column)})
  end

  def constraint_name(table, column)
    "fk_#{table}_#{column}"
  end

end
```

This looks heavy because we're using raw SQL, but don't let it throw you. The trick is using the execute method that is available in all migration classes to run arbitrary SQL and stashing these details in one tidy module.

The fk method simply uses the execute method to add a foreign key constraint, and the drop_fk method does the opposite.

Next, we'll revise our migration for the line_items table to use the new fk and drop_fk methods.

FKConstraints/db/migrate/003_create_line_items.rb

```ruby
class CreateLineItems < ActiveRecord::Migration

  extend MigrationHelpers

  def self.up
    create_table :line_items do |t|
      t.integer :product_id, :null => false
      t.integer :order_id,   :null => false
    end
    fk :line_items, :product_id, :products
    fk :line_items, :order_id,   :orders
  end

  def self.down
    drop_fk :line_items, :order_id
    drop_fk :line_items, :product_id
    drop_table :line_items
  end
end
```

We've used extend to add the methods in the MigrationHelpers module to our migration class. When the migration is applied, we call fk to add foreign key constraints. And when the migration is rolled back, we call drop_fk to do the opposite.

Now if we try to delete a product that a line item is pointing to, we get an exception:

```
ActiveRecord::StatementInvalid: Mysql::Error: Cannot delete or update
a parent row: a foreign key constraint fails
(`buffet_development/line_items`, CONSTRAINT `fk_line_items_product_id`
FOREIGN KEY (`product_id`) REFERENCES `products` (`id`)):
DELETE FROM `products` WHERE `id` = 1
```

That's exactly what we want to happen. When a foreign key constraint fails, we've broken a fundamental truth (an invariant) in our business logic.

When that happens, we need to take explicit action to deal with it.

Discussion

As of Rails 2.0, referential integrity checking is disabled while test fixtures are being created. That means you don't necessarily have to load test fixtures in a specific order when you're using foreign key constraints.

Also See

You might also consider checking out the Foreign Key Migration plugin.[1]

---

1. http://www.redhillonrails.org/#foreign_key_migrations

Write Custom Validations

By Matthew Bass (http://matthewbass.com)
Matthew is an independent software developer who has been enjoying the freedom of Ruby for many years now. He is a speaker, agile evangelist, and Mac addict. He co-organizes the Ruby Meetup in his hometown of Raleigh, North Carolina.

Problem

You need to write application-specific model validations and share them across models.

Solution

Rails gives us a basic set of model validations right out of the box. Say we have a Student model that validates the presence of a name and the format of the Social Security number is ###-##-#### (where each number sign is a number). The Student model looks like this:

```ruby
class Student < ActiveRecord::Base
  validates_presence_of :name
  validates_format_of :ssn,
                      :with => /^[\d]{3}-[\d]{2}-[\d]{4}$/,
                      :message => "must be of format ###-##-####"
end
```

Now imagine we add a new Teacher model and teachers also need to have valid Social Security numbers (SSNs). We *could* handle this by copying and pasting the SSN validation, but as advanced programmers we know better. Instead, we'd like to write a validates_ssn method we can declare in any model, like so:

```ruby
validates_ssn :ssn
```

And while we're asking for stuff, we might as well handle multiple SSN attributes:

```ruby
validates_ssn :lost_ssn, :replacement_ssn
```

OK, how do we get there? First, we need to create a class-level method that can be invoked from any subclass of ActiveRecord::Base. We will encapsulate all the details of calling validates_format_of in that class method, calling it once per attribute.

Our class method, by itself, looks like this:

```
def self.validates_ssn(*attr_names)
  attr_names.each do |attr_name|
    validates_format_of attr_name,
                        :with => /^[\d]{3}-[\d]{2}-[\d]{4}$/,
                        :message => "must be of format ###-##-####"
  end
end
```

Next, we need to get this method into the ActiveRecord::Base class. We have several options for going about this. One way is to open up the ActiveRecord::Base class and define our class method inline:

```
class ActiveRecord::Base
  def self.validates_ssn(*attr_names)
    attr_names.each do |attr_name|
      validates_format_of attr_name,
                          :with => /^[\d]{3}-[\d]{2}-[\d]{4}$/,
                          :message => "must be of format ###-##-####"
    end
  end
end
```

This isn't necessarily a bad option, but it can be somewhat difficult to test. Instead, by sticking our class method in its own module and then extending that module, we accomplish the same goal without encumbering testability. We'll do this by creating a CustomValidations module in the lib directory:

CustomValidations/lib/custom_validations.rb

```
module CustomValidations
  def validates_ssn(*attr_names)
    attr_names.each do |attr_name|
      validates_format_of attr_name,
                          :with => /^[\d]{3}-[\d]{2}-[\d]{4}$/,
                          :message => "must be of format ###-##-####"
    end
  end
end
ActiveRecord::Base.extend(CustomValidations)
```

At the end, we use the extend method to add the methods of our Custom-Validations module to the ActiveRecord::Base class. This is a better design because we can mix in our custom validation methods only when we need them. It also leads to better code organization. If we ever decide to write more validation methods, we can simply add them to the Custom-Validations module, and they'll be available in all Active Record models.

Now it's time to put our nifty new validations to use. To do that, we just need to require it in our environment.rb file:

`CustomValidations/config/environment.rb`

```
require 'custom_validations'
```

Then we can start using the validates_ssn method in all our Active Record models:

`CustomValidations/app/models/student.rb`

```
class Student < ActiveRecord::Base
  validates_presence_of :name
  validates_ssn :ssn
end
```

`CustomValidations/app/models/teacher.rb`

```
class Teacher < ActiveRecord::Base
  validates_presence_of :name
  validates_ssn :ssn
end
```

Finally, we'll test all this. We can sidestep the database completely by just calling valid? and optionally checking the errors collection. Here's the StudentTest, for example:

`CustomValidations/test/unit/student_test.rb`

```
require File.dirname(__FILE__) + '/../test_helper'

class StudentTest < ActiveSupport::TestCase

  def test_validation_succeeds
    s = Student.new(:name => "Charlie Brown", :ssn => "123-12-1234")
    assert s.valid?
  end

  def test_validation_fails
    s = Student.new(:name => "Linus", :ssn => "1234")
    assert !s.valid?
    assert_equal "must be of format ###-##-####", s.errors[:ssn]
  end
end
```

Encapsulating validations like this leads to far more readable model classes, not to mention that warm feeling you get when you realize your code is DRY.

Take Advantage of Master/Slave Databases

By Rick Olson (http://activereload.net/)
Thanks to Rick for technical help with this recipe.

Problem

Scalability is one of those fighting words. (In fact, if you really want to see how well your blog scales, just write a post stating that Rails can't possibly scale.) On a practical note, you have a number of knobs to turn and levers to pull to help your application scale.

One naive approach to improving scalability is to throw more Mongrel processes into the mix. But that's futile if your database is the real bottleneck. In that situation, after tuning your SQL queries, you may want to partition database access into read and write operations using master/slave database replication. But once you've set that up at the database level, how do you arrange things in your application to take advantage of it?

Ingredients

- Rick Olson's masochism plug-in:

  ```
  $ script/plugin install http://ar-code.svn.engineyard.com/plugins/masochism/
  ```

Solution

Imagine we have an application that lets people give shout-outs to the world. You know, something like Twitter. When someone shouts, we want it to go to the master (write) database. The database server will then take care of replicating the shout record down to our slave database. Lots of people listen for shouts from their friends, so we want reading shout records to go through the slave database.

Once we've configured replication at the database server level,[1] the masochism plug-in lets us seamlessly take advantage of the master/

---

1. Because database replication is very specific to your database, it's beyond the scope of this recipe. See *Deploying Rails Applications* [ZT08] for how to configure MySQL master/slave replication.

slave database arrangement. First, we need to configure the master and slave database in our config/database.yml file:

```
master_database:
  adapter: mysql
  database: the_master_database
  host: master.host.name
  ...

production:
  adapter: mysql
  database: the_slave_database
  host: slave.host.name
  ...
```

By default, the masochism plug-in will use the database labeled master_database for update operations, operations in a transaction, and reloads. It'll use whichever database you have configured for your current environment as the read-only/slave database. In this case, if we're running in production, the slave database will be the_slave_database. In production we'd likely set up the slave database on a different host than the master. The masochism plug-in makes all this transparent by automatically swapping the database connections depending on the underlying Active Record operation.

Next, we need to set up the connection proxy by adding this snippet to our config/environments/production.rb file:

```
config.after_initialize do
  ActiveReload::ConnectionProxy.setup!
end
```

Great, so how do we test this? One easy way is to try it without database replication being configured. If we write a Shout record, it should show up only in the master database. Let's try that in the console with our production environment:

```
$ ruby script/console -e production
>> Shout.create :name => "Rick", :shout => "Just ate some sushi!"
=> #<Shout id: 3...>
>> Shout.find(:all)
=> []
```

As expected, we gave a shout-out, and it was written to the master database. However, because we haven't configured database replication between the master and slave, calling find doesn't find the shout. This tells us that the find is using the slave database. Now we know our Active Record operations are flowing to the appropriate database.

Finally, once we configure master/slave replication at the database level, we should end up with shout records in the slave database:

```
>> Shout.find(:all)
=> [#<Shout id: 3 ...]
```

Now we can distribute the bulk of the database load across a number of slave databases and let the master database focus on handling write operations.

Discussion

Using slave databases has some disadvantages, primarily the replication lag. While the replication is in progress, the slave database won't have the latest data. If you need to have the latest data in some parts of your app, you can make the finders fall back to the master database by wrapping the call in a transaction:

```
>> Shout.transaction { Shout.find(:all) }
=> [#<Shout id: 3 ...]
```

If you have a model that should use the master database for *all* operations, just change the model to subclass ActiveReload::MasterDatabase:

```
class SuperShout < ActiveReload::MasterDatabase
end
```

Siphon Off SQL Queries

By Pierre-Alexandre Meyer (http://www.mouraf.org)
Pierre-Alexandre is a 21-year-old French application developer specializing in Ruby on Rails. He's currently pursuing a master's degree at Cornell University.

Problem

You're ready to deploy your application to the big, bold world. Before you pull the trigger, you want to analyze your database queries to see whether there are obvious optimizations you can make.

You could do that by walking through the main pages of your app and watching the SQL that gets spewed out in the log file. But you already have integration tests for the well-worn paths in your application. It would be really convenient if you could extract the SQL scenarios from those tests and use them with your favorite SQL benchmarking tools.

Solution

First, we need to collect all the SQL generated by Active Record. That seems difficult to do across all databases, given that Rails uses database-specific adapters to execute SQL operations.

However, capturing the SQL turns out to be remarkably easy. Every database adapter logs the SQL being run by calling the log_info method in the AbstractAdapter class. We'll just intercept that call and squirrel away the SQL statements. We'll do that by opening up the Abstract-Adapter class in an initializer file:

`SiphonSql/config/initializers/core_extensions.rb`

```ruby
if RAILS_ENV == "test"
  class ActiveRecord::ConnectionAdapters::AbstractAdapter
    @@queries = []
    cattr_accessor :queries

    def log_info_with_trace(sql, name, runtime)
      return unless @logger and @logger.debug?
      self.queries << sql
      log_info_without_trace(sql, name, runtime)
    end

    alias_method_chain :log_info, :trace
  end
end
```

We've essentially decorated the log_info method with some additional behavior using alias_method_chain. This is effectively the same as writing this:

```
alias_method :log_info_without_trace, :log_info
alias_method :log_info, :log_info_with_trace
```

Whenever the log_info method is called, the log_info_with_trace method will be executed first, and then the log_info_without_trace method (which is an alias for the original log_info method) is called.

Although we could capture all the queries in memory all the time, it's probably not wise in production. We just want to know which SQL statements were run during our integration tests. To do that, notice that we've wrapped the AbstractAdapter class definition in a condition so that we hook into the log_info method only when we're in test mode. OK, let's see how this works by running some queries in the console:

```
$ ruby script/console test
Loading test environment (Rails 2.0.1)
>> ActiveRecord::ConnectionAdapters::AbstractAdapter::queries
=> []
>> Order.find :first
=> #<Order id: 1...>
>> Order.find_by_name('Pierre-Alexandre')
=> #<Order id: 1...>
>> ActiveRecord::ConnectionAdapters::AbstractAdapter::queries
=> ["SET NAMES 'utf8'", "SET SQL_AUTO_IS_NULL=0", "SELECT * FROM `orders`
   LIMIT 1", "SHOW FIELDS FROM `orders`", "SELECT * FROM `orders`
   WHERE (`orders`.`name` = 'Pierre-Alexandre')  LIMIT 1"]
```

Great, we're capturing SQL behind Active Record's back. The last statement just dumps out the SQL statements that were stored in our queries class variable.

Next, we'll modify our integration tests to siphon off the SQL statements into a file. To do that, we'll wrap the test_create_order method in a trace_sql block. Here are the relevant parts:

SiphonSql/test/integration/story_test.rb

```
class StoryTest < ActionController::IntegrationTest

  def test_create_order
    trace_sql do
      go_to_orders
      place_order :name => 'Pierre-Alexandre', :total => 25.00
    end
  end
end
```

```ruby
private

  def trace_sql
    yield
    File.open("#{RAILS_ROOT}/log/integration.sql", "w") do |file|
      queries = ActiveRecord::ConnectionAdapters::AbstractAdapter::queries.
                join("\n")
      file.write queries
    end
  end
end
```

The trace_sql method simply dumps the SQL statements in our queries class variable into a file after the block has finished. After running our integration test, the SQL appears in the log/integration.sql file:

```sql
SET NAMES 'utf8'
SET SQL_AUTO_IS_NULL=0
BEGIN
SELECT * FROM `orders`
INSERT INTO `orders` (`city`, `name`, `updated_at`, `country`, `total`,
`created_at`) VALUES(NULL, NULL, '2007-12-14 07:22:45', NULL, NULL,
'2007-12-14 07:22:45')
```

Now we have an automated way to generate SQL statements from a tested use case. The only manual step is slurping this file into our SQL benchmarking tools.

Discussion

This technique of opening up Rails internal classes and hooking into methods (often called *monkey patching*) is powerful and at the same time potentially dangerous. Future versions of Rails may change internal workings and break our code. In this case, log_info is a public method of a heavily used API. It's unlikely that this method would change significantly, but it's always possible.

Also See

Two plug-ins in particular use a similar technique to give you insight into database activity:

- The query_trace plug-in[1] dumps the stack trace of where your application is at when a SQL statement is run. It's a great plug-in for pinpointing the exact location of a problematic query.

- The query_analyzer plug-in[2] prints out the MySQL execution plan in your logs (using the MySQL EXPLAIN statement).

---

1. http://terralien.com/projects/querytrace/
2. http://svn.nfectio.us/plugins/query_analyzer

Use Fixtures for Canned Datasets

By Marty Haught and Andrew Kappen (http://martyhaught.com)
Having worked for several start-ups and consulting firms, Marty has happily settled into independent software consulting focusing on agile development with Ruby and Ruby on Rails. He lives a contented life with his lovely wife and two children in Longmont, Colorado. Between being an active father, husband, and outdoorsman, he finds time to run the Boulder Ruby group in Boulder, Colorado.

After working for a series of start-up companies to deliver video-related applications, Andrew escaped neither burnt out nor dot-com rich. Much wiser for the experience, he currently leads a very pleasant life writing web applications under contract from his home in Lawrence, Kansas.

Problem

You want to stockpile multiple, distinct sets of data and easily load them into your database for different situations: impressive-looking data for sales demos, vast quantities of data for stress testing, real-life data for production seeding, and so on.

Ingredients

• The dataset plug-in:[1]

```
$ script/plugin install svn://code.logicleaf.com/rails-plugins/dataset
```

Solution

Rails test fixtures have taken a lot of flack, and rightfully so. They can be a royal pain to create by hand and maintain. However, they work quite well for managing multiple sets of data. And it turns out we can let the database do all the dirty work for us.

It doesn't take much to start using fixture files for more than testing. We'll use the Rake tasks that come with the dataset plug-in, but you can easily use this as a springboard to write your own custom tasks.

For example, say we've used our web application to whip up some slick data for an upcoming sales demo. We've created new accounts, added

---

1. http://www.logicleaf.com/open_source.html

some goodies to each account, and formed other model relationships. Now we just need to preserve the state of the database in a set of fixtures (a dataset). Here's the Rake task that automates that chore:

`Datasets/vendor/plugins/dataset/tasks/dataset_tasks.rake`

```
# this must contain the Session and any other models you wish to ignore
MODELS_TO_IGNORE = ["CGI::Session::ActiveRecordStore::Session"]

task :dump_fixtures => :environment do
  require 'dataset'
  Dir.glob('app/models/*.rb').each { |file| require file }

  path = dataset_path
  FileUtils.mkdir_p path

  models_to_include = ENV['INCLUDE'] ? ENV['INCLUDE'].split(',') : []

  ActiveRecord::Base.send(:subclasses).each do |ar|
    if !MODELS_TO_IGNORE.include?(ar.to_s) &&
        ((models_to_include.empty? ) ||
         models_to_include.include?(ar.to_s))
      ar.to_fixture(path)
    end
  end
end
```

To dump the dataset from our development database, we use this:

```
$ rake db:dataset:dump_fixtures DATASET=demo
```

This dumps a set of Active Record models into the appropriate fixtures in the db/dataset/demo directory. It starts by using the subclasses method on ActiveRecord::Base to iterate over each model. Two options are used to limit which models get dumped: INCLUDE is a distinct list of models to dump (which we didn't use this time), and MODELS_TO_IGNORE is an array of model names we don't want to dump out. (Stuff like the Session and models participating in single-table inheritance should be ignored.) Finally, it delegates the job of dumping each model to a fixture file using the to_fixture method in the dataset.rb file.[2]

OK, now we want to turn around and slurp all this data back into the database running on the laptop we'll use for the sales demo. We've added the fixture files to version control, so we start by checking them out. Then we need a Rake task to import the data.

---

2. If you have millions of rows of data and need only a small subset, you can pass a limit as the second argument to to_fixture.

Here's an example:

`Datasets/vendor/plugins/dataset/tasks/dataset_tasks.rake`

```ruby
task :load_fixtures => 'db:schema:load' do
  require 'active_record/fixtures'
  path = dataset_path
  fixtures_to_ignore = ENV['IGNORE'] ? ENV['IGNORE'].split(',') : []

  ActiveRecord::Base.establish_connection(RAILS_ENV.to_sym)
  Dir.glob(path + '/*.yml').each do |fixture_file|
    fixture_name = File.basename(fixture_file, '.*')
    next if fixtures_to_ignore.include?(fixture_name)
    puts "Loading fixture #{fixture_file.to_s}" unless keep_quiet
    Fixtures.create_fixtures(path, fixture_name)
  end
end
```

To import the dataset into our production database, we use this:

```
$ RAILS_ENV=production rake db:dataset:load_fixtures DATASET=demo
```

This task starts by invoking the db:schema:load task to load the database schema from the schema.rb file. Then it establishes a connection to the database and loads all the YAML files in the specified dataset directory using the Fixtures.create_fixtures method.

When we're done with the demo, we can clean out all the fixtures of the dataset using this:

```
$ RAILS_ENV=production rake db:dataset:clobber DATASET=demo
```

And that's all there is to it! With a couple of custom Rake tasks (or using those included in the dataset plug-in), you can dump and load arbitrary datasets across databases with ease.

Discussion

There are cases where this falls down. First, it's fairly slow when dealing with larger tables (more than 20,000 rows). In those cases, you may want to investigate the load and dump tasks in the dataset plug-in. Those tasks use native SQL and database commands to dump and load the data in a SQL format. This is more efficient in time both to dump and to load, as well as managing the datasets in version control.

We've also created a migrate task that will take a dataset, load it into a test database, perform migrations, and then dump it out. This is a handy task to run when you plan to keep your datasets current over the project life span.

Part III

User-Interface Recipes

Handle Multiple Models in One Form

By Ryan Bates (http://railscasts.com/)
Ryan has been involved in web development since 1998. In 2005 he started working professionally with Ruby on Rails and is now best known for his work on Railscasts, the free Ruby on Rails screencast series.

Problem

Most of the form code you see handles one model at a time. That's not always practical. Sometimes you need to create and/or update two (or more) models in a single form, where there is a one-to-many association between them.

Solution

Let's say we're keeping track of tasks we need to do on projects. When we create or update a project, we'd like to add, remove, and update its tasks in a single form. Here's what we're aiming for:

New Project

Name: [Yard Work]

Task: [rake the leaves]   remove

Task: [paint the fence]   remove

Task: [clean the gutters]   remove

Add a task

(Submit)

Let's start by creating a has_many relationship between Project and Task. To keep things simple, we'll give each model a required attribute called name.

```ruby
class Project < ActiveRecord::Base
  has_many :tasks, :dependent => :destroy
  validates_presence_of :name
end
```

```
class Task < ActiveRecord::Base
  belongs_to :project
  validates_presence_of :name
end
```

We'll be using the Prototype JavaScript library, so before we go any further, let's make sure it's loaded in our layout file:

MultiModelForm/app/views/layouts/application.html.erb

```
<%= javascript_include_tag :defaults %>
```

Now we turn our attention to the form for creating a project along with its associated, multiple tasks. When dealing with multiple models in one form, it's helpful to make one model the primary focus and build the other models through the association.

In this case, we'll make Project the primary model and build its tasks through the has_many association. So in the new action of our ProjectsController, we create a Project object like normal. However, we also initialize a new Task (in memory) that's associated with the Project so that our form has something to work with:

MultiModelForm/app/controllers/projects_controller.rb

```
def new
  @project = Project.new
  @project.tasks.build
end
```

The form template is a bit tricky since we need to handle fields for the Project model and each of its Task models. So, let's break the problem down a bit by using a partial to render the Task fields and an add_task_link helper to create the link that adds a new task:

MultiModelForm/app/views/projects/_form.html.erb

```
<%= error_messages_for :project %>

<% form_for @project do |f| -%>
  <p>
    Name: <%= f.text_field :name %>
  </p>
  <div id="tasks">
    <%= render :partial => 'task', :collection => @project.tasks %>
  </div>
  <p>
    <%= add_task_link "Add a task" %>
  </p>
  <p>
    <%= f.submit "Submit" %>
  </p>
<% end -%>
```

The new and edit templates simply render this form partial so that we have a consistent form for creating and updating a project. The form partial turns around and renders a task partial for each of the project's tasks. Before we get into the contents of the task partial, let's take a look at that add_task_link helper method:

MultiModelForm/app/helpers/projects_helper.rb

```ruby
def add_task_link(name)
  link_to_function name do |page|
    page.insert_html :bottom, :tasks, :partial => 'task', :object => Task.new
  end
end
```

When we click the "Add a task" link, we want a new set of task fields to appear at the bottom of the existing task fields in the form. Rather than bother the server with this, we can use JavaScript to add the fields dynamically. The link_to_function method accepts a block of RJS code. We usually associate RJS code with asynchronous calls back to the server. But in this case the RJS code generates JavaScript that gets executed in the browser immediately when the user clicks the link. The upshot is rendering the fields for adding a new task does not require a trip back to the server, which leads to faster response times.

Looking back to the form partial, we're using form_for to dedicate the form to the @project model. How then do we add fields for each of the project's tasks? The task partial holds the answer:

MultiModelForm/app/views/projects/_task.html.erb

```erb
<div class="task">
<% new_or_existing = task.new_record? ? 'new' : 'existing' %>
<% prefix = "project[#{new_or_existing}_task_attributes][]" %>

<% fields_for prefix, task do |task_form| -%>
  <p>
    Task: <%= task_form.text_field :name %>
    <%= link_to_function "remove", "$(this).up('.task').remove()" %>
  </p>
<% end -%>
</div>
```

The key ingredient here is the fields_for method. It behaves much like form_for but does not render the surrounding form HTML tag. This lets us switch the context to a different model in the middle of a form—as if we're embedding one form within another.

The first parameter to fields_for is very important. This string will be used as the prefix for the name of each task form field. Because we'll be using this partial to also render existing tasks—and we want to keep them separate when the form is submitted—in the prefix we include an indication of whether the task is new or existing. (Ideally we'd create the prefix string in a helper, but we've inlined it here to avoid further indirection.)

The generated HTML for a new task name input looks like this:

```
<input name="project[new_task_attributes][][name]" size="30" type="text"/>
```

If this were an existing task, Rails would automatically place the task ID between the square brackets, like this:

```
<input name="project[existing_task_attributes][7][name]" size="30" type="text"/>
```

Now when the form is submitted, Rails will decode the input element's name to impose some structure in the params hash. Square brackets that are filled in become keys in a nested hash. Square brackets that are empty become an array. For example, if we submit the form with two new tasks, the params hash looks like this:

```
"project" => {
  "name" => "Yard Work",
  "new_task_attributes" => [
    { "name" => "rake the leaves" },
    { "name" => "paint the fence" }
  ]
}
```

Notice that the attributes for the project *and* each task are nestled inside the project hash. This is convenient because it means the create action back in our controller can simply pass all the project attributes through to the Project model without worrying about what's inside:

MultiModelForm/app/controllers/projects_controller.rb

```
def create
  @project = Project.new(params[:project])
  if @project.save
    flash[:notice] = "Successfully created project and tasks."
    redirect_to projects_path
  else
    render :action => 'new'
  end
end
```

This looks like a standard create action for a single-model form. However, there is something subtle happening here. When we call Project.new(params[:project]), Active Record assumes that our Project model has a corresponding attribute called new_task_attributes because it sees a key called new_task_attributes in the params(:project) hash. That is,

Active Record will try to mass assign all the data in the params(:project) hash to corresponding attributes in the Project model. But we don't have a new_task_attributes attribute in our Project model.

One convenient way to keep all this transparent from the controller's perspective is to use a virtual attribute. To do that, we just create a setter method in our Project model called new_task_attributes=, which takes an array and builds a task for each element:

MultiModelForm/app/models/project.rb

```ruby
def new_task_attributes=(task_attributes)
  task_attributes.each do |attributes|
    tasks.build(attributes)
  end
end
```

It may not look like these tasks are being saved anywhere. In fact, Rails will do that automatically when the project is saved because both the project and its associated tasks are new records.

That's it for creating a project; now let's move on to updating one.

Just like before, we need to be able to add and remove tasks dynamically, but this time if a task already exists, it should be updated instead. The controller actions need to be concerned only about the project, so they're fairly conventional. As before, the updating of the tasks will be handled in the Project model:

MultiModelForm/app/controllers/projects_controller.rb

```ruby
def edit
  @project = Project.find(params[:id])
end

def update
  params[:project][:existing_task_attributes] ||= {}

  @project = Project.find(params[:id])
  if @project.update_attributes(params[:project])
    flash[:notice] = "Successfully updated project and tasks."
    redirect_to project_path(@project)
  else
    render :action => 'edit'
  end
end
```

One important note: The first line of the update action sets the existing_task_attributes parameter to an empty hash if it's not set already. Without this line, there would be no way to delete the last task from a project. If there are no task fields on the form (because we removed them all with JavaScript), then existing_task_attributes() won't be assigned by the form, which means our Project#existing_task_attributes= method won't be invoked. By assigning an empty hash here if existing_task_attributes() is empty, we ensure the Project#existing_task_attributes= method is called to delete the last task.

The form partial can stay the same. However, when we submit the form with existing tasks, the params(:project) hash will include a key called existing_task_attributes. That is, when we update the project, the POST parameters will look like this:

```
"project" => {
  "name" => "Yard Work",
  "existing_task_attributes" => [
    {
      "1" => {"name" => "rake the leaves"},
      "2" => {"name" => "paint the fence"},
    }
  ]
  "new_task_attributes" => [
    { "name" => "clean the gutters" }
  ]
}
```

To handle that, we need to add an existing_task_attributes= method to our Project model, which will take each existing task and either update it or destroy it depending on whether the attributes are passed:

MultiModelForm/app/models/project.rb

```
after_update :save_tasks

def existing_task_attributes=(task_attributes)
  tasks.reject(&:new_record?).each do |task|
    attributes = task_attributes[task.id.to_s]
    if attributes
      task.attributes = attributes
    else
      tasks.delete(task)
    end
  end
end

def save_tasks
  tasks.each do |task|
    task.save(false)
  end
end
```

Notice that we're saving the tasks in an after_update callback. This is important because, unlike before, the existing tasks will not automatically be saved when the project is updated.[1] And since callbacks are wrapped in a transaction, it will properly roll back the save if an unexpected problem occurs.

Passing false to the task.save method bypasses validation. Instead, to ensure that all the tasks get validated when the project is validated, we just add this line to the Project model:

```
validates_associated :tasks
```

This ensures everything is valid before saving. And if validation fails, then the use of error_messages_for :project in the form template includes the validation errors for the project and any of its tasks.

So now we can create and edit projects and their tasks in one fell swoop. And by using virtual attributes, we kept the controller code happily ignorant that we were handling multiple models from a single form.

Discussion

Once you start putting more than one model in a form, you'll likely want to create a custom error message helper to do things such as ignore certain errors and clarify others. See Snack Recipe 17, *Customize Error Messages*, on page 91 for how to write a custom error_messages_for method.

Date fields cause problems because, for some reason, Rails removes the [] from the name of the field. This can be fixed by manually specifying the :index option and setting it to an empty string if the task is new:

```
<%= task_form.date_select :completed_at,
                          :index => (task.new_record? ? '' : nil) %>
```

Unfortunately, checkboxes won't work in this recipe because their value is not passed by the browser when the box is unchecked. Therefore, you cannot tell which task a given checkbox belongs to when a new project is created. To get around this problem, you can use a select menu for boolean fields:

```
<%= task_form.select :completed, [['No', false], ['Yes', true]] %>
```

---

1. This behavior can vary depending on the type of association and whether the records are new. It's a good idea to thoroughly test each combination to ensure every model is validated and saved properly.

Replace In-View Raw JavaScript

By Jared Haworth (http://www.alloycode.com/)

Jared is working to change the world as a senior software engineer at Education Revolution. He is also actively involved in Rails advocacy through his company Alloy Code (http://www.alloycode.com/), a North Carolina–based web development shop.

Sometimes it's convenient to be able to use the familiar RJS syntax in your views to generate JavaScript. It turns out to be really easy. Say, for example, we need to toggle the visibility of an event_details div. Rather than writing raw JavaScript, we can mix a link_to_function call with an update_page method:

> ReplacingRawJSWithRJS/app/views/venues/show.html.erb

```
<p>
  <%= link_to_function "Show Event Details",
                       update_page { |page| page[:event_details].toggle } %>
</p>
<div id="event_details" style="display: none;">
  <%= render :partial => 'event', :collection => @venue.events %>
</div>
```

The link_to_function (and button_to_function) helper happily takes any JavaScript as the function parameter. The often-overlooked update_page method spits out Prototype-flavored JavaScript, which is substituted back into the view at the time the page is rendered. The page object in this case is a JavaScript generator. It's the same generator we use in RJS files.

This is a step in the right direction, but inline code like this can get messy quickly. So, let's take this a step further by bottling up the toggling code (with a highlight effect) as a helper method in the application_helper.rb file:

> ReplacingRawJSWithRJS/app/helpers/application_helper.rb

```
def toggle_div(div)
  update_page do |page|
    page[div].toggle
    page[div].visual_effect :highlight
  end
end
```

As if by design, the update_page method can be called from a helper. This makes sense because view helpers are a good place to stockpile reusable view code.

Then we'll update our view to call the helper:

`ReplacingRawJSWithRJS/app/views/venues/show.html.erb`

```
<p>
  <%= link_to_function "Show Event Details", toggle_div(:event_details) %>
</p>
<div id="event_details" style="display: none;">
  <%= render :partial => 'event', :collection => @venue.events %>
</div>
```

Now that our toggle code has found a comfy home, we can toggle an element from any view without the DRY police crying foul. Where it makes sense, we can also call these helpers from controllers in response to a full Ajax request.

Validate Required Form Fields Inline

By Jarkko Laine (http://jlaine.net)

Jarkko is one of the earliest Rails evangelists in Europe, with more than two years of experience in teaching and giving talks about Rails. He wrote *Beginning Ruby on Rails E-Commerce: From Novice to Professional* (HL06) (Apress) with Christian Hellsten and is the founder of the Finnish Rails user community. He currently works as a senior developer for http://dotherightthing.com, a site for rating and discussing the social performance of the world's businesses. In his free time, Jarkko runs through forests like a gnu and writes about anything he finds interesting on his weblog.

Problem

Rails has powerful and easy-to-use form validation mechanisms on the server side. However, from the user-interface perspective, it would be nice to catch at least the most obvious input errors—such as missing elements that are required—before the form is even submitted.

Ingredients

- Michael Schuerig's validation_reflection plug-in:

```
$ script/plugin install ↵
    svn://rubyforge.org//var/svn/valirefl/validation_reflection/trunk
```

Solution

Let's assume we have an account sign-up form that asks for an e-mail address and a password. We want to automatically mark those form fields as being required and validate that they contain values *before* the user clicks the submit button.

We'll tackle the solution in two steps. First, we'll extract validation information from a Rails model. Then, we'll write a custom form builder (see Recipe 30, *Keep Forms DRY and Flexible*, on page 175) to automatically decorate the required fields and validate them inline.

Models carry around a lot of useful information. For example, our User model knows that the email and password fields are mandatory because we said so:

```
class User < ActiveRecord::Base
  validates_presence_of :email, :password
end
```

The validation_reflection plug-in lets us tease this information out. For example, we can call the reflect_on_validations_for method to see the validations for a specific field of our User model:

```
$ ruby script/console
>> User.reflect_on_validations_for(:email)
=> [#<ActiveRecord::Reflection::MacroReflection:0x1834a40
   @macro=:validates_presence_of, @name=:email, @options=nil,
   @active_record=User(id: integer, login: string, email: string,
   password: string, created_at: datetime, updated_at: datetime)>]

>> User.reflect_on_validations_for(:password)
=> [#<ActiveRecord::Reflection::MacroReflection:0x1834464
   @macro=:validates_presence_of, @name=:password, @options=nil,
   @active_record=User(id: integer, login: string, email: string,
   password: string, created_at: datetime, updated_at: datetime)>]
```

Let's use this knowledge to write a custom ValidatingFormBuilder form builder. Here's what it looks like:

InlineFormValidations/lib/validating_form_builder.rb

```ruby
class ValidatingFormBuilder < ActionView::Helpers::FormBuilder

  helpers = field_helpers +
            %w(date_select datetime_select time_select) -
            %w(hidden_field label fields_for)

  helpers.each do |name|
    define_method(name) do |field, *args|
      options = args.last.is_a?(Hash) ? args.pop : {}

      if %w(text_field password_field).include?(name) && required_field?(field)
        options[:onblur] = "checkPresence('#{field_name(field)}')"
      end

      @template.content_tag(:p,
                            label(field, label_text(field)) + " " +
                            super(field, options))
    end
  end

private

  def field_name(field)
    "#{@object_name.to_s.underscore}_#{field.to_s.underscore}"
  end

  def label_text(field)
    "#{field.to_s.humanize}#{required_mark(field)}"
  end
```

```ruby
  def required_mark(field)
    required_field?(field) ? ' (*)' : ''
  end

  def required_field?(field)
    @object_name.to_s.camelize.constantize.
               reflect_on_validations_for(field).
               map(&:macro).include?(:validates_presence_of)
  end
end
```

At a first glance, this looks just like a normal form builder. However, we've added the required_field? method to check whether a given field is required. If so, we include a simple indicator (an asterisk) in the field's label text. We also added a check to see whether the helper we're creating is a required text or password field. If so, we add an onblur event handler that calls our checkPresence JavaScript function whenever the focus is moved away from the form field.[1]

Then we'll add the checkPresence JavaScript function to our application.js file:

InlineFormValidations/public/javascripts/application.js

```javascript
function checkPresence(field) {
 var hint = $F(field).length == 0 ? "Try again!" : "Right on!";
 if ($(field + '_hint')) {
   $(field + '_hint').update(hint);
 } else {
   content = '<span class="validation" id="' + field + '_hint">' +
            hint + '</span>';
   new Insertion.After(field, content);
 }
}
```

This function checks whether a field is empty and inserts an appropriate message after the form field.

Finally, we'll update our sign-up form to use our custom form builder:

InlineFormValidations/app/views/users/new.html.erb

```erb
<% form_for(@user, :builder => ValidatingFormBuilder) do |f| -%>
  <%= f.text_field :login %>
  <%= f.text_field :email %>
  <%= f.text_field :password %>
  <%= f.submit 'Create' %>
<% end -%>
```

---

1. We use an inline event handler here instead of less obtrusive methods for the sake of brevity.

The generated form looks like this:

```
<form action="/users" method="post">
  <p>
    <label for="user_login">Login</label>
    <input id="user_login" name="user[login]" size="30" type="text" />
  </p>
  <p>
    <label for="user_email">Email (*)</label>
    <input id="user_email" name="user[email]"
           onblur="checkPresence('user_email')" size="30" type="text" />
  </p>
  <p>
    <label for="user_password">Password (*)</label>
    <input id="user_password" name="user[password]"
           onblur="checkPresence('user_password')" size="30" type="text" />
  </p>
  <p>
    <input name="commit" type="submit" value="Create" />
  </p>
</form>
```

The email and password fields include asterisks in their labels. When the user tabs through those fields (for example), the phrase "Right on!" or "Try again!" appears below the input field.

Here's the best part: because this functionality is tucked away in our custom form builder, it applies to all forms that use the builder.

Discussion

You could easily extend the validation to also cater to more advanced validation such as text length or format (for example, for e-mail addresses). This way you could easily make your forms more user-friendly and at the same time save a few request cycles down to the server. You could also extend the form builder so that it would make Ajax requests check whether a given unique login name is already taken, for example.

Create Multistep Wizards

By Mike Hagedorn (http://www.silverchairsolutions.com)
Mike is a freelance web developer and founder of Silverchair Solutions, an agile methods consulting firm located in Houston, Texas. Mike has a long history of enterprise development dating back to the bad old days of Java 1.0 and has been actively doing work in Rails since late 2005. He has implemented solutions in Java, Cocoa (Objective-C), and C#. To round things out, he also moonlights as a professional musician and spends as many weekends as possible backpacking.

Problem

You've used a wizard before; it's those series of screens with Previous and Next buttons at the bottom. You can go backward and forward as many times as you like until you get things just right. Indeed, a good wizard takes a user by the hand and guides her through a step-by-step process.

Unfortunately, wizards aren't trivial to implement in web-based applications because the Web is a stateless world. And in order to know which step you're on in a multistep process, state is the very thing you need most. So, just how do you roll your own wizard?

Ingredients

* The acts_as_state_machine plug-in:

```
$ script/plugin install ↩
    http://elitists.textdriven.com/svn/plugins/acts_as_state_machine/trunk
```

Solution

Let's say we want to create an application that lets users take a short, three-question quiz. We'll need to keep track of which step of the quiz a user is currently on and therefore which question to present to the user next (or previous). Here's an example question:

What do you like to drink?

Saki

(← Previous) (Next →)

Of course, lots of people will take our quizzes, and sometimes they'll need to step away to ponder a particularly tough question, but we'll let them pick up right where they left off:

Quizzes

Player	Current Question	Last Played	
1	q30	2 minutes ago	Continue Where You Left Off...
2	q10	2 minutes ago	Continue Where You Left Off...
3	q20	1 minute ago	Continue Where You Left Off...
4	q10	less than a minute ago	Continue Where You Left Off...

Take the quiz!

Now that we know what we want, let's start with the models and migrations we'll need. A quiz has many associated answers and questions, and it remembers its current state:

Wizard/app/models/quiz.rb

```
class Quiz < ActiveRecord::Base
  has_many :answers, :dependent => :destroy
  has_many :questions
end
```

Wizard/db/migrate/001_create_quizzes.rb

```
create_table :quizzes do |t|
  t.string :state
  t.timestamps
end
```

And a question has many answers—one for each person who took the quiz—plus the question text and some metadata we'll get to later:

Wizard/app/models/question.rb

```
class Question < ActiveRecord::Base
  belongs_to :quiz
  has_many :answers
end
```

Wizard/db/migrate/003_create_questions.rb

```
create_table :questions do |t|
  t.string  :type, :text, :tag
  t.integer :quiz_id
  t.timestamps
end
```

And finally an answer reciprocates the relationships and has a value for the answer:

Wizard/app/models/answer.rb

```ruby
class Answer < ActiveRecord::Base
  belongs_to :question
  belongs_to :quiz
end
```

Wizard/db/migrate/002_create_answers.rb

```ruby
create_table :answers do |t|
  t.string   :value
  t.integer  :question_id, :quiz_id
  t.timestamps
end
```

That's fairly straightforward. Now, how are we going to tie all the questions together so that they get asked in a certain order? Well, we could use foreign keys in the database to point to the next and previous questions. But managing all that can get complicated as our quizzes become more involved.

Thankfully, there's a simpler, more elegant way: a finite state machine (FSM). Using an FSM lets us break down the problem into a small number of *states* (the current question) and then move between the states when an event is encountered (when the Next or Previous button is clicked).

The mere thought of using an FSM sounds intimidating (and may trigger flashbacks to a time when you thought real programmers would never use them), but they're really easy. Let's start by looking at our quiz application's states and transitions graphically:

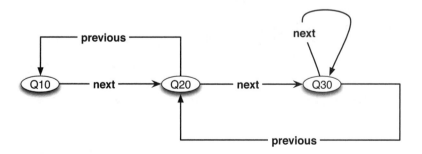

A quiz has three states with each state corresponding to a question to be posed.

This small diagram completely defines what our three-question quiz application should do when a next or previous event occurs.

- If you're in the first state (Q10) and you receive a next event, then transition to the next question (Q20).
- If you're in the second-question state (Q20) and you receive a next event, then transition to the third-question state (Q30). However, if you receive a previous event while in state Q20, go back to the first question (Q10).
- If you're in the third-question state (Q30) and receive a next event, do nothing. But if you receive a previous event, back up to question Q20.

That makes sense conceptually, but now how do we write code to make it work? Ah, that's where the acts_as_state_machine plug-in really pays off. Next, we'll express the states and transitions from our diagram right in our Quiz model, like so:

Wizard/app/models/quiz.rb

```ruby
class Quiz < ActiveRecord::Base
  has_many :answers, :dependent => :destroy
  has_many :questions

  acts_as_state_machine :initial => :q10

  state :q10, :after => :current_question
  state :q20, :after => :current_question
  state :q30, :after => :current_question

  event :next do
    transitions :to => :q20, :from => :q10
    transitions :to => :q30, :from => :q20
  end

  event :previous do
    transitions :to => :q10, :from => :q20
    transitions :to => :q20, :from => :q30
  end

  def current_question
    @current_question ||= find_question(self.current_state)
  end

  private

  def find_question(state)
    Question.find_by_tag(state.to_s)
  end
end
```

We've added the acts_as_state_machine declaration and set the initial state to q10 (which is just a name). Then we defined the names of our three states and associated a method to call after transitioning into that state. In this case, the current_question method will turn around and query the database for the Question that has the same tag as the name of the current state. This is the key that makes the correct question pop up whenever a user hits the Next or Previous button. Then, for each event (next and previous), we describe the transitions based on the current state.

Let's play around in the console a bit to get a feel for what's going on:

```
$ ruby script/console
>> quiz = Quiz.create
```

Notice that we didn't call the new method on Quiz. We have to use the create method in order for the acts_as_state_machine magic to kick in and set the initial state properly. Let's check that:

```
>> quiz.state
=> "q10"
```

OK so far; that is indeed our first state. Let's move to the next state (which, remember, is the same thing as stepping to the next question). To do that, we can use the next! method because we defined next as an event:

```
>> quiz.next!
=> true
>> quiz.state
=> "q20"
```

Great, now let's go backward using the previous! method:

```
>> quiz.previous!
=> true
>> quiz.state
=> "q10"
```

Then if we fast-forward to the end, we loop back on the last state:

```
>> quiz.next!
>> quiz.next!
>> quiz.next!
>> quiz.state
=> "q30"
```

Hey, that's pretty neat! But quizzes are more fun if we have different types of questions: short answers, true or false, and so on. Each of those requires a custom template to prompt the user accordingly. To keep things flexible, we will use single-table inheritance (STI) on the

Question model. Then we can have each question type provide its own template for viewing purposes, and the rest of the system will be none the wiser.

Next we'll create two subclasses of Question: one for short-answer questions and the other for true/false questions:

Wizard/app/models/short_answer_question.rb

```
class ShortAnswerQuestion < Question
end
```

Wizard/app/models/true_false_question.rb

```
class TrueFalseQuestion < Question
end
```

Since we defined the Quiz class with states q10, q20, and q30, we need to create records in the questions table that have these tag values. Let's do that from the console, too:

```
$ ruby script/console
>> ShortAnswerQuestion.create(:text => "What's your name?",
                              :tag  => "q10")
>> TrueFalseQuestion.create(:text => "Do you like wasabi?",
                            :tag  => "q20")
>> ShortAnswerQuestion.create(:text => "What do you like to drink?",
                              :tag  => "q30")
```

Then, over in a view helper, we'll write a helper figure out which question template to use when showing a particular question. To keep things simple, we'll just use the convention of naming the template (we'll use partials) based on the class name of the current question. Here's the helper:

Wizard/app/helpers/quizzes_helper.rb

```
module QuizzesHelper
  def question_template(question)
    "questions/#{question.class.name.underscore}"
  end
end
```

Let's go ahead and create the two partials that correspond to our two question types. These need to go in the app/views/questions directory according to our naming convention. Here's what the partial for short-answer questions looks like:

Wizard/app/views/questions/_short_answer_question.html.erb

```
<label for="answer_value"><%= question.text %></label>
<%= text_field :answer, :value %>
```

And here's the true/false-question partial:

`Wizard/app/views/questions/_true_false_question.html.erb`

```
<label for="answer_value"><%= question.text %></label>
<%= select :answer, :value,
           {"Yes" => "true", "No" => "false"},
           :selected => answer.value %>
```

The last piece to tie this all together is the QuizzesController, where all the interesting stuff happens. Let's generate it with four actions:

```
$ script/generate controller quizzes index new edit update
```

Then update our config/routes.rb file to use the RESTful conventions:

`Wizard/config/routes.rb`

```
map.resources :quizzes
map.resources :answers
```

We need to write two actions in the QuizzesController: edit and update. The edit action lets a user continue an existing quiz:

`Wizard/app/controllers/quizzes_controller.rb`

```
def edit
  @quiz   = Quiz.find(params[:id])
  @answer = @quiz.answers.
              find_by_question_id(@quiz.current_question.id) || Answer.new
end
```

Then, in the template for the edit action, we'll render the partial for the current question, handing it the question and the previous answer in the :locals hash:

`Wizard/app/views/quizzes/edit.html.erb`

```
<% form_for(@quiz) do |f| -%>
  <fieldset>
    <%= render :partial => question_template(@quiz.current_question),
               :locals => {
                 :question => @quiz.current_question,
                 :answer   => @answer
               } %>
  </fieldset>
  <%= hidden_field_tag :direction, "next" %>
  <hr/>
  <table class="controls">
    <tr>
      <td>
        <%= button_to_function "&#8592; Previous",
              "$('direction').value = 'previous'; this.form.submit();" %>
      </td>
      <td>
        <%= submit_tag "Next &#8594;" %>
```

```
          </td>
        </tr>
      </table>
<% end -%>
```

We use a direction hidden field here to indicate which direction we're going. Hitting the Next button just posts to the update action (because @quiz has already been saved) with the hidden field value set to next. The Previous button works slightly differently: before posting to the update action, it changes the hidden field value to previous, so we'll end up transitioning back one state.

Then we'll write the update action to handle the Previous or Next button:

Wizard/app/controllers/quizzes_controller.rb

```ruby
def update
  @quiz = Quiz.find(params[:id])
  @answer = @quiz.answers.find_by_question_id(@quiz.current_question)

  if @answer
    @answer.update_attribute(:value, params[:answer][:value])
  else
    @answer = Answer.new(:value    => params[:answer][:value],
                         :question => @quiz.current_question)
    @quiz.answers << @answer
  end

  case params[:direction]
  when 'next'
    @quiz.next!
  when 'previous'
    @quiz.previous!
  else
    flash[:error] = "Invalid direction!"
  end

  redirect_to :action => :edit
end
```

Every time a user hits the Previous or Next button, they'll transparently cycle through the update action. Their answer gets updated (if they've posted an answer before) or gets created (if they haven't given an answer yet). Depending on the value of the :direction parameter (the hidden field value), we fire an event on the quiz—next! or previous! is called on the quiz. After the transition, the quiz loads the corresponding next or previous question. Finally, the action re-renders the edit template to show the question.

Now all we have to do is fire up our browser, create a new quiz, and start stepping through the wizard!

What if you're not building an online quiz game? Instead, you have something with a few (or a lot) more states and transitions. That's all the more reason to find the back of a napkin, draw your state transition diagram, and start implementing it with acts_as_state_machine. Then walk through your diagram using the console, and when you have it working, write some unit tests that give you automated examples. By breaking it down this way, the final solution will likely be easier (and more elegant) than you may have imagined.

It would be fairly easy to extend this example to handle other question types, such as multiple-choice questions, by defining new Question subclasses and including corresponding templates in the questions directory. You could also generalize the question template that's used by adding a view_template attribute to Question and allowing that field value to override the default template name.

Customize Error Messages

By Mark Bates (http://www.markbates.com)
Mark is currently the director of architecture for Helium (http://helium.com). Mark spends his days fighting the establishment and wishing he'll be called up as the next front man for Van Halen. In addition to knowing the true meaning of Arbor Day, Mark also knows who let the dogs out, where the beef is, and who shot J.R.

The error_messages_for method provided by Rails is a great way to quickly put error messages on a form page. And if you don't mind working with some constraints, you can pass various options to error_messages_for to stylize the HTML that gets generated.

However, sometimes you (or your web designer) need to color outside the lines to help set your application apart from the crowd. Writing your own version of error_messages_for is easier than you might think. For the ultimate design flexibility, let's write a version that gives our web designer complete freedom to customize the error messages in his own special way in a partial template. We'll just slip this code into an initializer file:

`ErrorMessages/config/initializers/core_extensions.rb`

```ruby
module ActionView
  module Helpers
    module ActiveRecordHelper
      def error_messages_for(*params)
        options = params.extract_options!.symbolize_keys
        objects = params.collect {|name| instance_variable_get("@#{name}") }
        error_messages = objects.map {|o| o.errors.full_messages}
        unless error_messages.flatten!.empty?
          if options[:partial]
            render :partial => options[:partial],
                   :locals  => {:errors => error_messages}
          else
            header = "Whoops! Please correct the following errors:"
            error_list = error_messages.map {|m| content_tag(:li, m)}
            contents = ''
            contents << content_tag(:h2, header)
            contents << content_tag(:ul, error_list)
            content_tag(:div, contents,
                        :class => 'errorExplanation',
                        :id    => 'errorExplanation')
          end
        else
          ''
        end
      end
    end
  end
end
```

The trick is to use instance_variable_get to grab the model object corresponding to each name and then pull out all the error messages. After that, it's simply a matter of web design. The default behavior renders some pretty generic HTML. But we can specify a partial using the :partial option, like this:

```
<%= error_messages_for :user, :partial => 'application/error_messages' %>
```

Now your web designer can have a partial that displays errors on pop-ups, another partial that's used to display errors for certain sections of your site, and yet another partial that gets used only on the third Friday of every month that ends in *ber*. Best of all, you don't have to recode anything.

If you want an off-the-shelf solution with a few more options, check out the error_messages_for gem.[1]

---

1. gem install error_messages_for

Upload Images with Thumbnails

By Rick Olson (http://entp.com)

Rick has been an active contributor to the Rails community for more than three years. He has released numerous open source plug-ins and applications such as Mephisto and Altered Beast. He currently spearheads Rails R&D at entp.com, driving the innovation behind the Lighthouse and Warehouse applications.

Problem

You want to let users upload images (or any media file) as an "attachment" to one of your models. In the case of images, you also want to generate a variety of thumbnails for use around your site.

Ingredients

- The attachment_fu plug-in:

  ```
  $ script/plugin install ↩
      http://svn.techno-weenie.net/projects/plugins/attachment_fu/
  ```

- One of the following image-processing libraries and any libraries on which they depend:

  - *ImageScience:*[1] A lightweight inline-Ruby library that resizes only images. It wraps the FreeImage library, which you'll also need.

  - *RMagick:*[2] The granddaddy, both in terms of advanced image-processing features and memory usage. It wraps the ImageMagick library, which you'll also need.

  - *minimagick:*[3] This is much easier on memory than RMagick because it runs the ImageMagick command in a shell. You'll also need ImageMagick installed.

Image processing is best handled by native code. Regardless of the image processor you choose, you'll end up either building a native

---

1. http://seattlerb.rubyforge.org/ImageScience.html
2. http://rmagick.rubyforge.org/
3. http://rubyforge.org/projects/mini-magick/

library or downloading a prebuilt library specific to your operating system. Then you generally install a Ruby library (gem) that wraps the image-processing library with a Ruby API. If you already have one of these installed, go with it!

Solution

Suppose we're building an online jukebox and we need to upload cover images for the albums. While we're at it, we'd like to generate a few cover image thumbnails of varying sizes to sprinkle around the site. Here's where the attachment_fu plug-in really shines. Rather than groveling around at the API level of whatever Ruby image library we have installed, we can simply declare how we want files to get processed and let attachment_fu work out the details.

Let's start with what we need in the database. Now, we could try to cram all the album and cover information into one database table. But that gets messy, so instead we'll split them up into two tables. First, we need a database table to store information about the cover image: its size, where it lives, which album it belongs to, and so on. We won't actually store the cover image itself in the database, just its metadata. Here's the migration for the Cover model:

UploadImages/db/migrate/002_create_covers.rb

```ruby
class CreateCovers < ActiveRecord::Migration
  def self.up
    create_table :covers do |t|
      t.integer :album_id, :parent_id, :size, :width, :height
      t.string  :content_type, :filename, :thumbnail
      t.timestamps
    end
  end

  def self.down
    drop_table :covers
  end
end
```

The attachment_fu plug-in requires all these columns, with the exception of the album_id column, which is specific to our application. In particular, note that the parent_id column is not a foreign key to an album. Rather, it's a foreign key used by thumbnails to point to their parent cover images in the same covers table. Again, the covers table just stores the information about the cover, not the actual cover image.

When an image is uploaded, its location will be stored in the covers table, and the actual file data will be stored somewhere else (we'll get to *where* in a minute). Next, we need a Cover model (no, not that kind!). Here's what it looks like:

UploadImages/app/models/cover.rb

```
class Cover < ActiveRecord::Base
  belongs_to :album

  has_attachment :content_type => :image,
                 :storage      => :file_system,
                 :max_size     => 500.kilobytes,
                 :resize_to    => '384x256>',
                 :thumbnails   => {
                   :large =>  '96x96>',
                   :medium => '64x64>',
                   :small =>  '48x48>'
                 }

  validates_as_attachment
end
```

There's a lot of magic happening here. In the has_attachment method, we tell attachment_fu what to do with the uploaded image via a number of options:

- :content_type specifies the content types we allow. In this case, using :image allows all standard image types.

- :storage sets where the actual cover image data is stored. So, in fact, we could have stored the covers in the database (:db_file), but the filesystem is easier to manage.

- :max_size is, not surprisingly, the maximum size allowed. It is always good to set a limit on just how much data you want your app to ingest (the default is 1 megabyte).

- :resize_to is either an array of width/height values (for example, :resize_to => [384, 286]) or a geometry string for resizing the image. Geometry strings are more flexible but not supported by all image processors. In this case, by using the > symbol at the end, we're saying that the image should be resized to 384 by 286 only if the width or height exceeds those dimensions. Otherwise, the image is not resized.

- :processor sets the image processor to use: ImageScience, Rmagick, or MiniMagick. As we haven't specified one, attachment_fu will use whichever library we have installed.

- :thumbnails is a hash of thumbnail names and resizing options. Thumbnails won't be generated if you leave off this option, and you can generate as many thumbnails as you like simply by adding arbitrary names and sizes to the hash.

After describing how the image should be processed, we call the validates_as_attachment method to prevent image sizes out of range from being saved. (They're still uploaded into memory, mind you.) In addition, because we set an image content type, WinZip files won't be welcome, for example.

Of course, we'll also need an Album model to "attach" a Cover object to, but there's not much to it:

UploadImages/app/models/album.rb

```
class Album < ActiveRecord::Base
  has_one :cover, :dependent => :destroy
end
```

OK, with our models created, we turn our attention to the form used to upload the cover image file when we create a new Album:

UploadImages/app/views/albums/new.html.erb

```
<%= error_messages_for :album, :cover %>

<% form_for(@album, :html => { :multipart => true }) do |f| %>
  <p>
    <%= label :album, :title %>
    <%= f.text_field :title %>
  </p>
  <p>
    <%= label :album, :artist %>
    <%= f.text_field :artist %>
  </p>
  <p>
    <%= label :album, :cover %>
    <%= file_field_tag :cover_file %>
    <span class="hint">
      We accept JPEG, GIF, or PNG files up to 500 KB.
    </span>
  </p>
  <p>
    <%= f.submit "Create" %>
  </p>
<% end %>
```

It's a fairly standard form, but it has three important ingredients. First, to allow the form to accept files as POST data, the form_for includes the

:multipart => true option. (If you forget to add this, you're in for a long afternoon of debugging.)

Second, the form uses the file_field_tag helper (instead of f.file_field) to generate a Choose File button on the form. In this case, the name of the file input field will be :cover_file.

Finally, the error_messages_for method handles the @album and @cover objects so that it displays errors related to both objects.

So far, so good. Next, we need to do something with the cover image that gets uploaded. Specifically, we need to use its file data to create a Cover object and attach it to the Album being created. This gets a bit tricky: we're creating two models from one form. So, to keep the create action of our AlbumsController clean, we're going to introduce a new AlbumService class and let it do the grunt work. Here's the create action:

UploadImages/app/controllers/albums_controller.rb

```ruby
def create
  @album = Album.new(params[:album])
  @cover = Cover.new(:uploaded_data => params[:cover_file])

  @service = AlbumService.new(@album, @cover)

  respond_to do |format|
    if @service.save
      flash[:notice] = 'Album was successfully created.'
      format.html { redirect_to(@album) }
      format.xml  { render :xml     => @album,
                           :status   => :created,
                           :location => @album }
    else
      format.html { render :action => :new }
      format.xml  { render :xml     => @album.errors,
                           :status => :unprocessable_entity }
    end
  end
end
```

This populates the album-specific fields—name, artist, and so on—into an Album model. Then it assigns the value of the :cover_file parameter (the file data) to the :uploaded_data attribute of the Cover model. This is a virtual attribute that was added to the Cover model when we declared has_attachment. The create action then creates a new AlbumService with the album and cover and attempts to save it.

All the good stuff happens in the AlbumService model. Here's what it looks like:

Uploadimages/app/models/album_service.rb

```ruby
class AlbumService

  attr_reader :album, :cover

  def initialize(album, cover)
    @album = album
    @cover = cover
  end

  def save
    return false unless valid?
    begin
      Album.transaction do
        if @cover.new_record?
          @album.cover.destroy if @album.cover
          @cover.album = @album
          @cover.save!
        end
        @album.save!
        true
      end
    rescue
      false
    end
  end

  def valid?
    @album.valid? && @cover.valid?
  end
end
```

This class looks like an Active Record model: it has a save method and a valid? method. However, it doesn't subclass ActiveRecord::Base. It's just a plain ol' Ruby class that manages two Active Record models. You can name these methods however you like. I just find it easier to use conventional names.

The save method needs to save both the album and its cover. Now, attachment_fu hooks into the life cycle of the Cover model to do lots of special processing. For example, the thumbnails are automatically generated after the cover has been saved. Things can go wrong when a cover is being saved, in which case attachment_fu will raise an exception. We handle that by wrapping the saving of both the cover and the album in a transaction block. If an exception is raised in the block, all

the database operations are rolled back. That way, we don't end up with
one model being saved without the other.

Next, we need to deal with updating an album and potentially its cover
image. The form for updating an album looks just like the form for
creating one. There's nothing new there. However, the update action of
the AlbumsController needs to use the AlbumService, too.

UploadImages/app/controllers/albums_controller.rb

```ruby
def update
  @album = Album.find(params[:id])
  @cover = @album.cover

  @service = AlbumService.new(@album, @cover)

  respond_to do |format|
    if @service.update_attributes(params[:album], params[:cover_file])
      flash[:notice] = 'Album was successfully updated.'
      format.html { redirect_to @album }
      format.xml  { head :ok }
    else
      @cover = @service.cover
      format.html { render :action => :edit }
      format.xml  { render :xml     => @album.errors,
                            :status => :unprocessable_entity }
    end
  end
end
```

The update action starts by creating an AlbumService for the album
we're editing and its current cover. Then it simply throws the album
form parameters, including the :cover_file parameter, into the AlbumSer-
vice#update_attributes method. Here's what that method looks like:

UploadImages/app/models/album_service.rb

```ruby
def update_attributes(album_attributes, cover_file)
  @album.attributes = album_attributes
  unless cover_file.blank?
    @cover = Cover.new(:uploaded_data => cover_file)
  end
  save
end
```

When we're editing an album, we may want to keep its existing cover
image by not choosing a new file on the edit form. Then, when update_
attributes is called, the cover_file parameter will be blank. In that case,
the save method simply saves the album and leaves its current cover
intact.

However, we may want to change an album's cover by uploading a new cover image file. In that case, the value of the cover_file parameter will reference the file data when update_attributes is called. Because it's not blank, a new @cover object is created with the file data. Then, when save is called, it'll destroy the album's existing cover (and its thumbnails) and save the new cover (and generate its thumbnails). All this happens within a transaction, just as it does when creating a new album.

OK, now we're off to the races: we select a cover file using the Choose File button on the form, the cover image is uploaded to a file on our server, and the file metadata is stored in the covers database table. We end up with four rows in the covers table: one for the resized original (parent) image and one for each of the three thumbnails. The thumbnails have their parent_id column set to the primary key of the cover from which they were created.

Each image also has a base filename recorded in the covers table. The public_filename method uses this information to give us the public path to the resized original file. Let's inspect our images in the console:

```
$ ruby script/console
>> c = Cover.find :first
=> #<Cover id: 1, album_id: 1, parent_id: nil, size: 72620, width: 201,
    height: 201, content_type: "image/png",
    filename: "foo_fighters.png", thumbnail: nil>
>> c.public_filename
=> "/covers/0000/0001/foo_fighters.png"
```

The public_filename method also takes the name of a thumbnail we used in the :thumbnails hash:

```
>> c.public_filename(:small)
=> "/covers/0000/0001/foo_fighters_small.png"
>> c.public_filename(:medium)
=> "/covers/0000/0001/foo_fighters_medium.png"
>> c.public_filename(:large)
=> "/covers/0000/0001/foo_fighters_large.png"
```

Since we're using the filesystem as storage, our cover image files are stored relative to the RAILS_ROOT/public directory on our server.[4] The thumbnail files have a suffix that corresponds to the name we used in the :thumbnails hash.

---

4. The default path prefix for the filesystem is public/#{table_name}. This can be changed by using the :path_prefix option on the has_attachment method.

Finally, let's write a view helper so we can easily show covers in various sizes (and linked to the full-size image) around our jukebox site:

UploadImages/app/helpers/albums_helper.rb

```ruby
module AlbumsHelper
  def cover_for(album, size = :medium)
    if album.cover
      cover_image = album.cover.public_filename(size)
      link_to image_tag(cover_image), album.cover.public_filename
    else
      image_tag("blank-cover-#{size}.png")
    end
  end
end
```

Then we can use the cover_for helper to list all the albums and their covers:

UploadImages/app/views/albums/index.html.erb

```erb
<table>
<% for album in @albums -%>
  <tr>
    <td><%= cover_for(album, :large) %></td>
    <td>
      <strong><%= link_to album.title, album %></strong>
      by <%= h album.artist %>
    </td>
  </tr>
<% end -%>
</table>
```

Now we can create and update an album and its cover image. The creation step was fairly straightforward, but dealing with two models had the added complication of using a transaction. The update step added a bit more degree of difficulty in deleting the old cover images. By introducing an AlbumService class, we were able to encapsulate this complexity in one place and keep the controller clean. If other controllers need to manipulate covers, they can reuse AlbumService to do the heavy lifting.

Discussion

If you want to customize the validations that attachment_fu performs, you can write you own custom validations rather than using the validates_as_attachment convenience method.

For example, if you wanted to completely change the error messages, you could remove the call to validates_as_attachment in the Cover model and add the following:

`UploadImages/app/models/cover.rb`

```ruby
validate :attachment_valid?

def attachment_valid?
  unless self.filename
    errors.add_to_base("No cover image file was selected")
  end

  content_type = attachment_options[:content_type]
  unless content_type.nil? || content_type.include?(self.content_type)
    errors.add_to_base("Cover image content type must an image")
  end

  size = attachment_options[:size]
  unless size.nil? || size.include?(self.size)
    errors.add_to_base("Cover image must be 500-KB or less")
  end
end
```

Also See

Although the attachment_fu plug-in provides support for storing attachments on Amazon's S3 web service, I've found it better to do that in an out-of-band process. See Recipe 42, *Send Lightweight Messages*, on page 233 for how to hook into attachment_fu and upload files to S3 using a queue server.

Snack Recipe 76, *Preserve Files Between Deployments*, on page 399 describes how to keep uploaded images stored on the filesystem from disappearing between deployments.

Decouple JavaScript with Low Pro

By Adam Keys (http://therealadam.com)
Adam is a connoisseur of code, dachshunds, and existentialism jokes.

Problem

Rails gives you some great shortcuts that make building interactive web applications with Ajax really easy. However, the Rails Ajax helpers leave something to be desired when it comes to keeping the JavaScript unobtrusive.

How do you structure your JavaScript logic and easily apply it to your pages while at the same time supporting users who have JavaScript turned off?

Ingredients

• The Low Pro[1] JavaScript library (lowpro.js) in your public/javascripts directory

Solution

It turns out that abandoning Rails' Ajax helpers in favor of using Java-Script directly is pretty easy. And it's doubly so if we use Dan Webb's fantastic Low Pro library.

Low Pro lets us write JavaScript *behaviors* that handle the various events an HTML element can emit—events such as onclick, keydown, and onsubmit. We can then bind those behaviors to specific HTML elements in our page using CSS selectors. It is a delightful way to incrementally add the interactive bits of our application, so let's get right to it.

Let's say we've built a lovely little Rails application for tracking our friends and all their contact information. It doesn't have any JavaScript and thus feels sort of bland, so let's add some fanciness to it.

---

1. http://lowprojs.com

Before we get started, we need to include the Low Pro JavaScript library. The trick here is that it must be loaded *before* our application-specific JavaScript but *after* the Prototype library. For this reason, we can't use the default JavaScript includes. Instead, we'll include the JavaScript files in this order:

Lowpro/app/views/layouts/application.html.erb

```
<%= javascript_include_tag 'prototype', 'effects',
                           'lowpro', 'application' %>
```

The first thing we'll do is take the somewhat boring index page and add some interactivity to it. When we list our friends, the generated HTML looks like this:

```
<ul class="people_list">
  <li>
    <a href="/people/1">Adam Keys</a>
    <span class="preview">http://therealadam.com</span>
  </li>
</ul>
```

We want to change this so that the person's URL is shown only when we mouse over the person. Now, we could add the JavaScript code directly into the HTML, but we'd rather treat the JavaScript as a separate layer on top of our already working application.

We're already giving our HTML elements id and class attributes, so we'll just start attaching behaviors to them. To do that, first we add a simple Low Pro behavior in our application.js file:

```
var PeoplePreview = Behavior.create({

  initialize: function() {
    this.element.down('.preview').hide();
  },

  onmouseover: function() {
    this.element.down('.preview').show();
  },

  onmouseout: function() {
    this.element.down('.preview').hide();
  }
});
```

Let's take this apart. We're creating a Low Pro behavior by calling Behavior.create. Think of this like a method that creates an object for us, because that is exactly what it does. The methods on the object we pass can have any name we like, but since we're writing a behavior, we should probably throw in some event handlers like onmouseover and onmouseout. If we specify an initialize method, it gets called when the behavior is attached to an actual element.

Within the methods of our behavior, this refers to our behavior object. The Low Pro library arranges for this.element to refer to the element to which this behavior was attached. With the element in hand, we can proceed to do anything we can do in Prototype, such as calling hide() or show() on an element.

Next, in our application.js file, we'll attach the behavior to all the HTML elements matching the CSS selector .people_list li like so:

```
Event.addBehavior({
  '.people_list li': PeoplePreview
});
```

That's all there is to it. The behavior is attached as soon as the DOM is loaded, unobtrusively, so there's no need to call this JavaScript from our views.

Before we proceed, let's clean up what we already have. Instead of inlining the CSS class to use for previews, we can pass it in to the behavior when it's created. This lets us hide the incantation for finding the element behind an accessor so our code is nice and DRY. Here's the cleaned-up version:

`Lowpro/public/javascripts/application.js`

```
var PeoplePreview = Behavior.create({
  preview: null,

  initialize: function(preview_selector) {
    this.preview = this.element.down(preview_selector);
    this.preview.hide();
  },

  onmouseover: function() {
    this.preview.show();
  },

  onmouseout: function() {
    this.preview.hide();
  }
});
```

It's a few lines longer, but changing the code will prove much easier in the future. Note that we can create instance variables if we want, and that arguments to PeoplePreview() are passed into the behavior when it's created.

Then we'll close the loop by updating our behavior to pass in the CSS class for our preview:

```
Event.addBehavior({
  '.people_list li': PeoplePreview('.preview')
});
```

Now let's make deleting a person more interesting. What we'll do is intercept clicks on the Delete button and prompt the user for confirmation. To the user, this will look just like Rails' built-in helper for confirming an action. However, our implementation will not insert JavaScript into the HTML we render, giving us a nice little unobtrusive implementation.

First, we'll change our view to render our own form instead of using the button_to helper. Our Delete button now looks like this:

Lowpro/app/views/people/_person.html.erb

```
<% form_for person,
            :html => {:class => dom_class(person, 'delete'),
                      :method => :delete} do |f| -%>
  <p>
    <%= f.submit "Delete #{person.name}" %>
  </p>
<% end -%>
```

Note that we use the dom_class helper to generate a delete_person class for our delete form. We also have to set the HTML method to :delete to let Rails know we want to emulate a DELETE request. Now that our form is in place, we'll write a behavior for it:

Lowpro/public/javascripts/application.js

```
var DeleteConfirmation = Behavior.create({
  onsubmit: function(evt) {
    if (confirm('Really delete this item?')) {
      return true; // Allow the delete
    } else {
      evt.stop();
      return false;
    }
  }
});
```

This behavior is a little different from our first in that we're declaring our handler, onsubmit, as taking an event parameter. (All event handlers are passed this event object; we just didn't need it in the first example.) This object contains information on the HTML element that the event occurred on, mouse coordinates at the time of the event, any key-press events, and other information. Prototype kindly wraps this all up for us so we can just treat it as an Event object, rather than the various unfriendly objects browsers would pass to us.

The crux of our behavior is prompting the user to see whether they *really* want to delete this person. If they click OK, our behavior returns true, and the browser will continue to submit the form. However, if the user clicks Cancel, we stop the event by calling evt.stop() and returning false from our handler. The form is never submitted, and the user's data is safe!

Next, we'll attach this behavior to the entire form. That way we can catch submit events generated by mouse clicks *and* keyboard events (such as the user tabbing through the page or hitting the Submit button). Here are the behaviors we've attached so far in our application.js file:

```
Event.addBehavior({
  '.people_list li': PeoplePreview('.preview'),
  '.delete_person': DeleteConfirmation
});
```

Finally, let's add some unobtrusive Ajax. Right now, when we edit a person, it triggers a full page reload to render the form. We'd like to change the Edit link to issue an Ajax request that slips the edit form into the page behind the scenes. That's where Low Pro's Remote behavior comes in. Using Remote, we just need to specify which links and forms are "remote." The behavior takes care of performing the Ajax requests for us.

Let's see how this works. Here's what the Edit link currently looks like:

Lowpro/app/views/people/_person.html.erb

```
<%= link_to "Edit", edit_person_path(person),
            :class => dom_class(person, 'edit') %>
```

We want to make that link a remote Ajax call, if the user has JavaScript turned on. To do that, we'll add a behavior rule that matches the link with the edit_person class.

Here's our final list of behaviors:

`Lowpro/public/javascripts/application.js`

```
Event.addBehavior.reassignAfterAjax = true;
Event.addBehavior({
  '.people_list li': PeoplePreview('.preview'),
  '.delete_person': DeleteConfirmation,
  '.edit_person': Remote
});
```

The last rule matches our Edit link and attaches the Remote behavior to it. Now, when it's clicked, a new Prototype Ajax.Request object is created that requests the URL specified by our link, /people/1/edit, for example.

Then we'll use RJS to modify the page, in this case placing an edit form in place of the display markup:

`Lowpro/app/views/people/edit.rjs`

```
page[dom_id(@person)].replace_html :partial => "person_form", :object => @person
page[dom_id(@person, 'edit')].visual_effect :highlight
```

At this point, our edit form is in place. When the user submits it, we'd like to use Ajax to send the request and then replace the form with the updated person. The great thing about Remote is that it's really a helper on top of Remote.Link and Remote.Form. So, you can attach Remote to a link or a form, and it will do the right thing.

Since the form we insert into the page has the same CSS class as our link, we don't need another rule to add the behavior. We do, however, need to tell Low Pro to reload all its behavior rules after every Ajax request. We do this before we declare our behavior rules by setting Event.addBehavior.reassignAfterAjax to true. For performance reasons, the author of Low Pro doesn't recommend this for all applications. However, for our little application, it's the simplest way to accomplish what we need.

Now our address book is a lot more interesting, and it still works great for folks who don't have JavaScript enabled. Plus, we don't have JavaScript lurking in our HTML, saving us from long nights tracking down logic. Low Pro makes all that easy. Behaviors give you a great way to get everything working without JavaScript first and then progressively enhance the user experience with Ajax and other JavaScript behaviors.

Also See

We didn't cover things like building composed behaviors or some of the other interesting behaviors that ship with Low Pro. If you're itching to learn more, get yourself to http://lowprojs.com, and dig in!

Format Dates and Times

You want to customize the format of dates and times displayed in your application. The text you see when you convert a Ruby date or time to a string is usually good enough for us programmers but often too impersonal for your average web surfer. You'd like to dress up the text a bit, preferably without fiddling around with the strftime method in every case. Then, when you inevitably change your mind and need to tweak a format that's used on multiple pages of the application, you want to make the change in just one place.

Dates and times are ubiquitous in web applications: the day an article was posted, the last time you logged in, how long you'll have to wait before your Wii order ships, and so on. Rails already includes a few predefined date and time formats to help get you started. You use them by calling the to_s method on a Date or Time object and passing in the name of the format. And if you fancy creating custom formats, you can do that too.

As always, the console is a great place to experiment, so let's go there for some examples. If we want to get the current time in a format that's compatible with our database, we use the :db format:

```
$ ruby script/console
>> Time.now.to_s(:db)
=> "2008-03-04 12:41:44"
```

Or if we want to show today's date in a long format, we use the :long option:

```
>> Date.today.to_s(:long)
=> "March  4, 2008"
```

In addition to :db and :long, Rails includes formats named :short and :rfc822. You can also use the :time format on DateTime objects to just get the time part of the date and time.

Now let's suppose we need to trick out an existing format or, better yet, create a new one altogether. Say, for example, we want to render the time an order was placed using a custom format name, like so:

```
<%= order.placed_at.to_s(:chatty) %>
```

And we want the resulting time formatted like this:

```
03:45 PM MST on November 06, 2007
```

To make that work, we need to register our custom format by adding the :chatty format to the hash of predefined time conversions. We'll put this code in an initializer file to ensure it's automatically loaded. Here's what it looks like:

`buffet/config/initializers/date_time_formats.rb`

```
ActiveSupport::CoreExtensions::Time::Conversions::DATE_FORMATS.merge!(
  :chatty => "%I:%M %p %Z on %B %d, %Y"
)
```

Similarly, we can define custom formats for dates. Suppose we display the date a product will become available in various places in our application. Using a named format means we don't have to remember the formatting details when we're writing the code or reading it. We just have to remember the name of the format:

```
<%= product.available_on.to_s(:weekday) %>
```

This time we need to add the :weekday format to the hash of predefined date conversions:

`buffet/config/initializers/date_time_formats.rb`

```
ActiveSupport::CoreExtensions::Date::Conversions::DATE_FORMATS.merge!(
  :weekday => "%A: %B %d, %Y"
)
```

The resulting date looks like this:

```
Tuesday: November 06, 2007
```

Taking it a step further, we can encapsulate the calls to our formatters inside view helper methods. Here's an example:

```
module ProductsHelper
  def available_on(product)
    product.available_on.to_s(:weekday)
  end
end
```

So now we have more freedom on two axes of change. If we need to change what it means for *any* object to be represented in the weekday format, we modify the value of that format in our initializer file. If we need to specifically change the date format for a product's availability, we modify the view helper method. And that's what being DRY is all about.

Discussion

As a matter of style, consider always defining your own formats that have semantic, rather than format-related, meaning. For example, :short implies "display in this format," whereas using :order_date in your application is more meaningful.

We didn't go into detail about the strftime[1] method. It has a number of single-character directives for formatting dates and times into strings. A few minutes reviewing the documentation (run ri strftime) is, er, time well spent.

---

1. http://ruby-doc.org/core/classes/Time.html#M000297

Support an iPhone Interface

By Ben Smith (http://www.slashdotdash.net)
Ben discovered Ruby on Rails more than two years ago, quickly realizing it was the future for agile web development. Only recently did he start working professionally with Rails after escaping the world of enterprise .NET development.

Problem

You've finally launched that killer web application, and now you want to increase its reach by creating a version optimized for the iPhone. Even though your site may already work perfectly with the iPhone (after all, it's just Safari), the benefits of an iPhone-specific version provide a native feel to your site and tiny transfer sizes to make the site snappy, even on GPRS.

Ingredients

* The iUI library:[1]

  ```
  $ wget http://iui.googlecode.com/files/iui-0.13.tar.gz
  ```

  This recipe was originally baked with version 0.13.

Solution

The iUI framework, based on Joe Hewitt's iPhone navigation work, aims to provide a more iPhone-like experience to web apps. We'll use it as our main ingredient, along with a custom Rails MIME type to send iPhone content to Mobile Safari browsers: the iPhone and iPod Touch.

Before we get started, do yourself a favor and snag a copy of iPhoney.[2] It's an indispensable (and free) tool for aiding the development of an iPhone-specific site.

To focus on the extra steps required to support an iPhone version of an application, we're going to keep the application itself simple. For this example, we'll assume we have a to-do list manager with a standard HTML interface that we want to optimize for the iPhone.

---

1. http://code.google.com/p/iui/
2. http://www.marketcircle.com/iphoney/

First, we'll copy the iUI JavaScript, CSS, and image files to their respective directories in our Rails application:

```
$ cp iui/iui.js public/javascripts/iui.js
$ cp iui/iui.css public/stylesheets/iui.css
$ cp iui/*.png public/images/
```

We also need to change the image URLs in the iui.css style sheet to point to our images directory (for example, url(/images/xxx.png)).

Next, we'll add an iPhone MIME type alias to the config/initializers/mime_types.rb file so that we can set the format for an incoming Rails request:

iPhone/config/initializers/mime_types.rb

```ruby
Mime::Type.register_alias "text/html", :iphone
```

When requests come into our application from an iPhone or iPod Touch (a Mobile Safari device), we need to render special iPhone-specific templates. To do that, we'll need a way to detect requests from Mobile Safari devices. A global before_filter and a couple simple methods will do the trick. We'll add them to ApplicationController:

iPhone/app/controllers/application.rb

```ruby
class ApplicationController < ActionController::Base
  before_filter :adjust_format_for_iphone

  helper_method :iphone_user_agent?

protected

  def adjust_format_for_iphone
    # iPhone sub-domain request
    # request.format = :iphone if iphone_subdomain?

    # Detect from iPhone user-agent
    request.format = :iphone if iphone_user_agent?
  end

  # Request from an iPhone or iPod touch?
  # (Mobile Safari user agent)
  def iphone_user_agent?
    request.env["HTTP_USER_AGENT"] &&
    request.env["HTTP_USER_AGENT"][/(Mobile\/.+Safari)/]
  end

  def iphone_subdomain?
    return request.subdomains.first == "iphone"
  end
end
```

This code uses a before_filter to run the :adjust_format_for_iphone method. We have a couple options here for adjusting the format. We can create an iPhone-specific subdomain[3] (http://iphone.todo.com, for example) and adjust the format when the incoming request comes from that subdomain. Or we can sniff the user agent looking for Mobile Safari devices.[4] In this case, we do that latter in the iphone_user_agent? method. Regardless of the option we use, the important step is to set request.format to :iphone.

Once the request format is set, we'll make sure that the actions in our ListsController handle an iphone format in their respond_to block. For example, here are the index and show actions:

iPhone/app/controllers/lists_controller.rb

```
class ListsController < ApplicationController
  def index
    @lists = List.find(:all)

    respond_to do |format|
      format.html # index.html.erb
      format.iphone # index.iphone.erb
      format.xml  { render :xml => @lists }
    end
  end

  def show
    @list = List.find(params[:id])

    respond_to do |format|
      format.html # show.html.erb
      format.iphone { render :layout => false } # show.iphone.erb
      format.xml  { render :xml => @list }
    end
  end

  # other CRUD actions
end
```

Next, we'll create iPhone-specific view templates and a layout file. When we're responding to iPhone requests, Rails will go looking for templates and layouts ending with .iphone.erb.

_____

3. Recipe 83, *Give Users Their Own Subdomain*, on page 425 describes how to create subdomains.
4. If you're using iPhoney, make sure the user agent is set to iPhone User Agent in the main menu item.

Here's our layout file:

iPhone/app/views/layouts/application.iphone.erb

```
<!DOCTYPE html PUBLIC "-//W3C//DTD XHTML 1.0 Strict//EN"
"http://www.w3.org/TR/xhtml1/DTD/xhtml1-strict.dtd">

<html xmlns="http://www.w3.org/1999/xhtml" xml:lang="en">
<head>
  <meta http-equiv="content-type" content="text/html; charset=utf-8" />
  <meta id="viewport" name="viewport"
        content="width=320; initial-scale=1.0; maximum-scale=1.0;
                 user-scalable=0;" />
  <title>TODO - iPhone version</title>
  <%= stylesheet_link_tag 'iui' %>
  <%= javascript_include_tag 'iui', 'prototype', 'application' %>
</head>
<body>
  <div class="toolbar">
    <h1 id="pageTitle"></h1>
    <a id="backButton" class="button" href="#"></a>
  </div>
  <%= yield %>
</body>
</html>
```

Notice that it's using the iUI JavaScript and style sheet. To take advantage of the iUI styling, we need to make sure to assign the correct element IDs and CSS styles. For example, creating a toolbar div gives us an iPhone toolbar for navigation.

Here's the index template for showing all the to-do lists:

iPhone/app/views/lists/index.iphone.erb

```
<ul title="TODO" selected="true">
  <% for list in @lists -%>
    <li><%= link_to h(list.title), list_path(list) %></li>
  <% end -%>
  <li class="group">Actions</li>
  <li>
    <%= link_to 'Add list', new_list_path %>
  </li>
</ul>
```

The value of the title attribute on the list will get substituted into the pageTitle header in our layout file. Setting selected="true" on an element determines which one is shown first. Standard hyperlinks are loaded using Ajax, and they slide into the view. Links can optionally be prefixed with target="_self" to replace the entire page (external links) or target="_replace" to replace the element with the response (using Ajax).

Finally, we'll need to update the new template to add a new to-do item to a list:

`iPhone/app/views/items/new.iphone.erb`

```
<% form_for(@item, :url => list_item_path(@list, @item),
                   :html => {:class => 'panel',
                             :selected => 'true',
                             :title => 'Add task'}) do |f| -%>
  <fieldset>
    <div class="row">
      <label for="title">Title</label>
      <%= f.text_field :title %>
    </div>
  </fieldset>

  <a class="whiteButton" type="submit" href="#">Add</a>
<% end -%>
```

We can again let iUI do the styling for us. Notice that the form uses the panel CSS class, which is defined by the iUI style sheet. To display a button in the iUI style, we assign the correct CSS class and use a hyperlink with an attribute of type="submit".

Following these iUI styles, we end up with an iPhone-friendly interface!

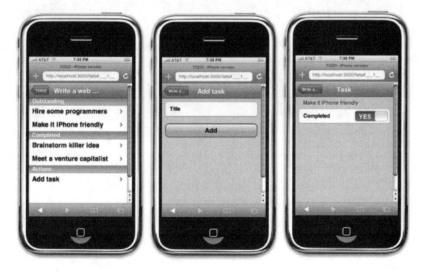

Discussion

We've looked at only the basics for creating an iPhone-optimized site. We haven't made use of the iPhone except as a web browser when it could be used to integrate with other iPhone applications by adding phone, mail, map, and YouTube links.

It's important to remember that iUI will load content using Ajax; thus, you need to render a layout (such as application.iphone.erb) only for the first request or page of your iPhone site. All subsequent requests should use render :layout => false (unless loaded into a new page with target="_replace"). If you experience any weird rendering issues, it's most likely because of this irregularity.

Part IV

Search Recipes

Improve SEO with Dynamic Metatags

By Dan Benjamin (http://hivelogic.com)
Dan is a software developer, interface designer, writer, and business strategist. Dan has more than fifteen years of experience building applications and leading development efforts for companies such as Capgemini, Happy Cog, Halogen Guides, Convergys, MCI, and Vitalsource.

Problem

You want to dynamically, and consistently, set HTML metatags across your app to help search engines guide people to your site.

Solution

A good start is to put relevant titles, descriptions, and keywords on each page for the search engines to snarf up. It doesn't guarantee better rankings, but it sure can't hurt to use the HTML markup the way it was intended. With a few instance variables and simple helpers, we can quickly add metatag consistency in the top of our application layout, like so:

`DynamicMetaTags/app/views/layouts/application.html.erb`

```
<%= page_title %>
<%= meta "description", meta_description %>
<%= meta "keywords", meta_keywords %>
```

Let's visit each helper method in turn.

Search engines love a good title tag, and it helps people using our site, too. So, we'll start by writing the page_title helper to generate an appropriate title for each page. We'll put this and other metatag helpers in our ApplicationHelper module:

`DynamicMetaTags/app/helpers/application_helper.rb`

```
def page_title
  title = @page_title ? "| #{@page_title}" : ''
  %(<title>Bookstore #{title}</title>)
end
```

If we don't want the default page title ("Bookstore," in this case), we just set the @page_title instance variable. It turns out that a layout template has access to all the instance variables that are set in the action and template that renders the page. The template seems like a natural place to set up an HTML page title. If a page is showing a book, we'll set @page_title to the book's title in the show template:

DynamicMetaTags/app/views/books/show.html.erb

```
<% @page_title = @book.title %>
```

Next come the metatags. Let's start with a little helper that takes the metatag name and its content and then generates the actual HTML:

DynamicMetaTags/app/helpers/application_helper.rb

```
def meta(name, content)
  %(<meta name="#{name}" content="#{content} />")
end
```

That lets us write this in our layout file:

```
<%= meta "description", "A Book" %>
```

Except if the current page is showing a book (that is, we have an @book instance variable set), then the description should include the title and author. So, next we write a special helper to generate the description metatag content:

DynamicMetaTags/app/helpers/application_helper.rb

```
def meta_description
  if @book and !@book.new_record?
    "Information about #{@book.title} by #{@book.author}."
  else
    "Books for programmers by programmers"
  end
end
```

Then we can mix the two helpers together to get this:

```
<%= meta "description", meta_description %>
```

Last, but by no means least, let's go for broke by filling in the keywords metatag with some of the book's attributes:

DynamicMetaTags/app/helpers/application_helper.rb

```
def meta_keywords
  if @book and !@book.new_record?
    [@book.title,
     @book.author,
     "#{@book.edition.ordinalize} Edition",
     @book.isbn,
     @book.pubdate.to_s(:month_year)].join(',')
  else
    %w(books programmers).join(',')
  end
end
```

Then back in the layout file it looks like this:

```
<%= meta "keywords", meta_keywords %>
```

With all these helpers in place, here's an example of the HTML generated for a book page:

```
<title>Bookstore | Agile Web Development with Rails</title>
<meta name="description" content="Information about Agile Web Development
                           with Rails by Dave Thomas." />
<meta name="keywords" content="Agile Web Development with Rails,
                   Dave Thomas,2nd Edition,
                   978-0-9776166-3-3,Nov 2007" />
```

Now we can rest easy knowing that all the book pages have meaningful metatags.

Build a Site Map

By Tony Primerano (http://tonycode.com/)
Tony is a system architect at AOL, where he has helped develop a variety of web applications over the past eight years (five of them as a manager). Prior to AOL, Tony developed software for Lockheed Martin's air-traffic control systems.

Problem

Search engines generally discover web pages by crawling through links within a site and from other sites that send it link love. The good news is your site's pages get indexed while you sleep. The bad news is you may have to wait a while for the crawler to stumble upon your site's pages. Of course, you really want search engines to find all your site's important pages and index them in a timely manner.

Solution

Thankfully, there's an easy way to help search engines do a better (faster) job of indexing your site: build a *site map*. A site map is simply an XML file that lists URLs for your site, with some helpful metadata about each URL, so that search engines can more intelligently crawl your site.

Let's suppose our marketing gurus just returned from an off-site strategy meeting (boondoggle) where they came up with this ingenious business model: let people create their own personal home page on our server and slap ads on each page. We make money only if search engines find these pages, and the sooner the better. So, we'll use a site map to help increase our ad revenue.

We could list any resource in our site map, but to keep it simple, we'll use a humble little home page:

```
$ script/generate scaffold homepage title:string content:text
```

To build a site map, we need a couple of basic ingredients: a controller action and a corresponding template that generates the site map XML document.

Let's start by creating the SitemapController:

`Sitemap/app/controllers/sitemap_controller.rb`

```ruby
class SitemapController < ApplicationController

  def sitemap
    @pages = Homepage.find_for_sitemap
    headers["Last-Modified"] = @pages[0].updated_at.httpdate if @pages[0]
    render :layout => false
  end

end
```

Not much to it, really. The Homepage model takes care of fetching all the home pages with the newest page first. We then use the newest page's updated_at time to set the Last-Modified header of the site map. This isn't required, but it's a nice touch because some search engines will send a HEAD request to determine whether they need to read the site map. To keep the controller skinny, we'll tuck the query back in the Homepage model:

`Sitemap/app/models/homepage.rb`

```ruby
class Homepage < ActiveRecord::Base
  def self.find_for_sitemap
    find(:all, :select => 'id, updated_at',
               :order  => 'updated_at DESC',
               :limit  => 50000)
  end
end
```

One thing to keep in mind is that site maps are allowed only to have up to 50,000 entries, and they must be less than 10 megabytes. So, to play it safe, we'll limit the number of home pages using the :limit option and pull back only the data needed in the site map using the :select option.

Next we'll use a small Builder template to generate an XML response in the Sitemap protocol (see http://www.sitemaps.org/protocol.php and https://www.google.com/webmasters/tools/docs/en/protocol.html.):

`Sitemap/app/views/sitemap/sitemap.builder`

```ruby
xml.instruct!
xml.urlset :xmlns => 'http://www.sitemaps.org/schemas/sitemap/0.9' do
  @pages.each do |page|
    xml.url do
      xml.loc homepage_url(page)
      xml.lastmod page.updated_at.xmlschema
    end
  end
end
```

The only required element of each home page entry is its fully qualified URL (<loc>), which the homepage_url method generates. We can help out the search engines a bit more by adding optional elements, such as the <lastmod> element.[1] Site maps expect the date to follow the ISO 8601 format, which the xmlschema method of the Time class gives us.

Finally, we'll add a route to the config/routes.rb file for our site map in the root directory, like so:

`Sitemap/config/routes.rb`

```
map.sitemap 'sitemap.xml', :controller => 'sitemap', :action => 'sitemap'
```

Now if we add some home pages and hit http://localhost:3000/sitemap.xml, we'll get a site map similar to the following:

```
<?xml version="1.0" encoding="UTF-8"?>
<urlset xmlns="http://www.sitemaps.org/schemas/sitemap/0.9">
  <url>
    <loc>http://localhost:3000/homepages/3</loc>
    <lastmod>2008-02-06T22:16:42-05:00</lastmod>
  </url>
  <url>
    <loc>http://localhost:3000/homepages/2</loc>
    <lastmod>2008-02-06T22:08:38-05:00</lastmod>
  </url>
  <url>
    <loc>http://localhost:3000/homepages/1</loc>
    <lastmod>2008-02-06T22:06:39-05:00</lastmod>
  </url>
</urlset>
```

Great, so now how do we tell the search engines where to find our site-map file? Well, we have a few options. First, it's wise to manually submit our site map to search engines that already support site maps. Google[2] and Yahoo[3] currently have web pages where you can inform them of your site map location.

Using these sites will also give us a heads-up if there are any errors in our site map, so it's worth the extra effort to manually submit our site map to one of these search engines.

Once we've done that, there's another option. Unlike the robots.txt file, search engines won't find our site-map file automatically.

---

1. You can also include the optional elements <priority> and <changefreq>. In this example, the content is user generated, so we don't know how often each page is likely to change, and they all have the same priority.
2. https://www.google.com/webmasters/tools/siteoverview
3. https://siteexplorer.search.yahoo.com/submit

But here's a neat trick: we simply add a reference to our site-map file in the robots.txt file, like this:

```
Sitemap: http://your-domain.com/sitemap.xml
```

Finally, there's a third option. Suppose we want to tell a search engine to read our site-map file right away *and* whenever a new home page is created. To do that, we can use the ping protocol. It's just a simple HTTP request, for example:

```
http://google.com/ping?sitemap=http://your-domain.com/sitemap.xml
```

Then if we combine that with a Homepage model observer, we have ourselves an automated site-map pinger:

Sitemap/app/models/homepage_observer.rb
```
require 'net/http'
require 'uri'

class HomepageObserver < ActiveRecord::Observer
  observe Homepage

  include ActionController::UrlWriter
  default_url_options[:host] = 'www.your-domain.com'

  def after_create(homepage)
    Net::HTTP.get('www.google.com',
                  '/ping?sitemap=' + URI.escape(sitemap_url))
  end

end
```

Note that we've used the sitemap_url method to generate the URL to our site-map file. It keeps things nice and dry, but for this to work, we had to include the ActionController::UrlWriter module and set a default host.

We also have to register the observer in the environment file:

Sitemap/config/environment.rb
```
config.active_record.observers = :homepage_observer
```

Now for the disclaimer (you knew this was coming): If you're sending thousands of pings a day, Google may end up blacklisting you. Also, although Google may index your pages within minutes of the ping, it may not update their live indexes right away.

Building a site-map file does not guarantee that your pages will in fact get indexed by search engines, but it's an easy way to give them hints for how best to crawl your site. And that just might give you a leg up on the competition.

Discussion

We could've put the after_create callback code in the Homepage model, but pinging search engines falls outside the primary role of a model. Observers, on the other hand, can link to a model and take on extra responsibilities via callbacks, such as in the after_create method.

If you're lucky enough to have a site with more than 50,000 items (the site-map limit), you'll need to create a siteindex.xml file that has pointers to one or more sitemap.xml files. This also makes it easy to create different site maps for different models. Here's an example, where sitemap.1.xml might have 50,000 entries and sitemap.2.xml may have only 100 entries:

```
<?xml version="1.0" encoding="UTF-8"?>
<sitemapindex xmlns="http://www.sitemaps.org/schemas/sitemap/0.9">
    <sitemap>
        <loc>http://localhost.com:3000/sitemap.1.xml</loc>
        <lastmod>2008-02-06T22:16:42-05:00</lastmod>
    </sitemap>
    <sitemap>
        <loc>http://localhost.com:3000/sitemap.2.xml</loc>
        <lastmod>2008-02-06T22:16:42-05:00</lastmod>
    </sitemap>
</sitemapindex>
```

Adding a Last-Modified header to your show actions can also help search engines. (By default your Rails application will not set this header.) Doing this ensures that when the search engine is given a modified date in the site map, it will match it up against the date it gets when it goes to the URL specified (invoking the show action). This will keep the search engine happy and put you on your way to indexing bliss.

If search engines are actively indexing your site, you may not need to implement an indexer and search of your own. For example, if a user is searching your site for the word *recipes*, the Google query is simply *site:your-domain.com recipes*.

Find Stuff (Quick and Dirty)

By Jason LaPier (http://offtheline.net)
Jason currently works at the University of Oregon as a system administrator and web developer. He is also the lead developer of Pioneers of Aethora, a browser-based role-playing game built on Rails (http://aethora.com). He lives in Portland, Oregon with his wife, Jennifer, and their two long-haired dachshunds.

Problem

You want to search multiple columns in your models for a keyword. You don't have the time (or the need) for a full-blown search engine right now, but you'd like to keep things DRY and leave the door open for one later, if necessary.

Solution

We could use Rail's dynamic finders (for example, Contact.find_by_last_name), but we'd need to know the specific field. The search query would also need to be an exact match for the record. Instead, we want to be able to enter any combination of fields into a search box to find a contact.

Since this is a fairly generic operation and we'll likely want to use it in multiple models, we'll start by writing a Searchable module. It goes in the lib/searchable.rb file:

`Searchable/lib/searchable.rb`

```
module Searchable

  def searchable_by(*column_names)
    @search_columns = []
    [column_names].flatten.each do |name|
      @search_columns << name
    end
  end

  def search(query, fields=nil, options={})
    with_scope :find => {
              :conditions => search_conditions(query, fields) } do
      find :all, options
    end
  end
```

```ruby
  def search_conditions(query, fields=nil)
    return nil if query.blank?
    fields ||= @search_columns

    # split the query by commas as well as spaces, just in case
    words = query.split(",").map(&:split).flatten

    binds = {}      # bind symbols
    or_frags = []   # OR fragments
    count = 1       # to keep count on the symbols and OR fragments

    words.each do |word|
      like_frags = [fields].flatten.map { |f| "LOWER(#{f}) LIKE :word#{count}" }
      or_frags << "(#{like_frags.join(" OR ")})"
      binds["word#{count}".to_sym] = "%#{word.to_s.downcase}%"
      count += 1
    end

    [or_frags.join(" AND "), binds]
  end
end
```

This is fairly straightforward but not very subtle. The `searchable_by` method just flattens out all the columns we want to search into an array. Then, in the `search_conditions` method, we check for each keyword in every field using LIKE, join those LIKEs together with ORs, and then join the chunks of ORs together with ANDs. A hash keeps track of the named bind variable (with a counter to keep it unique) and its corresponding "keyword," with all the OR fragments lined up in an array.[1] Finally, the `search` method uses `with_scope` to scope the find operation with the search conditions.

Next, we need to add these search-related methods to all our Active Record models. We'll do that by using `extend` in an initializer file:

Searchable/config/initializers/core_extensions.rb

```ruby
ActiveRecord::Base.extend Searchable
```

Then we can use the `searchable_by` method in our model, like so:

```ruby
class Contact < ActiveRecord::Base
  searchable_by :first_name, :last_name, :job_title, :department_name
end
```

To find a contact with "Robert" in any of the searchable fields, we just use this:

```ruby
Contact.search('Robert')
```

---

1. Yes, using bind variables ensures that the SQL is sanitized.

As an added bonus, since our search method uses with_scope, we can easily pass in typical find options. For example, to find a contact with "Robert" as the first or last name, with some extra find options, we use this:

```
Contact.search('Robert', [:first_name, :last_name],
  { :limit => 10, :order => 'last_name' })
```

Note that in this example we're assuming there won't be much overlap between first names and last names, because we're actually going to search each field for any of the keywords listed. It works for this example because we're aware of what our data might look like, but it's something to be wary of.

Now that we have our search strategy laid out in a nice DRY structure, it's fairly easy to add other capabilities, such as conditionals and quoted phrases.

Discussion

This simple technique is handy especially for string fields and works with text-based fields as well. String-based fields (for example, the MySQL VARCHAR type) can often be easily indexed directly in the database where appropriate. However, this technique suffers from performance problems when you start searching large text-based fields. Many plug-ins (such as the acts_as_fulltextable plug-in) speed up full-text searches by creating external indexes specifically for that purpose.

Also See

If and when performance becomes a problem, you can simply change the searchable_by declaration in your models to use the equivalent method described in Recipe 25, *Search Text with Ferret*, on page 137; Recipe 27, *Solr-Power Your Search*, on page 151; or Recipe 26, *Ultra-Search with Sphinx*, on page 143.

Search Text with Ferret

By Gregg Pollack and Mike Subelsky (http://www.railsenvy.com, http://www.subelsky.com/)
This recipe is a blend of ideas, code, and text contributed independently by Gregg and Mike. I mixed them together to bring you a tasty dish baked with the freshest ingredients.

Problem

At some point you're bound to need a search field. While single-column searches of more than 1,000 records is easy, things slow down when you start searching millions of records across multiple database tables and columns. All the big boys use optimized search applications, so why not you?

Ingredients

- The ferret gem:

  ```
  $ gem install ferret
  ```

- The acts_as_ferret plug-in:

  ```
  $ script/plugin install ↵
      svn://projects.jkraemer.net/acts_as_ferret/tags/stable
  ```

Solution

Admittedly, there's more than one way to skin this cat, but Ferret[1] is a lightweight, and yet high performance, text search engine derived from the well-known Java Lucene project (which is what all the Java big boys use). The acts_as_ferret plug-in gives us a simple interface so we can start creating complex search indexes before the database melts.

Let's say we're running a job hunting site. People like to search through job postings, if only to remind themselves that they know more acronyms than the recruiters who post the jobs. Here's what our JobPosting model's schema looks like:

`ActsAsFerret/db/migrate/001_create_job_postings.rb`

```ruby
create_table :job_postings do |t|
  t.string :name
  t.text   :requirements, :description
end
```

---

1. http://ferret.davebalmain.com/trac

First, we'll mix the acts_as_ferret goodies into our JobPosting model:

`ActsAsFerret/app/models/job_posting.rb`

```
class JobPosting < ActiveRecord::Base
  acts_as_ferret :fields => [ :name, :description, :requirements ],
                 :remote => true
end
```

Ferret can rapidly search through data because it builds optimized indexes on all search terms. If we don't specify which fields we'd like Ferret to index, it assumes we want to index all fields. This can be expensive, so instead we tell Ferret exactly which fields in our model we want to index (and do searches on).[2]

Take special note of the :remote => true option. If you leave that option out in production, you're in for a lot of pain! Ferret stores its indexes on the filesystem where the server is running, subdivided by environment. (By default, this is RAILS_ROOT/index/development/job_posting, for example.) If you have multiple Rails processes running index operations on that directory, you'll quickly wind up with a corrupted index. Using :remote => true causes your model to connect to a remote Ferret server for index-friendly search operations. Using a remote Ferret server in production *is a must!*

Next, we'll set up the remote Ferret server. The acts_as_ferret plug-in automatically rolled out a configuration file for the remote Ferret server in config/ferret_server.yml:

```
production:
  host: ferret.yourdomain.com
  port: 9010
  pid_file: log/ferret.pid
development:
  host: localhost
  port: 9010
  pid_file: log/ferret.pid
test:
  host: localhost
  port: 9009
  pid_file: log/ferret.pid
```

---

2. You generally want to index only those fields that have varying text content. It doesn't make sense to index fields that could be searched with less-expensive comparison searches that can already be done via Active Record's find method.

By default, the development and test sections are commented out. If acts_as_ferret can't find a configuration for its current environment, then it just won't use a remote server. We don't necessarily *need* a remote server unless we are in production, but it is good to test everything out locally anyway. So, we will go ahead and uncomment all the environments. You may want to change the name of the pid_file for the three environments so that you can run servers for each environment simultaneously.

Then, to start the Ferret server, we just run this:

```
$ script/ferret_server start
```

This will launch a distributed Ruby (dRuby) server that runs as a separate process on the configured port. And if all goes well, we'll see the following:

```
starting ferret server...
```

Now let's run some searches in the console. First, we'll create a couple of job postings:

```
$ ruby script/console
>> JobPosting.create(:name => "Rails Hacker",
             :description => "We have a foosball table",
             :requirements => "At least 10 years of Rails experience")
>> JobPosting.create(:name => "Ruby Hacker",
             :description => "We've seen the light",
             :requirements => "Can you explain what a symbol is?")
```

We have a few search methods at our fingertips, the first of which is find_id_by_contents. Let's use it to search all job postings for hackers:

```
>> total, jobs = JobPosting.find_id_by_contents('hacker')
=> [2, [{:score=>0.029847851023078, :data=>{}, :model=>"JobPosting", :id=>"1"},
        {:score=>0.029847851023078, :data=>{}, :model=>"JobPosting", :id=>"2"}]]
>> total
=> 2
```

We end up with two matches in the total variable, and in the jobs array we get the results with the IDs and search scores for each of them. Using find_id_by_contents is good for times when we don't want to fetch all the matching objects from our database but instead we just want to get their IDs and relevance scores. Then we could selectively pick the best results and how many we'll display.

Now let's say we want to display the job posting information. This is where find_by_contents comes in:

```
>> results = JobPosting.find_by_contents('hacker')
=> #<ActsAsFerret::SearchResults:0x193ab24 @total_pages=1,
   @results=[
     #<JobPosting id: 1, name: "Rails Hacker",
       description: "We have a foosball table",
       requirements: "Must have at least 10 years of Rails experience">,
     #<JobPosting id: 2, name: "Ruby Hacker",
       description: "We've seen the light",
       requirements: "Can you explain what a symbol is?">],
   @per_page=2, @current_page=nil, @total_hits=2>
```

The neat thing about this is the way it pulls in our JobPosting objects. Calling find_by_contents turns around behind the scenes and calls find_id_by_contents to get all the IDs from the search server. Then it issues one database query to select all job postings in that set of IDs.

That gives us everything we need to run efficient searches. All that's left is putting it on the Web. We'll create a search action like this:

> ActsAsFerret/app/controllers/job_postings_controller.rb

```
def search
  @results = JobPosting.find_by_contents(params[:term]).
               sort_by(&:ferret_rank)
end
```

Here we're sorting by ferret_rank, which refers to the sort order Ferret recommends for the hits, based on the relevance score.

Then we'll render our job postings with their scores:

> ActsAsFerret/app/views/job_postings/search.html.erb

```
<h1><%= pluralize(@results.size, 'result') %></h1>

<ul>
<% for job in @results %>
  <li><%= job.ferret_score %>: <%= link_to job.name, job %></li>
<% end %>
</ul>
```

Finally, to stop the remote Ferret server, we use this:

```
$ script/ferret_server stop
```

Now, back to searching for those humorous job postings....

Discussion

The find_id_by_contents and find_by_contents methods take two optional parameters after the query string that can greatly extend the power of your queries: limit and offset. These should look familiar and feel just like your normal Active Record find searches.

Other acts_as_ferret options allow you to search multiple models at once and share indexes among models.

Also See

- If Ferret just isn't a good fit for you or you need more faceted browsing features, see Recipe 26, *Ultra-Search with Sphinx*, on page 143 and Recipe 27, *Solr-Power Your Search*, on page 151.

- The acts_as_searchable plug-in adds full-text searching capabilities based on Hyper Estraier.

- The acts_as_tsearch plug-in gives you access to Postgres's T-search native text–indexing extension.

- The acts_as_fulltextable plug-in gives you easy access to the MySQL full-text search engine.

Ultra-Search with Sphinx

By Ben Smith (http://www.slashdotdash.net)
Ben discovered Ruby on Rails more than two years ago, quickly realizing it was the future for agile web development. Only recently did he start working professionally with Rails after escaping the world of enterprise .NET development.

Problem

You've tried some of the other search solutions, but for one reason or another they aren't what you're looking for. You want a fast, reliable search engine that's easy to use and yet sophisticated enough to let users filter results by category. Oh, and you don't mind compiling some code to get there.

Ingredients

- The Sphinx full-text search engine:

```
$ wget http://www.sphinxsearch.com/downloads/sphinx-<version>.tar.gz
$ tar xvf sphinx-<version>.tar.gz
$ cd sphinx-<version>
$ ./configure && make && sudo make install
```

- The Ultrasphinx plug-in:

```
$ script/plugin install svn://rubyforge.org/var/svn/fauna/ultrasphinx/trunk
```

- The chronic gem:

```
$ gem install chronic
```

- The hpricot gem:

```
$ gem install hpricot
```

- The will_paginate plug-in (optional):

```
$ script/plugin install svn://errtheblog.com/svn/plugins/will_paginate
```

This recipe was originally prepared with Sphinx 0.9.8 and Ultrasphinx 1.6.7.

Solution

Sphinx[1] is a stand-alone, full-text search engine that accesses MySQL or PostgreSQL directly. Some have called it the Nginx of the search world—it's fast and Russian. It was originally created way back in 2001 as a scratch-an-itch solution for improved search quality and speed.

Speaking of itches: Suppose we want to build a searchable interface to the Rails API documentation.[2] We'll import a local copy into our database and feed it to Sphinx so we can quickly build a search browser.

Let's start by configuring the Sphinx server. Don't worry, it'll take only a minute. We just copy the examples/default.base file from the Ultrasphinx plug-in to the config/ultrasphinx directory:

```
$ mkdir config/ultrasphinx
$ cp vendor/plugins/ultrasphinx/examples/default.base ⏎
    config/ultrasphinx/default.base
```

The default configuration is pretty close to what we need but requires a couple of minor tweaks. The searchd section sets up the Sphinx daemon to run on a host and port. We'll update it as follows to make sure the log and PID files end up in the log directory:

```
searchd
{
  address = 0.0.0.0
  port = 3312
  log = log/searchd.log
  query_log = log/query.log
  read_timeout = 5
  max_children = 300
  pid_file = log/searchd.pid
  max_matches = 100000
}
```

Then we'll update the index section to set the index path to the sphinx directory in our Rails app, like so:

```
index {
  path = sphinx
  ...
}
```

---

1. http://www.sphinxsearch.com/
2. http://api.rubyonrails.org

Finally, to improve search accuracy on the Rails API (in HTML format), we'll update the source section to strip HTML:

```
source {
  strip_html = 1
  ...
}
```

Given this base configuration file, we're ready to create our application-specific version:

```
$ rake ultrasphinx:configure
```

This task generates a config/ultrasphinx/development.conf file, which contains the actual SQL query that will be run when we build our database indexes later.

Next, we'll generate the Rails API HTML files locally. To do that, we'll run two Rake tasks: the first to put Rails in the vendor/rails directory and the second to generate the documentation based on that version of Rails:

```
$ rake rails:freeze:gems
$ rake doc:rails
```

This task may take a minute or so to finish, but eventually the generated documentation should end up in the doc/api directory. We'll move it into the public directory so we can serve it up:

```
$ mv doc/api public/
```

Then we'll create a Document model to manage all that good content. Scaffolding gives us a jump-start on the model and migration. Before running the migration, though, we'll need to make sure our database configuration is using MySQL or PostgreSQL. SQLite (the Rails default) doesn't work with Sphinx.

```
$ script/generate scaffold document title:string file_path:string ↩
    category:string content:text
$ rake db:migrate
```

At this point, we're ready to import all the HTML files from the public/api directory into our documents table. To do that, we'll write a Rake task that uses the Hpricot[3] HTML parser to bust through all the documentation and create Document objects.

---

3. http://code.whytheluckystiff.net/hpricot/

Here's what it looks like:

`Sphinx/lib/tasks/rails_api.rake`

```
require 'hpricot'
require 'open-uri'

ENV['RAILS_ENV'] ||= "development"

namespace :rails_api do

  desc "Import the Rails API docs"
  task :import => :environment do
    Dir['public/api/**/*.html'].each do |file|
      doc = Hpricot(open(file))
      title = (doc/"title").text

      category = ''
      if title =~ /\AClass\: /
        category = 'Class'
      elsif title =~ /\AModule\: /
        category = 'Module'
      elsif title =~ /\AFile\: /
        category = 'File'
      end

      Document.create!(:title     => title,
                       :category  => category,
                       :file_path => file,
                       :content   => File.read(file))
    end
  end
end
```

Then, of course, we need to actually run the import task:

```
$ rake rails_api:import
```

Now we have some documents we can start searching. This is where the Ultrasphinx plug-in comes into play. We'll just add the is_indexed method into our Document model, with a list of fields to index:

```
class Document < ActiveRecord::Base
  is_indexed :fields => ['title', 'content']
end
```

Depending on how your models are related, you may also want to include a field via an association using the :include option, restrict the available records with the :conditions option, or even concatenate a number of fields from a single or associated record using the :concatenate key. Go ahead, get crazy with options if it makes you feel better.

Next, we'll build the database indexes (they'll end up in the sphinx directory) and fire up the Sphinx search daemon using a couple Rake tasks:

```
$ rake ultrasphinx:index
$ rake ultrasphinx:daemon:start
```

(If you're into shortcuts, these three Rake tasks can be run together using the ultrasphinx:bootstrap task.)

Now it's time to play. We'll start searching the API in the console using Ultrasphinx's Search class:

```
$ ruby script/console
>> search = Ultrasphinx::Search.new(:query => 'find')
=> #<Ultrasphinx::Search:0x1709da0 ...>
>> search.run
=> #<Ultrasphinx::Search:0x187fba8 ...>
>> search.total_entries
=> 42
>> search.results
=> [#<Document id: 400, title: "File: CHANGELOG",
    file_path: "public/api/files/vendor/rails/activerecord/CHANGELO...",
    category: "File", content: "<?xml...]
```

Hey, this is coming together. Now let's plumb it back into our Rails application. There's nothing new when it comes to creating the search form:

Sphinx/app/views/layouts/application.html.erb

```erb
<% form_tag search_documents_path, :method => :get do -%>
  <div id="search">
    <%= text_field_tag :q, params[:q], :class => 'text' %>
    <%= submit_tag 'Go', :class => 'button' %>
  </div>
<% end -%>
```

It posts to a search action using a GET request so the search results can be easily bookmarked. That means we need to add a route extension in the config/routes.rb file:

```
map.resources :documents, :collection => {:search => :get}
```

The search action simply populates @documents with the results of running the search query (runtime field weighting is used for the title field):

Sphinx/app/controllers/documents_controller.rb

```
def search
  @search = Ultrasphinx::Search.new(:query => params[:q],
                                    :weights => { 'title' => 2.0 },
                                    :per_page => 50)

  @search.run
  @documents = @search.results

  respond_to do |format|
    format.html # search.html.erb
  end
end
```

Here's the template for rendering the search results:

Sphinx/app/views/documents/search.html.erb

```
<h1>Search results for '<%= h params[:q] %>'</h1>
<% unless @documents.empty? -%>
  <ul>
    <% for document in @documents -%>
      <li><%= link_to document.title, "/#{document.file_path}" %></li>
    <% end -%>
  </ul>
  <%= will_paginate @search %>
<% else -%>
  <p>No documents were found!</p>
<% end -%>
```

In the search action, we overrode the default page size (20), so in this case the @documents variable contains the fifty most relevant documents. Yeah, but we want pagination! You got it: the @search variable can be used directly with the will_paginate plug-in's view helper for pagination bliss.

Finally, let's use facets to filter search results by category. To do that, we just specify the facet fields in the model, like so:

Sphinx/app/models/document.rb

```
class Document < ActiveRecord::Base
  is_indexed :fields => ['title', 'content',
    {:field => 'category', :facet => true}]
end
```

We've changed the field configuration, so we need to reconfigure Sphinx and manually restart the daemon (Sphinx won't reload the configuration file automatically).

Then, to run a facet-field search, we specify which facets to include. Using the facets method shows us how our results break out into the categories:

```
$ ruby script/console
>> search  = Ultrasphinx::Search.new(:query => 'error', :facets => ['category'])
>> search.run
>> search.facets
=> {"category"=>{""=>2, "Module"=>22, "Class"=>19, "File"=>7}}
```

Better yet, we can let the user filter the initial results by including the facet in the query string:

```
>> search  = Ultrasphinx::Search.new(:query => 'error category:Module')
>> search.run
>> search.total_entries
=> 22
>> search.results
=> [#<Document id: 71, ...]
```

Last, but by no means least, to stop the Sphinx daemon we use another Rake task:

```
$ rake ultrasphinx:daemon:stop
```

The combination of Sphinx and Ultrasphinx gives you a fast, stable, full-text solution without a lot of fuss. Keep in mind that before you deploy this to a production server, you'll need to configure and index Sphinx for the production environment.

Discussion

What about real-time updates? Well, Sphinx is fast enough at indexing data that you don't really need to worry about observing updates to your models. Instead, you can simply reindex everything at an appropriate interval. Depending upon the data size and expected update frequency, this may be hourly or daily, for example. To rotate the index, just use this:

```
$ rake ultrasphinx:index
```

Ideally, reindexing would be done automatically via a cron job. Here's an example cron entry to reindex every two hours:

```
* */2 * * *  cd /path/to/rails_app/current; ↩
             rake ultrasphinx:index RAILS_ENV=production
```

Ultrasphinx also provides a number of useful bonus features including excerpt highlighting, memcached integration, and query spell check via raspell. The search query string supports boolean operation, parentheses, phrases, and field-specific search, plus ranged queries.

Also See

- If Sphinx just isn't a good fit for you, see Recipe 25, *Search Text with Ferret*, on page 137.

- If you need more faceted browsing features, see Recipe 27, *Solr-Power Your Search*, on the next page.

- The acts_as_sphinx and sphincter plug-ins provide similar functionality for Sphinx searching.

Solr-Power Your Search

By Erik Hatcher (http://code4lib.org/erikhatcher)

Erik, besides lamely playing with rucene and ruby-lucene for years, coauthored *Lucene in Action* (GH04). He speaks passionately around the world on varying technical topics of interest, most recently on this very combination of Solr and Ruby at RailsConf and Ruby-Conf 2007. Erik has worked at the University of Virginia's Applied Research in Patacriticism to shine Solr's light onto the 19th-century world of art and poetry and now works full-time on Lucene and Solr technologies for a start-up company.

Problem

Your content needs to be full-text searchable (not in the puny SQL LIKE %whatever% way), and you want to allow what's called *faceted browsing*[1] to help users narrow down results into meaningful categories. At the same time, you want Active Record creates, updates, and deletes to "just work" with the least amount of, er, work.

Ingredients

- The Java Runtime Environment (JRE) 1.5

- Solr, which can be downloaded from:

  `http://www.apache.org/dyn/closer.cgi/lucene/solr/`

- The solr-ruby gem:[2]

  ```
  $ gem install solr-ruby
  ```

- The acts_as_solr plug-in:

  ```
  $ script/plugin install ↵
      svn://svn.railsfreaks.com/projects/acts_as_solr/trunk
  ```

This recipe was prepared with Solr 1.2 and solr-ruby 0.0.5.

---

1. Faceted browsing is a way of navigating search data by way of various sets of associated attributes. For example, an online bookstore might classify searches for books by subject, publisher, and date published with counts for each of the various attributes.
2. http://wiki.apache.org/solr/solr-ruby

Solution

We're going to pull out the big cooking utensils in this recipe, because we want a solution that is fast and scalable (and we set the bar unreasonably high by calling SQL "puny" in the problem statement).

Solr[3] is an open source search server based on the tried and true Lucene[4] search library. Solr was created for CNET and open sourced to an active community, and it has gained mind share by the bulk of the expert information retrieval folks in the world. Solr runs in a Java servlet container, but don't worry about that—setting it up won't slow us down a bit.

We're going to jump right into a fairly enterprise adventure searching one of the most wonderful human inventions: books. We'll use the example Solr server that comes with the Solr release, which includes a built-in Jetty web server.

After downloading Solr, we first need to create a Solr schema for the book dataset we will be using. Solr's schema.xml file defines the field names, types, and analysis/tokenization configuration. We'll save the original schema for posterity and replace it with a prebuilt schema file on the Web. (Note that the base directory name may vary depending on the version of Solr you downloaded.)

```
$ cd apache-solr-<version>/example/
$ rm -rf solr/data
$ mv solr/conf/schema.xml solr/conf/orig-schema.xml
$ curl http://svn.apache.org/repos/asf/lucene/solr/↩
            trunk/client/ruby/solr-ruby/solr/conf/schema.xml \
                > solr/conf/schema.xml
```

We just replaced Solr's example product data-related schema with a general-purpose schema useful for basic full-text search and faceting. To really become a Solr whiz, you'll want to spend some time understanding Solr's schema configurability, which is well documented as comments in the built-in example schema.xml, as well as on the Solr wiki.[5]

Then we'll go ahead and fire up the Solr server:

```
$ java -jar start.jar
```

---

3. http://lucene.apache.org/solr/
4. http://lucene.apache.org
5. http://wiki.apache.org/solr/SchemaXml

Next, we need to import some book data into the Solr server. I've pre-pared a tab-delimited file of book information exported from my Deli-cious Library.[6] We'll just slurp it down into a local sample_export.txt file:

```
$ curl http://svn.apache.org/repos/asf/lucene/solr/trunk/client/↩
      ruby/solr-ruby/examples/delicious_library/sample_export.txt \
              > sample_export.txt
```

Bringing this data into Solr is mostly a field name mapping exercise. Thankfully, the solr-ruby library provides a handy general-purpose data mapping facility that makes this exercise trivial. We'll write a small Ruby program that imports (indexes) the data in the sample_export.txt file into the running Solr server:

SolrPoweredSearch/script/import_books.rb

```ruby
require 'rubygems'
require 'solr'

delimited_file = 'sample_export.txt'
books = Solr::Importer::DelimitedFileSource.new(delimited_file)

mapping = {
  :id              => :asin,
  :author_text     => :author,
  :title_text      => :fullTitle,
  :publisher_facet => :publisher,
  :category_facet  =>
    Proc.new { |data| data[:genre].split('/').map {|s| s.strip}},
  :year_facet      =>
    Proc.new { |data| data[:published].scan(/\d\d\d\d/)[0] }
}

indexer = Solr::Indexer.new(books, mapping)
indexer.index
```

Notice that we've done some custom mapping here to massage the field names of the original dataset into Solr field names. The mapping hash uses the Solr field names as keys and the original data's field names as values.

We've also had to scrub the genre and published columns a bit. Our origi-nal book data has a single genre field that contains slash-separated val-ues. For example, the original *Rails Recipes* [Fow06] book's genre field is "Object-Oriented Design/Internet" (blame Amazon). What we want, though, is for that field to be split into separate individual category val-ues. So, we've used a Proc to run arbitrary code during the mapping

---

6. Delicious Library is a cool Mac OS X personal book library manager that scans book bar codes from an iSight camera and looks up data through Amazon web services.

process to massage the data. Similarly, we used a Proc to extract the first four consecutive digits from the published field of the original data.

OK, after running that import program, we're ready to do some searching. We'll do that in a good ol' irb session. First we need to connect with the Solr server:

```
$ irb
>> require 'rubygems'
>> require 'solr'

>> solr = Solr::Connection.new('http://localhost:8983/solr')
=> #<Solr::Connection:0x1340b10 ...>
```

Then we'll use the connection to search for some "pragmatic" books:

```
>> response = solr.query('pragmatic')
=> #<Solr::Response::Standard:0x133a0e4 ...>

>> docs = response.hits
=> [{"score"=>1.3403791, "category_facet"=>["Object-Oriented Design", ...
>> docs.size
=> 9
>> docs[0]
=> {"score"=>1.3403791, "category_facet"=>["Object-Oriented Design",
    "Internet"], "author_text"=>["Chad Fowler"], "id"=>"0977616606",
    "publisher_facet"=>["Pragmatic Bookshelf"],
    "title_text"=>["Rails Recipes (Pragmatic Programmers)"],
    "year_facet"=>["2006"]}
```

The resulting docs variable is simply an array of hashes. Each hash is a "document" of book data that matches the search criteria. In this case, we have nine matching books.

Now let's say we're looking for all publishers of pragmatic books, and we're also interested in knowing how many of those books each publisher has published. This time we'll run a *faceted search* on the publisher_facet field:

```
>> response = solr.query('pragmatic',
                :facets => {:fields => ['publisher_facet'], :mincount => 1})
>> docs = response.hits
=> [{"score"=>1.3403791, "category_facet"=>["Object-Oriented Design", ...

>> response.field_facets('publisher_facet')
=> [#<struct Solr::Response::Standard::FacetValue
            name="Pragmatic Bookshelf", value=5>,
        #<struct Solr::Response::Standard::FacetValue
            name="The Pragmatic Programmers", value=3>,
        #<struct Solr::Response::Standard::FacetValue
            name="Addison-Wesley Professional", value=1>]
```

We've used the field_facets method to get the name of each publisher and the count of pragmatic books for that publisher. A custom array data structure is returned to preserve Solr's sort order. That is, rather than returning an array of hashes, it's an array of more sensible structs.

OK, so solr-ruby gives us a Ruby API for interacting with the Solr server. Now, how do we integrate this into our Rails application? Well, if we want the full power of the Solr server, we'd continue building on the solr-ruby API. We'd likely wrap all these calls up into a search method and call it from a search action in one of our Rails controllers, for example. Then, in the search results template we'd style up the collection of "documents" (hashes of data) matching the search criteria that solr-ruby returns. There's even a Rakefile that comes with the solr-ruby gem to convert itself into a Rails plug-in.

However, sometimes you just want to quickly get started using Solr in your Rails app. Specifically, you want to search your Active Record models. That's where the acts_as_solr plug-in comes in. It uses the solr-ruby library as a substrate, which is why it's worth learning at least a little bit about solr-ruby first.

Now we're going to switch gears. Rather than using the imported book data, we'll hook acts_as_solr into a Rails model so we can create and search books transparently from our Rails app. We'll also switch to using the Solr server that comes with the acts_as_solr plug-in.

Let's start with the Rails models. Say we have books and categories in a has_and_belongs_to_many embrace. The only interesting migration file is for the books table. Here are the book columns we can search on:

`SolrPoweredSearch/db/migrate/001_create_books.rb`

```ruby
class CreateBooks < ActiveRecord::Migration

  def self.up
    create_table :books do |t|
      t.string :title, :asin, :author, :publisher
      t.date   :published_date
    end
  end

  def self.down
    drop_table :books
  end
end
```

With the acts_as_solr plug-in installed, we will go ahead and add Solr support to our Book model by (you guessed it) adding a acts_as_solr declaration:

```
class Book < ActiveRecord::Base
  acts_as_solr

  has_and_belongs_to_many :categories
end
```

Now it's time to fire up the Solr server. When we installed the acts_as_solr plug-in, it added a handful of Rake tasks to manage the server. Here it goes:[7]

```
$ rake solr:start
```

The plug-in also dropped a config/solr.yml file that tells Solr which URL and port to run on. Similarly, it tells our Book model how to summon the mighty search server. The default development port is 8982 (it's 8983 for production). With the server started, we can walk right up to it and start submitting searches via the web interface:

```
http://localhost:8982/solr/
```

Next, let's create a new Book and start searching it. We'll start by adding a book and its categories in the console:

```
$ ruby script/console
>> book = Book.new(:title => "Solr Recipes",
                   :published_date => Date.today,
                   :publisher => "See The Light Publishing")
>> book.categories << Category.new(:name => "Yummy")
>> book.categories << Category.new(:name => "Information Retrieval")
>> book.save
```

When save is called, the book information is automatically indexed in the Solr server. Then, still in the console, we can turn around and use the Book.find_by_solr method to find all the books with "recipe" in any column:

```
>> results = Book.find_by_solr('recipe')
=> #<ActsAsSolr::SearchResults:0x2552ea8 ...>

>> results.docs
=> [#<Book id: 1, title: "Solr Recipes", asin: nil, author: nil,
publisher: "See The Light Publishing", published_date: "2008-02-28">]
```

---

7. The solr:start task relies on the fork method, which doesn't work on Windows. One workaround is to change the task to use exec instead of fork.

Notice we searched for "recipe" (singular), and it matched the Book we indexed with "Recipes" (plural) in the title. Thanks to Solr's schema.xml configuration, the text was normalized by lowercasing on both indexing and querying, and stemming was also performed. Stemming reduces words to their simplest form, typically removing the endings. For example, using basic English stemming built into Solr, "pragmatic," "pragmatics," and "pragmatically" all stem to the same form ("pragmat").

Next, we'll run faceted searches on publishers. To do that, we just add a facet for the publisher attribute in the acts_as_solr declaration:

```
class Book < ActiveRecord::Base
  acts_as_solr :facets => [:publisher]

  has_and_belongs_to_many :categories
end
```

Changing the acts_as_solr configuration may require reindexing, which we can do using the rebuild_solr_index method for the model that has changed. Back in the console, we'll rebuild the book index:

```
>> reload!
>> Book.rebuild_solr_index
```

Then we'll run the same query, but this time telling find_by_solr that we're interested in knowing the count of "recipe" books by publisher (using the publisher facet):

```
>> results = Book.find_by_solr("recipe", :facets => {:fields => [:publisher]})
=> #<ActsAsSolr::SearchResults:0x1a46950 ...>
>> results.total
=> 1
>> results.facets
=> {"facet_queries"=>{},
    "facet_fields"=>{"publisher_facet"=>{"See The Light Publishing"=>1}}}
```

The facets method breaks down the results into their respective buckets (facets). Faceted searching like this can help provide a richer browsing experience for users—the kind of drill down through categories that you might see on a shopping site, for example. We could also use Solr's filter query capability to further constrain results by selected facets, like we saw in the solr-ruby example.

Now let's say we want to add the book category and year published as facets. This requires a few magic incantations, but we're feeling lucky.

First, we'll change our Book model to look like this:

SolrPoweredSearch/app/models/book.rb

```
class Book < ActiveRecord::Base
  acts_as_solr :facets => [:publisher, :category, :year],
               :additional_fields => [:category, :year]

  has_and_belongs_to_many :categories

  def category
    categories.collect {|c| c.name }
  end

  def year
    published_date ? published_date.year : nil
  end
end
```

We have added a couple of accessor methods—category and year—to bundle up lower-level data. The :additional_fields option tells acts_as_solr to pull in these "synthetic" fields. We also specify those same field names as facet fields, which causes them to be named and treated differently by Solr.

Unless otherwise specified, all fields are assumed to be text fields (*_t in the acts_as_solr version of the Solr schema). Fields specified in the :facets array are named *_facet in the Solr documents. The acts_as_solr plug-in expends great effort to map field names automatically between Active Record and Solr, but the Solr facet field names leak through acts_as_solr, as shown with the _facet suffixes.

Then, we'll run Book.rebuild_solr_index to rebuild the index and have a look at the new facets in the console:

```
>> reload!
>> Book.rebuild_solr_index
>> results = Book.find_by_solr("solr",
:facets => {:fields => [:category, :year]})
=> #<ActsAsSolr::SearchResults:0x17b883c...>

>> results.facets
=> {"facet_queries"=>{}, "facet_fields"=> {
      "category_facet"=>{"Information Retrieval"=>1, "Yummy"=>1},

    "year_facet"=>{"2008"=>1}}}
```

Finally, all that's left is putting the search results on the Web. That's the easy part. We just create a *search* action like this:

SolrPoweredSearch/app/controllers/books_controller.rb

```ruby
def search
  @results = Book.find_by_solr(params[:q],
              :facets => {:fields => [:publisher]})

  if @results
    @publisher_facet = @results.facets['facet_fields']['publisher_facet']
  end

  respond_to do |format|
    format.html # search.html.erb
  end
end
```

Then we'll render our search results, with a breakdown of how many matching books belong to each publisher, like so:

SolrPoweredSearch/app/views/books/search.html.erb

```erb
<h1>Search results for '<%= h params[:q] %>'</h1>

<strong>Publisher:</strong>
<% @publisher_facet.each do |name, count| -%>
  <%= name %> (<%= count %>)
<% end -%>
<ul>

<% for book in @results.docs -%>
  <li><%= link_to book.title, book %></li>
<% end -%>
</ul>
<% end -%>
```

To stop the Solr server, we use this:

```
$ rake solr:stop
```

When tinkering around, you may want to start with a fresh Solr index. The search index data resides in vendor/plugins/acts_as_solr/solr/solr/data by default. To start with a fresh index, stop Solr, delete that directory, and restart Solr.

We've put together full-text searching *with* faceting in fairly short order, with very little changes to our Active Record models.

Two additional bells and whistles in acts_as_solr are worth mentioning:

- Autocommit control, so batch indexing can commit to Solr at the end instead of for every record
- Multimodel search, allowing full-text searches to span ActiveRecord models

Solr Flare[8] is a Rails plug-in that gives you a general-purpose faceted browser with all the power of Solr. It works well for immediately bringing up a nicely featured findability tool on an instance of Solr. Features include the following:

- Ajax suggest in a full-text search field
- Additive session-based constraints, including example session-based saved searches
- Invertible constraints
- In-place full-text constraint editing
- SIMILE Timeline and Exhibit integration
- Query term highlighting

---

8. http://wiki.apache.org/solr/Flare

Also See

- If running a JVM gives your IT department grief, see Recipe 25, *Search Text with Ferret*, on page 137.

- If Solr just isn't a good fit for you, see Recipe 26, *Ultra-Search with Sphinx*, on page 143.

Part V

Design Recipes

Freshen Up Your Models with Scope

By Dan Manges (http://www.dcmanges.com)
Dan is a passionate programmer who focuses on Ruby and Rails development. He enjoys giving back to the community by working on open source projects. After successfully bringing Rails into the enterprise at JPMorgan Chase, he is now a developer with ThoughtWorks.

Problem

You need to use a similar set of database query conditions in multiple scenarios—and even mix and match them with other conditions—all without creating a duplication nightmare.

Ingredients

* Rails 2.1, but only if you want to use one new feature at the end of the recipe

Solution

Let's say we're designing an online newspaper system. Reporters draft articles and can schedule them to be publicly viewable later. We need to make sure only the finished and ready-for-publish articles are shown on the site. If we try to filter articles in the controller, we end up with this maintenance nightmare:

```ruby
class ArticlesController < ApplicationController
  def index
    @articles = Article.find(:all,
                  :conditions => ["draft = ? AND publish_date <= ?",
                                  false, Time.now])
  end

  def show
    @article = Article.find(params[:id],
                  :conditions => ["draft = ? AND publish_date <= ?",
                                  false, Time.now])
  end
end
```

The first step toward removing the duplication is to push the conditions back into the Article model where they belong. After all, the Article model is the sole authority on what it means for an article to be publicly viewable. This is called *encapsulation*, and it's our best defense against brittle (and ugly) code.

We'll start by refactoring our Article model to look like this:

```
class Article < ActiveRecord::Base

  def self.find_all_publicly_viewable
    find(:all, :conditions => ["draft = ? AND publish_date <= ?",
                               false, Time.now])
  end

  def self.find_publicly_viewable(id)
    find(id, :conditions => ["draft = ? AND publish_date <= ?",
                             false, Time.now])
  end
end
```

All we did was move code around—the details are now hidden behind custom finder methods. It doesn't seem like much progress, but it cleans up our controller considerably:

```
class ArticlesController < ApplicationController

  def index
    @articles = Article.find_all_publicly_viewable
  end

  def show
    @article = Article.find_publicly_viewable(params[:id])
  end
end
```

That's a good start. However, we can do better, and we will! Our Article model still has duplication in the :conditions option. Also, our custom finder methods are currently limited in that we can't pass in additional find options for ordering, limiting, and so on.

Next, we'll refactor to use with_scope to surround a single find method:

```
class Article < ActiveRecord::Base

  def self.find_publicly_viewable(*args)
    with_scope(:find =>
                  {:conditions => ["draft = ? AND publish_date <= ?",
                                   false, Time.now]}) do
      find(*args)
    end
  end
end
```

The with_scope method simply uses the options passed to it to set the scope of the database operations within its block. In other words, it *scopes* the find operation to all publicly viewable articles. That also means we can pass additional options into our custom finder without bothering to merge our options with the default options. For example, now our controller can use the same custom finder, but with different options depending on the action:

```
class ArticlesController < ApplicationController
  def index
    @articles =
      Article.find_publicly_viewable(:all,
                                     :order => 'publish_date DESC')
  end

  def show
    @article = Article.find_publicly_viewable(params[:id])
  end
end
```

Now let's suppose we need to get a count of the total number of publicly viewable articles or calculate the average number of pages (again, just for publicly viewable articles). The find method in the block of with_scope won't work.

Instead, we'll extract the with_scope part of the finder method into its own method so we can reuse it. Here's the revised model:

```
class Article < ActiveRecord::Base

  def self.find_publicly_viewable(*args)
    with_publicly_viewable { find(*args) }
  end

  def self.calculate_publicly_viewable(*args)
    with_publicly_viewable { calculate(*args) }
  end

  def self.with_publicly_viewable
    with_scope(:find =>
                 {:conditions => ["draft = ? AND publish_date <= ?",
                                  false, Time.now]}) do
      yield
    end
  end
end
```

The with_publicly_viewable method just sets the scope and then yields control over to a block. Inside the block, we can run a find or a calculate method and know that the resulting database operations are properly scoped.

Now, to get a count or average of all publicly viewable articles, we'd use this:

```
Article.calculate_publicly_viewable(:count, :all)
Article.calculate_publicly_viewable(:avg, :pages)
```

Things get even more interesting when we start stacking with_scope blocks to mix and match conditions. For example, let's say we have a scope for articles that are premium (you have to log in to read them) in a method called with_premium:

```
def self.with_premium
  with_scope(:find => {:conditions => {:premium => true}}) do
    yield
  end
end
```

To define publicly viewable *and* premium articles, we'll simply stack the scopes, like this:

```
def self.find_publicly_viewable_premium_articles(*args)
  with_publicly_viewable do
    with_premium do
      find(*args)
    end
  end
end
```

Active Record will happily continue merging conditions throughout the chain of with_scope blocks. In other words, if we're applying more than one with_scope block and specifying an option in the find call that was also in a with_scope block, the value in the find wins. All options can be overwritten except for the :conditions option, which merges using an AND operator.

This is a major improvement over the original code! Indeed, it's about as DRY as we can make our model using standard Rails facilities. However, we can further simplify the definition of these scopes using the new named_scope method in Rails 2.1. Here's our revised Article model using named_scope:

```
class Article < ActiveRecord::Base

  named_scope :publicly_viewable,
    lambda { {:conditions => ["draft = ? AND publish_date <= ?",
                              false, Time.now]} }

  named_scope :premium,
              :conditions => {:premium => true}
end
```

The publicly_viewable scope needs to be defined using a lambda because of the dynamic use of time for the publish date. Otherwise, the time would always be set to the time when the Article class was loaded.

Now to find all the publicly viewable or premium articles, we can use class methods that match the named scope:

```
>> Article.publicly_viewable
=> [#<Article id: 1,...]
>> Article.premium
=> [#<Article id: 2,...]
```

To find all publicly viewable *and* premium articles, we can nest the scopes:

```
>> Article.publicly_viewable.premium
=> [#<Article id: 1,...>, #<Article id: 2,...> ]
```

Fresh, clean, and (most important) easy to maintain.

Discussion

Class-level finder methods also work through association proxies. For example, let's say we have a Reporter model that has_many :articles. With the scopes defined in this recipe, we could do this:

```
Reporter.find_by_name('Dan').articles.find_publicly_viewable(:all)
```

It may be tempting to use with_scope in an around_filter in your controller or override the default find to apply this scope. However, these techniques are not recommended because they hide your scope and add unexpected behavior to a method familiar to all Rails developers.

Also See

- Thanks to Chris Wanstrath for the blog post "with_scope with scope."[1]

---

1. http://errtheblog.com/post/41

Create Meaningful Relationships Through Proxies

You find yourself writing lots of custom finder methods to constrain your model associations based on a variety of scenarios—finding all paid registrations for a given event, for example. As a result, your model code has gradually turned into something you're not proud of, and you'd like to clean it up.

Let's walk through a series of code refactorings, starting with the following relationship:

```ruby
class Event < ActiveRecord::Base
  has_many :registrations
end
```

We'd like to add some code that returns just the registrations that have been paid. Where do we put that code? To answer that, let's first dig deeper into the association:

```
$ ruby script/console
>> e = Event.find :first
=> #<Event id: 1...>
>> e.registrations
=> []
>> e.registrations.class
=> Array
```

Here's where things get interesting. The registrations method returns something that looks like an array and acts like an array, but in fact it's *not* an array. It's really an *association proxy* in disguise. Among its other special powers, it lets us call Active Record class methods on the association:

```
>> e.registrations.create(:name => 'Fred', :paid_at => Time.now, :price => 5.00)
=> #<Registration id: 1...>

>> e.registrations.find(:all, :conditions => "paid_at is not null")
=> #<Registration id: 1...>
```

```
>> e.registrations.sum(:price)
=> #<BigDecimal:190c92c,'0.5E1',4(8)>
```

Interestingly, the association is proxying method calls—create, find, and sum—through to the Registration class. But, and here's the really important part, it scopes any database operations to the root object (an event in this case). Here's the SQL generated by the methods we just ran:

```
INSERT INTO `registrations` (`event_id`, `name`, `price`, `paid_at`)
  VALUES(1, 'Fred', '5.0', '2007-12-14 09:42:15')
SELECT * FROM `registrations` WHERE (registrations.event_id = 1
  AND (paid_at is not null))
SELECT sum(price) AS sum_price FROM `registrations`
  WHERE (registrations.event_id = 1)
```

So if we can proxy calls through to the Registration class, then we could put the conditions for finding paid registrations in a class method:

```
class Registration < ActiveRecord::Base
  belongs_to :event

  def self.paid
    find :all, :conditions => "paid_at is not null"
  end
end
```

The paid method lets us find all paid registrations for a specific event:

```
>> e.registrations.paid
=> [#<Registration id: 1...]
```

However, since we're always scoping paid registrations to the event, we'll go ahead and transform the code into a well-named association (paid_registrations) on the Event class itself:

```
class Event < ActiveRecord::Base

  has_many :registrations

  has_many :paid_registrations,
           :class_name => "Registration",
           :conditions => "paid_at is not null"
end
```

It's the same underlying database operation, but the call is a bit more meaningful:

```
>> e.paid_registrations
=> [#<Registration id: 1...]
```

Now we have the code where we want it, but it's inconvenient to maintain two associations: the unpaid and paid registrations. Instead, we will pass a block to the registrations association that defines methods just for that association. Here's the same code, this time using just one association:

```
class Event < ActiveRecord::Base
  has_many :registrations do
    def paid
      find(:all, :conditions => "paid_at is not null")
    end
  end
end
```

Now the call looks like something we've seen before:

```
>> e.registrations.paid
=> [#<Registration id: 1
```

With all design decisions, there's a trade-off. The call to e.registrations caches the results—it'll hit the database only the first time. However, calling e.registrations.paid isn't cached. It falls out of bounds of Active Record default caching. Let's fix that by introducing a reload flag:[1]

```
class Event < ActiveRecord::Base
  has_many :registrations do
    def paid(reload=false)
      @paid_registrations = nil if reload
      @paid_registrations ||= find(:all, :conditions => "paid_at is not null")
    end
  end
end
```

Now we have a simple but effective association proxy cache that we can expire by passing in true. Named associations like this go a long way toward making code more expressive and maintainable.

---

1. Thanks to Mike Mangino for this tip.

Keep Forms DRY and Flexible

By Mike Mangino (http://www.elevatedrails.com)
Mike is the founder of Elevated Rails. He lives in Chicago with his wife, Jen, and their two Samoyeds.

Problem

Your nonview code is DRY and beautiful, but you cringe every time you look at your forms. You have variations of the same few lines all over the place. You want to move your forms to a standards-based layout—and perhaps even change the layout in one place later—but you can't stand the thought of changing all that code.

Solution

It's quick and painless to DRY up our forms using a custom form builder and get lots of other goodies along the way. It turns out we've been using a form builder all along, every time we use form_for, without even knowing it. Here's one:

`KeepFormsDry/app/views/people/new.html.erb`

```erb
<% form_for(@person) do |f| -%>
  <p>
    <%= label :person, :first_name %>
    <%= f.text_field :first_name %>
  </p>
  <p>
    <%= label :person, :last_name %>
    <%= f.text_field :last_name %>
  </p>
  <p>
    <%= label :person, :birthday %>
    <%= f.date_select :birthday %>
  </p>
  <p>
    <%= label :person, :sex %>
    <%= f.select :sex, Person::SEX %>
  </p>
  <p>
    <%= label :person, :bio %>
    <%= f.text_area :bio %>
  </p>
  <p>
    <%= f.submit 'Create' %>
  </p>
<% end -%>
```

The f block parameter that form_for yields is a FormBuilder instance. The default builder doesn't do very much, but it does let us skip referencing the @person object in every form field. Indeed, some duplication has been removed, but there's still quite a bit left.

Let's start drying this up by creating a custom FormBuilder to evaporate all those label and paragraph tags. Here's a simple implementation of our LabelFormBuilder:

KeepFormsDry/lib/label_form_builder.rb

```
class LabelFormBuilder < ActionView::Helpers::FormBuilder

  helpers = field_helpers +
            %w(date_select datetime_select time_select) +
            %w(collection_select select country_select time_zone_select) -
            %w(hidden_field label fields_for)

  helpers.each do |name|
    define_method(name) do |field, *args|
      options = args.last.is_a?(Hash) ? args.pop : {}
      @template.content_tag(:p, label(field) + super)
    end
  end
end
```

This isn't much code, but it does a lot for us: it wraps each form element in a p tag *and* creates an appropriately named label tag for it. Notice that our custom form builder is a subclass of ActionView::Helpers::FormBuilder. This means that our form builder can generate the standard form elements (the fields it's wrapping) simply by calling the super method.

The code starts by building up the helpers variable with the names of form helpers we want to decorate: the default form helpers, plus a few that aren't included in the defaults and minus a few that don't need labels. Then we loop through the helper names and use define_method to create a method for each one. If we wanted to define one of these methods explicitly, it would look like this:

```
def text_field(field, *args)
  @template.content_tag(:p, label(field) + super)
end
```

The @template variable inside our form builder is a reference to the view context in which a form element is being executed.

Calling the content_tag method on the template just slaps in the content (our label and input field) surrounded by a tag (the paragraph). The call to super turns around and calls the regular text_field method to generate a plain input field.

The label method used here is slightly different from the one we used in our original form. Specifically, this version of label doesn't need the object because the form builder already has a reference to the object instance that was passed to the form_for method (the @person). Simply by giving it the field, it'll generate the label tag with an appropriate for attribute (person_first_name, for example).

Now we can reduce our original form to this:

KeepFormsDry/app/views/people/new.html.erb

```
<% form_for(@person, :builder => LabelFormBuilder) do |f| -%>
  <%= f.text_field  :first_name %>
  <%= f.text_field  :last_name %>
  <%= f.date_select :birthday %>
  <%= f.select      :sex, Person::SEX %>
  <%= f.text_area   :bio %>
  <%= f.submit 'Create' %>
<% end -%>
```

That's definitely an improvement, but we lost some flexibility. It would be nice if we could override the field labels, for instance. While we're at it, we might as well add better highlighting of fields and error messages. To do that, we'll leave our LabelFormBuilder and create a new ErrorHandling-FormBuilder:

KeepFormsDry/lib/error_handling_form_builder.rb

```
class ErrorHandlingFormBuilder < ActionView::Helpers::FormBuilder

  helpers = field_helpers +
    %w(date_select datetime_select time_select collection_select) +
    %w(collection_select select country_select time_zone_select) -
    %w(label fields_for)

  helpers.each do |name|
    define_method name do |field, *args|
      options = args.detect {|argument| argument.is_a?(Hash)} || {}
      build_shell(field, options) do
        super
      end
    end
  end
end
```

```ruby
def build_shell(field, options)
  @template.capture do
    locals = {
      :element => yield,
      :label   => label(field, options[:label])
    }
    if has_errors_on?(field)
      locals.merge!(:error => error_message(field, options))
      @template.render :partial => 'forms/field_with_errors',
                       :locals  => locals
    else
      @template.render :partial => 'forms/field',
                       :locals  => locals
    end
  end
end

def error_message(field, options)
  if has_errors_on?(field)
    errors = object.errors.on(field)
    errors.is_a?(Array) ? errors.to_sentence : errors
  else
    ''
  end
end

def has_errors_on?(field)
  !(object.nil? || object.errors.on(field).blank?)
end
end
```

Here we see our friend @template again. This time it's doing a bit more. We're using its render method to render one of two partial templates depending on whether the field being generated has errors. Because of the way we're using @template, instance variables won't be passed to the partials. So, we use the :locals hash to pass in the underlying input field text and its label. The result of rendering the template is captured in the template using the capture method.

This version is quite an improvement now that we've moved our presentation into templates where it belongs. Our form-handling logic is separate from the layout and style of the views. Inside the form field template, we can access the local variables to render the label and form element:

KeepFormsDry/app/views/forms/_field.html.erb

```erb
<p>
  <span class="field_label">
    <%= label %>
  </span>
```

```
<span class="form_field">
  <%= element %>
</span>
</p>
```

The template for a form element with errors is similar but includes the error below each form element and a CSS class for painting it a jarring color:

KeepFormsDry/app/views/forms/_field_with_errors.html.erb

```
<p>
  <span class="field_label">
    <%= label %>
  </span>
  <span class="form_field">
    <%= element %>
    <span class="form_error_message">
      <%= error %>
    </span>
  </span>
</p>
```

Now that our forms are nice and DRY, let's clean up having to constantly specify a :builder parameter when calling form_for. To do that, we'll write a helper method that automatically adds our ErrorHandling-FormBuilder as the default:

KeepFormsDry/app/helpers/application_helper.rb

```
def error_handling_form_for(record_or_name_or_array, *args, &proc)
  options = args.detect { |argument| argument.is_a?(Hash) }
  if options.nil?
    options = {:builder => ErrorHandlingFormBuilder}
    args << options
  end
  options[:builder] = ErrorHandlingFormBuilder unless options.nil?
  form_for(record_or_name_or_array, *args, &proc)
end
```

It took a while to get here, but the reward is a bone-dry form:

KeepFormsDry/app/views/people/new.html.erb

```
<% error_handling_form_for(@person) do |f| -%>
  <%= f.text_field :first_name %>
  <%= f.text_field :last_name, :label => 'Family Name' %>
  <%= f.date_select :birthday %>
  <%= f.select      :sex, Person::SEX %>
  <%= f.text_area  :bio %>
  <%= f.submit 'Create' %>
<% end -%>
```

The internals of a form builder can feel really messy. It's metaprogramming, subclassing, and groveling around in view internals all rolled into one. Thankfully, it's localized to just one file. The big payoff comes when you want to change the way all your forms look (and handle errors). You just tweak the form builder, and away you go!

Discussion

You could easily subclass this form builder if you wanted to have different looks for different forms. You could also dynamically change forms based upon an input option.

Prevent Train Wrecks

By Hugh Bien (http://hughbien.com)
Hugh is a web programmer who likes working with agile languages. He uses Rails at his day job and keeps himself busy with fun side projects.

Problem

ActiveRecord associations make it easy to traverse model relationships; just add one more dot. But go too far, and you often end up with long method chains that access attributes through a relationship:

```
account.subscription.free?
account.subscription.last_payment.overdue?
```

Some people call this object-oriented programming. We call it a train wreck. If the details of how a subscription handles its last payment change, for example, the whole thing goes off the rails. How do you clean this up?

Solution

Let's start by refactoring this method chain:

```
account.subscription.free?
```

One solution is to encapsulate far-reaching attributes in methods that delegate to other models, like so:

```
class Account < ActiveRecord::Base
  has_one :subscription

  def free?
    self.subscription.free?
  end
end
```

But there's an easier way. We'll use the delegate method to keep one object from knowing too much about its related objects. (It's a *shy* object.) Instead of defining a free? method in our Account class, we'll just delegate it straight to the account's subscription.

Delegate/app/models/account.rb

```
class Account < ActiveRecord::Base
  has_one :subscription
  delegate :free?, :to => :subscription
end
```

Then, given an Account object, we can see whether its subscription is free by calling the free? method directly, like so:

```
account.free?
```

If we also wanted to query the account's subscription to see whether it was a paid subscription, we could delegate the paying? method, too.

Delegate/app/models/account.rb

```
class Account < ActiveRecord::Base
  has_one :subscription
  delegate :free?, :paying?, :to => :subscription
end
```

We need to be a tad careful here. It's possible that an account won't have a subscription. In this case, we'll get a NoMethodError of a Nil object (sometimes called the *whiny nil*). We'll prevent this with a little hack:

Delegate/app/models/account.rb

```
delegate :free?, :paying?, :to => "subscription.nil? ? false : subscription"
```

Let's see how that works in the console without a subscription:

```
$ ruby script/console
>> a = Account.new
=> #<Account id: nil ...>
>> a.subscription
=> nil
>> a.free?
=> false
```

If no subscription exists, then free? returns false rather than nil. Then we'll assign a subscription to the account, and it delegates the call as expected:

```
>> a.subscription = Subscription.new(:free => true)
=> #<Subscription id: nil ...>
>> a.free?
=> true
```

Next, let's break up this nasty method chain:

```
account.subscription.last_payment.overdue?
```

In this case, we'll use delegate to traverse through more than one association:

Delegate/app/models/account.rb

```
delegate :overdue?, :to => "subscription.last_payment"
```

This code delegates the overdue? method to the last payment object of the account's subscription.

Using this simple technique, you can reduce unnecessary coupling across your codebase. Instead of having long method chains gumming up the works, you can refactor the code to use expressive, shy methods instead. That way, any changes to how your associations work will require just one change in your call to delegate.

Discussion

If you find yourself using delegate on a frequent basis, it may be a "smell," as they say. Too much delegation leads to tightly coupled clumps of objects that are difficult to reuse, test, and maintain. Before wielding the mighty delegate method, see whether there's a better way to arrange your objects so that they don't have to delegate.

Simplify Controllers with a Presenter

By Jay Fields (http://jayfields.com)
Jay is a software developer and consultant at ThoughtWorks. He has a passion for discovering and maturing innovative solutions. His most recent work has been delivering large enterprise applications utilizing Ruby and Rails. He is also very interested in maturing software design through software testing.

Problem

As your application has grown, so have your controllers. Rather than just orchestrating the work, they've taken on the responsibility of aggregating data from various objects to make life simpler for the views. As a result, maintainability has been compromised. You need to breathe new life into the controllers.

Solution

Imagine we have a controller that's responsible for creating, populating, and saving three models:

`PresenterPattern/app/controllers/orders_controller.rb`

```ruby
class OrdersController < ApplicationController

  def new
    @account    = UserAccount.new
    @address    = Address.new
    @credential = UserCredential.new
  end

  def create
    @account    = UserAccount.new(params[:account])
    @address    = Address.new(params[:address])
    @credential = UserCredential.new(params[:credential])

    account_saved = @account.save
    @address.user_account = @account
    @credential.user_account = @account
    if account_saved && @address.save && @credential.save
      redirect_to thank_you_url
    end
  end
end
```

And to collect all the data in one form, we have the following new.html.erb template:

```
<% form_tag(:action => 'create') do -%>
  <table>
    <tr><td colspan="2">Account Information:</td></tr>
    <tr>
      <td>Name</td>
      <td><%= text_field :account, :name %></td>
    </tr>
    <tr><td colspan="2">Address Information:</td></tr>
    <tr>
      <td>Address Line 1</td>
      <td><%= text_field :address, :line_1 %></td>
    </tr>
    <tr>
      <td>Address Line 2</td>
      <td><%= text_field :address, :line_2 %></td>
    </tr>
    <tr>
      <td>City</td>
      <td><%= text_field :address, :city %></td>
    </tr>
    <tr>
      <td>State</td>
      <td><%= text_field :address, :state %></td>
    </tr>
    <tr>
      <td>Zip Code</td>
      <td><%= text_field :address, :zip_code %></td>
    </tr>
    <tr><td colspan="2">Credential Information:</td></tr>
    <tr>
      <td>Username</td>
      <td><%= text_field :credential, :username %></td>
    </tr>
    <tr>
      <td>Password</td>
      <td><%= text_field :credential, :password %></td>
    </tr>
  </table>
  <%= submit_tag "Complete Order" %>
<% end -%>
```

This works, but the controller is an eyesore. Also, testing individual behaviors, such as that the redirect does not occur if the credential doesn't save correctly, is a bit of a pain.

The solution is to introduce an intermediate object—a *presenter*—to relieve some burden from the controller, while at the same time keeping the view simple.

First, we'll change the controller to be more concise and focused:

```ruby
def new
  @presenter = OrderPresenter.new(params[:presenter])
end

def create
  @presenter = OrderPresenter.new(params[:presenter])
  if @presenter.save
    redirect_to thank_you_url
  end
end
```

Now that we have only one instance variable being set in the controller, we'll change the view to use form_for and change each field's name to include that field's model name:

```erb
<% form_for :presenter,
            :url => {:action => 'create'} do |form| %>
  <table>
    <tr><td colspan="2">Account Information:</td></tr>
    <tr>
      <td>Name</td>
      <td><%= form.text_field :account_name %></td>
    </tr>
    <tr><td colspan="2">Address Information:</td></tr>
    <tr>
      <td>Address Line 1</td>
      <td><%= form.text_field :address_line_1 %></td>
    </tr>
    <tr>
      <td>Address Line 2</td>
      <td><%= form.text_field :address_line_2 %></td>
    </tr>
    <tr>
      <td>City</td>
      <td><%= form.text_field :address_city %></td>
    </tr>
    <tr>
      <td>State</td>
      <td><%= form.text_field :address_state %></td>
    </tr>
    <tr>
      <td>Zip Code</td>
      <td><%= form.text_field :address_zip_code %></td>
    </tr>
    <tr><td colspan="2">Credential Information:</td></tr>
```

```
    <tr>
      <td>Username</td>
      <td><%= form.text_field :credential_username %></td>
    </tr>
    <tr>
      <td>Password</td>
      <td><%= form.text_field :credential_password %></td>
    </tr>
  </table>
  <%= form.submit "Complete Order" %>
<% end %>
```

Then we'll write the OrderPresenter class. It's just a plain ol' Ruby class that encapsulates access to the three models we were previously using in our controller. Here's what it looks like:

PresenterPattern/app/presenters/order_presenter.rb

```
class OrderPresenter

  def initialize(params)
    params.each_pair do |attribute, value|
      self.send :"#{attribute}=", value
    end unless params.nil?
  end

  def account
    @account ||= UserAccount.new
  end

  def address
    @address ||= Address.new
  end

  def credential
    @credential ||= UserCredential.new
  end

  def save
    account_saved = account.save
    address.user_account = account
    credential.user_account = account
    account_saved && address.save && credential.save
  end

  def method_missing(model_attribute, *args)
    model, *method_name = model_attribute.to_s.split("_")
    super unless self.respond_to? model.to_sym
    self.send(model.to_sym).send(method_name.join("_").to_sym, *args)
  end
end
```

There's an interesting trick here. When we pluck the form parameters out of the presenter hash, the parameter keys will have a model name and a corresponding attribute name. So, for example, the value of the account name will be indexed by the account_name key. We need to unravel that so the value is assigned to the name attribute of the account object living inside the presenter.

To do that, we use method_missing to first intercept the call to account_name=, for example, and then forward it on to the account object. It keeps the presenter flexible, but it relies on the careful naming of the form fields.

One last step, and we're home free. We've added the presenter to the app/presenters directory, which Rails doesn't know about. We'll add this directory to the Rails load path in environment.rb:

PresenterPattern/config/environment.rb

```
config.load_paths += %W( #{RAILS_ROOT}/app/presenters )
```

We've lightened the load on our controller and gained a presenter object that aggregates view data and can be tested without any dependencies on Rails.

Discussion

Arguably we should push the logic of the OrderPresenter.save method back into one of the models, preferably wrapped in a transaction.

Part VI

Integration Recipes

Process Credit Card Payments

By Cody Fauser (http://www.codyfauser.com)

Cody lives in Ottawa, Canada, with his lovely wife, Maria. When not hacking on Shopify, he likes traveling, boxing training, yoga, ball hockey, and snowboarding. Cody is the author of *RJS Templates for Rails* (Fau06) and the PeepCode ActiveMerchant PDF, and he is currently working on the upcoming book *Rails in a Nutshell* for O'Reilly.

Problem

You have your shiny new Rails application ready to launch, with hundreds of excited beta testers ready to whip out their credit cards. There is just one small thing missing: a way for your customers to make payments.

To make matters worse, your customers will be making payments of different amounts each time, and you don't want them to have to punch in their credit card information for every transaction. You also don't want to be tied down to any particular payment gateway's implementation of a secure credit card storage system.

Instead, you want to create a simple yet flexible method of charging credit cards that is independent of any particular payment gateway provider and avoids the complexity of integrating a billing system into your existing application.

Ingredients

- The ActiveMerchant plug-in:[1]

  ```
  $ script/plugin install ↩
      http://activemerchant.googlecode.com/svn/trunk/active_merchant
  ```

---

1. http://www.activemerchant.org/

> **Solution**

A flexible credit card server can be quickly and easily created using Active Resource along with ActiveMerchant. ActiveMerchant is a payment gateway library that provides a common API to more than thirty payment gateways worldwide. It was originally extracted from Shopify[2] in 2005 by Tobias Lütke.

We're going to develop two applications: a card server and a simple card client. The card server will securely store cardholder information and allow purchases to be made on the cards. The card client will allow us to store credit cards on the card server and also make purchases on the stored cards. The credit card number will be secured using the U.S. government-standard AES encryption. Any attacker will need to penetrate both the card server and the card client in order to decrypt the credit card numbers.

Let's start with a fresh card_server application that has the ActiveMerchant plug-in installed. ActiveMerchant requires a bit of configuration to ensure that payment requests are sent to the appropriate payment gateway server depending on the environment. When we're doing development or testing, payment requests should be routed to the payment gateway's test server. We'll add the following configuration code to the config/environments/development.rb and config/environments/test.rb files:

```
config.after_initialize do
  ActiveMerchant::Billing::Base.mode = :test
end
```

When we're in production, payment requests should go to the payment gateway's production (live) server. We'll add the following to the config/environments/production.rb file:

```
config.after_initialize do
  ActiveMerchant::Billing::Base.mode = :production
end
```

Now that ActiveMerchant has been installed and configured, we'll generate the CreditCard resource for the application:

```
$ script/generate resource credit_card first_name:string ↩
    last_name:string data:binary salt:binary month:integer ↩
    year:integer last_digits:string brand:string
```

---

2. http://shopify.com

The CreditCard resource will securely store a customer's credit card information. This will simplify the client application because the charging of customer credit cards is completely abstracted. All the client application has to do is store the credit card IDs and then later charge them by creating purchases on the card server.

Next, we'll generate the Purchase resource:

```
$ script/generate resource purchase credit_card_id:integer ↵
  amount:decimal order:string description:string reference:string ↵
  message:string receipt:text test:boolean
```

The Purchase resource will interact with ActiveMerchant to charge credit cards and store the transaction information returned from the payment gateway for successful purchases.

We need to make one small modification to the generated migration file (db/migrate/002_create_purchases.rb) to set the desired precision and scale of the amount column.

The precision determines the total number of decimal digits that can be stored, and the scale specifies the number of decimals allowed. So, we'll change the amount column definition to include the following precision and scale:

ActiveMerchant/card_server/db/migrate/002_create_purchases.rb

```
t.decimal :amount, :precision => 8, :scale => 2
```

Then we'll run the migrations:

```
$ rake db:migrate
```

Now we're ready to start adding business logic to the CreditCard and Purchase resources to perform the actual charging of credit cards.

For starters, we need a means to use symmetric cryptography to encrypt and decrypt credit card numbers. We'll put that in an Encryption module in the app/models/encryption.rb file. (We could use acts_as_secure (see Recipe 67, *Encrypt Sensitive Data*, on page 361), but in this recipe we do the encryption manually.)

ActiveMerchant/card_server/app/models/encryption.rb

```ruby
module Encryption
  mattr_accessor :algorithm
  self.algorithm = 'aes-256-cbc'

  def encrypt(data, password, salt)
    cipher = OpenSSL::Cipher::Cipher.new(algorithm)
    cipher.encrypt
    cipher.pkcs5_keyivgen(password, salt)
    encrypted_data = cipher.update(data)
    encrypted_data << cipher.final
  end

  def decrypt(encrypted_data, password, salt)
    cipher = OpenSSL::Cipher::Cipher.new(algorithm)
    cipher.decrypt
    cipher.pkcs5_keyivgen(password, salt)
    data = cipher.update(encrypted_data)
    data << cipher.final
  end
end
```

The encrypt method accepts the data to be encrypted, the encryption password, and a salt. The data to be encrypted will be a credit card number, but it could be any data. The encryption password is the secret needed to decrypt the data. The salt is a randomly generated eight-octet string that makes recovering the password from the cipher text even more difficult than normal (which is more or less impossible).

The encrypt method creates a new instance of the chosen cipher. The AES block cipher has a 256-bit key and uses the CBC block cipher mode. Since block ciphers[3] encrypt only fixed-size blocks, the block cipher mode is the algorithm used for encrypting data that isn't exactly one block in size. The cipher is then initialized, and the data to be encrypted is added to the cipher. Finally, the encrypted data is returned by the method as a Base64-encoded string.

The decrypt method essentially does the reverse of the encrypt method. The same password and salt used to encrypt the data are used to decrypt the encrypted data. Finally, the original unencrypted string is returned by the method as a binary string.

---

3. For more information on block ciphers, see *Practical Cryptography* [FS03].

Next, we'll mix this Encryption module into our CreditCard model. We'll also include the CreditCardMethods module to pick up a few ActiveMerchant convenience methods for performing validations. Here's the full CreditCard implementation:

`ActiveMerchant/card_server/app/models/credit_card.rb`

```ruby
class CreditCard < ActiveRecord::Base
  include Encryption, ActiveMerchant::Billing::CreditCardMethods

  has_many :purchases
  cattr_accessor :password
  attr_accessor :number

  def verification_value?() false end

  def to_xml(options = {})
    super options.merge(:except => [:data, :salt])
  end

  def encrypt_number
    self.data = encrypt(number, password, salt)
  end

  def decrypt_number
    self.number = decrypt(data, password, salt)
  end

  private

  before_create :store_last_digits, :generate_salt, :encrypt_number

  def store_last_digits
    self.last_digits = self.class.last_digits(number)
  end

  def generate_salt
    self.salt = [rand(2**64 - 1)].pack("Q")
  end

  def validate
    errors.add(:year, "is invalid") unless valid_expiry_year?(year)
    errors.add(:month, "is invalid") unless valid_month?(month)
    errors.add(:number, "is invalid") unless self.class.valid_number?(number)
    if password.blank?
      errors.add_to_base("Unable to encrypt or decrypt data without password")
    end
  end

  validates_presence_of :first_name, :last_name, :brand
end
```

The verification_value? method is used by the ActiveMerchant payment gateways to check whether a CVV2 code has been provided. Since we're storing cardholder information—and it's forbidden by the Payment Card Industry Data Security Standard to store CVV2 codes—this will always be false.

The encrypt_number and decrypt_number methods simply delegate their work to the encrypt and decrypt methods in the Encryption module. The result of calling those methods is stored in the CreditCard object's attributes. The password that's required to encrypt and decrypt the card information is set with the CreditCard.password class accessor. This was done because the password is not stored in the application. The password will be provided by the client application and only temporarily stored in the class accessor, using an around_filter, during each request.

We're using two before_create callback methods to automatically generate a random salt and encrypt the card number before the CreditCard object is inserted into the database. The generate_salt method generates a salt in the format the Encryption module requires: an eight-octet byte string. The salt does not need to be kept secret, because its purpose is to make it harder to discover the password from the encrypted cipher text.

The client we'll be creating for the application will be an Active Resource client that consumes the card server's services through its XML API. We don't want to return the encrypted credit card data or the salt to the client application, so we override to_xml to exclude the data from the XML representation of the card.

The CreditCard class also defines a third before_create callback method, store_last_digits, to store the last four digits of the card number for display purposes. The last_digits class method is provided by the CreditCardMethods module.

Lastly, we have validations that ensure the credit card information provided by the client application is valid. The validations for the year, month, and number are provided by the CreditCardMethods module. The password is required, but the error message is added to the base because the password will be sent in the request headers from the client Active Resource application.

That takes care of the CreditCard class. Next we'll add the ability to charge stored credit cards by implementing the Purchase resource.

It goes in the app/models/purchase.rb file and looks like this:

ActiveMerchant/card_server/app/models/purchase.rb

```ruby
class Purchase < ActiveRecord::Base
  serialize :receipt
  belongs_to :credit_card

  def amount_in_cents
    (amount.round(2) * 100).to_i
  end

  private
  def charge_credit_card
    credit_card.decrypt_number

    response = gateway.purchase(amount_in_cents, credit_card,
                  :order_id => order,
                  :description => description
                )

    self.test = response.test?
    self.reference = response.authorization
    self.message = response.message
    self.receipt = response.params

    if !response.success?
      errors.add_to_base(message)
      return false
    end
  end

  def gateway
    @gateway ||= ActiveMerchant::Billing::BraintreeGateway.
                    new(:login => 'demo', :password => 'password')
  end

  before_create :charge_credit_card
  validates_presence_of :amount, :description, :order, :credit_card_id
end
```

The Purchase model really does only one thing: charge credit cards. We want this to happen when our client application creates a new Purchase with the amount, description, order reference, and credit card identifier. To do that, we've used a before_create callback to invoke the charge_credit_card method.

First, the charge_credit_card method decrypts the credit card number of the associated CreditCard object. This object must be present because the Purchase validates the presence of the credit_card_id attribute.

Next, the credit card is charged using the ActiveMerchant Braintree (http://www.braintreepaymentsolutions.com/) payment gateway. (Your choice of ActiveMerchant payment gateway could be substituted for the BraintreeGateway.) The gateway performs the purchase by passing in the amount_in_cents of the order, the CreditCard object, the order reference, and the description of the purchase.

The ActiveMerchant gateway returns an ActiveMerchant::Billing::Response object with all the details of the transaction. The details of the response are stored in the Purchase object for later reference. The reference attribute of the Purchase model is the transaction authorization returned by the payment gateway.

The reference is required in order to perform any future reference transactions, such as voiding the payment. The receipt contains a serialized hash of all parameters returned by the payment gateway. Recording all the returned response parameters is good for keeping a complete history of the transaction and for debugging purposes.

Finally, since we've decided to store only successful transactions to the database, we check whether the purchase was successful. If so, we allow the callback to complete and end up storing the purchase to the database. If the purchase was unsuccessful, we halt the callback chain by adding the message returned from the payment gateway to the errors collection.

With our models complete, we'll now move on to implementing the RESTful controllers that will give our Active Resource client application access to the card server. These controllers are really simple—we're going to implement only the create action because that's all we need!

First we need to add a global around filter in the ApplicationController that sets the encryption password on the CreditCard class for the duration of the request.

ActiveMerchant/card_server/app/controllers/application.rb

```
class ApplicationController < ActionController::Base
  around_filter :set_encryption_password

  private

  def set_encryption_password
    if request.headers['HTTP_X_PASSWORD'].blank?
      raise StandardError, "No password was provided"
    end
```

```
  begin
    CreditCard.password = request.headers['HTTP_X_PASSWORD']
    yield
  ensure
    CreditCard.password = nil
  end
end

end
```

If the HTTP_X_PASSWORD header is missing, then a StandardError will be raised, which causes a 500 error to be returned to the client. If the password has been provided, then it will be used for the duration of the request as the password for encrypting and decrypting credit card data.

Next, in the CreditCardsController, we'll define a standard RESTful create action:

```
ActiveMerchant/card_server/app/controllers/credit_cards_controller.rb
class CreditCardsController < ApplicationController

  filter_parameter_logging :credit_card

  def create
    @credit_card = CreditCard.new(params[:credit_card])

    respond_to do |format|
      if @credit_card.save
        format.xml { render :xml      => @credit_card,
                            :status   => :created,
                            :location => @credit_card }
      else
        format.xml { render :xml      => @credit_card.errors,
                            :status => :unprocessable_entity }
      end
    end
  end

end
```

It's important to note that we need to use filter_parameter_logging to filter the credit card POST parameters. Otherwise, credit card numbers will end up in our log files.

Likewise, we'll add a create action to the PurchasesController:

ActiveMerchant/card_server/app/controllers/purchases_controller.rb

```ruby
class PurchasesController < ApplicationController

  def create
    @purchase = Purchase.new(params[:purchase])

    respond_to do |format|
      if @purchase.save
        format.xml { render :xml     => @purchase,
                            :status   => :created,
                            :location => @purchase }
      else
        format.xml { render :xml    => @purchase.errors,
                            :status => :unprocessable_entity }
      end
    end
  end
end
```

We're on the home stretch! All we need now is a simple Active Resource client application. You'll likely plug this into a larger application, but to keep things simple, we've just created a new Rails application called card_client, for example.

Then we'll create the following three Active Resource models:

ActiveMerchant/card_client/app/models/card_server_resource.rb

```ruby
class CardServerResource < ActiveResource::Base
  self.site = 'http://localhost:3000'
  PASSWORD = 'My very long secret password'
end
```

ActiveMerchant/card_client/app/models/credit_card.rb

```ruby
class CreditCard < CardServerResource
  self.headers['X_PASSWORD'] = PASSWORD
end
```

ActiveMerchant/card_client/app/models/purchase.rb

```ruby
class Purchase < CardServerResource
  self.headers['X_PASSWORD'] = PASSWORD
end
```

The CardServerResource is a base class for the other two classes. It sets the site to the standard location where a Rails application runs in development mode. The password, which will be used to encrypt and decrypt the credit cards, is being sent to the card server in the HTTP header. The client and server would have to be connected using a secure

SSL connection in order to keep the password secure.[4] The password would also not be stored in the application but loaded securely from the server's filesystem.

Now we're ready to store a credit card and perform a purchase with the card server! We'll do that by firing up a console in the client application. First we'll store a new credit card on the card server:

```
$ ruby script/console
>> cc = CreditCard.create(:first_name => 'Cody', :last_name => 'Fauser',
                          :number => '4242424242424242', :month => 8,
                          :year => 2015, :brand => 'visa')
=> #<CreditCard:0x1359d54 ...>
```

Then we'll use the stored card to perform a purchase:

```
>> p = Purchase.create(:amount => 1.00, :description => "Subscription Fee",
                       :order => "#1000", :credit_card_id => cc.id)
=> #<Purchase:0x1289154 ...>
>> p.message
=> "This transaction has been approved"
>> p.reference
=> "599048703"
```

The credit card gets stored and a successful purchase is made using the card. If any of the resources fail validation, the errors will be returned to the Active Resource client as expected.

Discussion

This recipe provides an overall architecture for creating a credit card server that stores encrypted credit card numbers but is by no means an exhaustive implementation of a secure card server. There are many important aspects to the design and security of a card server that are not addressed by this recipe.

Your application will need to meet all the requirements of the Payment Card Industry Data Security Standard (PCI DSS).[5] The PCI DSS is the standard on which all the major credit card companies base their security requirements.

---

4. Recipe 5, *Authenticate REST Clients*, on page 29 describes how to authenticate an Active Resource client.
5. https://www.pcisecuritystandards.org/pdfs/pci_dss_v1-1.pdf

There are several important assumptions made in terms of architecture for the application:

- The password is not stored in the source code of the card client but is read from a secured location on the server.

- The communication channel between the card client and card server applications is SSL secured.

- The password sent in requests by the client is not logged in any way, shape, or form by the client or server. The password needs to be carefully guarded to ensure the safety of the stored credit card numbers.

- The card server is configured to allow only incoming connections from the card client application and especially does not accept connections from the Internet.

To ensure that your application is PCI compliant, you will need to enlist a Qualified Security Assessor.[6]

Also See

- The ActiveMerchant PeepCode PDF[7]

---

6. https://www.pcisecuritystandards.org/resources/qualified_security_assessors.htm
7. http://peepcode.com/products/activemerchant-pdf

Play Nice with Facebook

By Ezra Zygmuntowicz and Warren Konkel (http://brainspl.at, http://hungrymachine.com)

Ezra is a cofounder of EngineYard.com, a scalable Rails hosting service. He is the author of the book *Deploying Rails Applications* (ZT08) from the Pragmatic Bookshelf and has contributed many open source Ruby and Rails related projects, such as BackgrounDrb, ez-where, and Merb. Warren is a Washington, D.C., native and a developer at HungryMachine. His other projects include BountySource.com and Statisfy.net.

Rails and Facebook don't always agree; they both have their own strong opinions. For starters, all canvas page views are proxied through POST requests. That means resource routes were hopelessly broken, until the Facebook platform team was kind enough to add a new feature just for us Rails folks. They now send a signed parameter that indicates the original request type (POST vs. GET) against canvas pages.

To restore RESTful routes, just toss the following small patch into an initializer file, such as config/initializers/facebook_overrides.rb:

```
ActionController::AbstractRequest.class_eval do
  def request_method_with_facebook_overrides
    @request_method ||= begin
      case
        when parameters[:_method]
          parameters[:_method].downcase.to_sym
        when parameters[:fb_sig_request_method]
          parameters[:fb_sig_request_method].downcase.to_sym
        else
          request_method_without_facebook_overrides
      end
    end
  end
  alias_method_chain :request_method, :facebook_overrides
end
```

That'll get you by for a while, but a related problem will bite you once you start using Rails page caching with the popular Nginx web server. In particular, it doesn't allow serving a static file in response to a POST request. Instead, it returns a 405 error, and your Facebook app is left holding the bag.

To solve the caching problem, you need to handle the 405 error and serve up the page-cached file from disk while at the same time handling all the normal requests.

Add the following incantations to the bottom of your vhost server block in your Nginx configuration file:

```
error_page    405 =200 @405;
location @405 {
  index  index.html index.htm;
  # needed to forward user's IP address to rails
  proxy_set_header  X-Real-IP  $remote_addr;
  proxy_set_header  X-Forwarded-For $proxy_add_x_forwarded_for;
  proxy_set_header Host $http_host;
  proxy_redirect false;
  proxy_max_temp_file_size 0;
  proxy_next_upstream error;
  if (-f $request_filename) {
    break;
  }
  if (-f $request_filename.html) {
    rewrite (.*) $1.html break;
  }
  if (!-f $request_filename) {
    proxy_pass http://mongrel;
    break;
  }
}
```

This catches the 405 error with an error_page directive and changes it to a 200 response code. Then, after setting some proxy directives, it checks to see whether there's a page-cached file that matches the request. If so, the page is served straight from disk, and Facebook is none the wiser. However, if no page-cached file exists, then the regular stuff happens: Nginx handles requests for static .html files and falls back to Mongrel to handle dynamic Rails requests.

Tricks like these seem obvious once you get them working and step back, but they can take forever to figure out. Here's saving you the trouble!

Mark Locations on a Google Map

By Andre Lewis (http://earthcode.com)

Andre has been working with technology for the last nine years. His experience ranges from large-scale enterprise consulting with Accenture to start-up ventures and open source projects. He currently runs his own business, developing Ruby on Rails applications and consulting on Web 2.0 technologies. When he's not working with clients or exploring the latest technologies, he likes to mountain bike, camp, and ride his motorcycle.

Problem

Your application needs to find things based on a physical location and put them on a map. For example, you need to be able to find restaurants up to half a mile from some point and plot them on a Google map.

Ingredients

- The GeoKit plug-in:[1]
  ```
  $ script/plugin install svn://rubyforge.org/var/svn/geokit/trunk
  ```
- An API key for one or more geocoding web services (instructions included)
- A database that supports trigonometric functions (sorry, SQLite won't cut it)

Solution

When you're hungry for sushi, you need to find the nearest sushi bars...and fast! So, let's build an app that lets you punch in your current location and a radius, and in return you get a list of nearby sushi bars marked on a Google map.

---

1. http://geokit.rubyforge.org/

Here's the first part—the sushi finder:

Find Sushi Near You!

Address

9637 East County Line Road, Englewood, CO

Within

5 ⬍ miles

(Find Sushi)

To make this work, we obviously need a way to measure the distance from one street address (where we are) to another (where we could go). It turns out literal street addresses make for lousy distance calculations—latitude and longitude (lat/lng) are the way to go. Here's the really good news: we don't have to walk the entire surface of the earth while holding a GPS unit *or* do any math. Thankfully, a number of online geocoding services can handle that for us.

First, we need to create an account with a geocoding service: Google[2] and Yahoo[3] both provide free geocoding services. For this recipe, we'll use Google.

Once you've signed up for an account (don't worry, it's fairly painless), you'll end up getting a key that uniquely identifies your application. Depending on which version of the GeoKit plug-in you're using, it'll write its default configuration either in the config/environment.rb file or in the config/initializers/geokit.rb file. Just replace the default GeoKit::Geocoders:: google key with your account key:

```
GeoKit::Geocoders::google = 'REPLACE_WITH_YOUR_GOOGLE_KEY'
```

Now it's time to prime our database with some geocoded data: sushi longitude. We'll use scaffolding to create a Restaurant resource for that:

```
$ script/generate scaffold restaurant name:string  ↩
    address:string lat:float lng:float
$ rake db:migrate
```

This gives us everything we need to start creating restaurant data. However, we don't know the latitude and longitude for an address, and even

---

2. http://www.google.com/apis/maps/signup.html
3. http://developer.yahoo.com/wsregapp/

if we did, we wouldn't want to be typing them in. No worries—we'll let our geocoding service handle that. We'll just add the acts_as_mappable method with the auto_geocode option to our Restaurant model class:

Geocoding/app/models/restaurant.rb

```
class Restaurant < ActiveRecord::Base
  validates_presence_of :lat, :lng

  acts_as_mappable :auto_geocode => true
end
```

OK, now let's use the console to see whether we have everything wired together:

```
$ ruby script/console
>> r = Restaurant.create(:name => "Sushi Den",
                         :address => "1487 S Pearl St, Denver, CO")
=> #<Restaurant id: 9 ...>
>> r.lat
=> 39.689612
>> r.lng
=> -104.98041
```

Hey, look at that! When we created the Restaurant record, it automatically got saved with its latitude and longitude values.

Let us spend a minute walking through how that worked. The :auto_geocode=>true option to acts_as_mappable added a before_validation_on_create callback method to our Restaurant class. If we wanted to do the same thing manually (or we just wanted more fine-grained control), we could have left off the :auto_geocode=>true option and written this code instead:

```
class Restaurant < ActiveRecord::Base
  validates_presence_of :lat, :lng
  acts_as_mappable
  before_validation_on_create :geocode_address

private

  def geocode_address
    geo = GeoKit::Geocoders::MultiGeocoder.geocode(address)
    errors.add(:address, "Could not geocode address") unless geo.success
    self.lat, self.lng = geo.lat, geo.lng if geo.success
  end
end
```

The workhorse here is the MultiGeocoder class. When we create a new Restaurant object, the value of the address attribute (you can specify a different field name if needed) is transparently sent to whichever geocoding service we've configured. It then sends back the latitude and longitude values for the address, pokes them into our model attributes, and then carries on creating the record.

Now we're on to our next step: finding nearby sushi bars. This turns out to be trivial thanks to location-based find method options added by the GeoKit plug-in. Assuming we've entered a few more restaurants, we'll use the console to find restaurants ordered by distance from a given location, but only up to 5 miles away:

```
>> places = Restaurant.find :all,
    :origin => "9637 East County Line Road, Englewood, CO",
    :within => 5, :order => 'distance'
>> places.size
=> 3
>> places.first.distance
=> "0.8399105330356"
```

It's easy to gloss over what's happening here because it looks just like the Active Record find method we're already used to, with a couple location-specific options. But in fact there's a bit more going on behind the scenes.

First, the find sends off a request to our geocoding service to get the latitude and longitude values for the address string we used as our origin. Then, it computes the distance from the origin's latitude/longitude to the latitude/longitude of each of our restaurants by running a SQL query representing a trigonometric formula.[4] In the process of performing the query, a distance attribute is added to all the Restaurant objects returned by the find. The distance attribute represents the distance (in miles, by default) from the origin we used in the query.

If we're just looking for the closest sushi bar (the *I'm Feeling Lucky* of geocoding), we could use this:

```
Restaurant.find :closest,
               :origin => "9637 East County Line Road, Englewood, CO"
```

All we need now is a form that asks for the two variables—the address and the radius—and a controller action that runs the query.

---

4. The GeoKit plug-in uses the Haversine formula (http://en.wikipedia.org/wiki/Haversine_formula) to calculate the distance between two latitude/longitude points.

There's nothing interesting about the form. In the search action we'll use the find with the location-based options again:

Geocoding/app/controllers/restaurants_controller.rb

```ruby
def search
  @address = params[:address]
  @within  = params[:within]

  @restaurants = Restaurant.find :all,
                    :origin => @address,
                    :within => @within,
                    :order => 'distance'

  respond_to do |format|
    format.html # index.html.erb
    format.xml  { render :xml => @restaurants }
  end
end
```

To tidy this up, we could tuck all the options behind a custom finder method that we'd call like so:

```ruby
@restaurants = Restaurant.near(@address, @within)
```

Next, over on the search results page, we'll list the restaurants and put them on a Google map:[5]

Geocoding/app/views/restaurants/search.html.erb

```erb
<h1><strong><%= pluralize(@restaurants.size, 'sushi bar') %></strong>
within <strong><%= h @within %> miles</strong>:</h1>

<ul>
<% for restaurant in @restaurants -%>
  <li>
    <p>
      <strong><%= link_to restaurant.name, restaurant %></strong>
      at <%= h restaurant.address %><br/>
      <i>(<%= sprintf("%.2f", restaurant.distance) %> miles away)</i>
    </p>
  </li>
<% end -%>
</ul>

<div id="map" style="width:500px; height:300px;"></div>
```

Notice we've added an empty map div at the bottom of the search results page waiting to be filled in.

---

5. This assumes you signed up for a Google Maps API key in the first step.

To do that, first we'll add the following code to the <head> section of our layout file to include the Google Maps JavaScript code. It also outputs @restaurants as JSON if @restaurants is available:

Geocoding/app/views/layouts/restaurants.html.erb

```
<script type="text/javascript"
        src="http://maps.google.com/maps?file=api&amp;v=2&amp;
              key=<%= GeoKit::Geocoders::google %>" >
</script>
<% if @restaurants -%>
  <script type="text/javascript">
    var restaurants = <%= @restaurants.to_json %>;
  </script>
<% end -%>
<%= javascript_include_tag :defaults %>
```

Then we need a hunk of JavaScript to instantiate the map in our map div, loop through the restaurants (made available to the JavaScript code as JSON), and add the markers. We'll just toss all this into our public/javascripts/application.js file:

Geocoding/public/javascripts/application.js

```
function initialize() {
  if (GBrowserIsCompatible() && typeof restaurants != 'undefined') {
    var map = new GMap2(document.getElementById("map"));
    map.setCenter(new GLatLng(37.4419, -122.1419), 13);
    map.addControl(new GLargeMapControl());

    // Clicking the marker will hide it
    function createMarker(latlng, restaurant) {
      var marker = new GMarker(latlng);
      var html="<strong>"+restaurant.name+"</strong><br />"+restaurant.address;
      GEvent.addListener(marker,"click", function() {
        map.openInfoWindowHtml(latlng, html);
      });
      return marker;
    }

    var bounds = new GLatLngBounds;
    for (var i = 0; i < restaurants.length; i++) {
      var latlng=new GLatLng(restaurants[i].lat,restaurants[i].lng)
      bounds.extend(latlng);
      map.addOverlay(createMarker(latlng, restaurants[i]));
    }
    map.setCenter(bounds.getCenter(),map.getBoundsZoomLevel(bounds));
  }
}
window.onload=initialize;
window.onunload=GUnload;
```

Now when the search results page is rendered, we get a Google map with markers that shows the name and address of nearby restaurants.

3 sushi bars within 5 miles:

- **Yuki Sushi** at 9447 Park Meadows Dr, Lone Tree, CO
  (0.84 miles away)

- **Sushi Wave** at 9555 E Arapahoe Road, Greenwood Village, CO
  (1.99 miles away)

- **Sushi Terrace** at 8162 S Holly St, Littleton, CO
  (2.42 miles away)

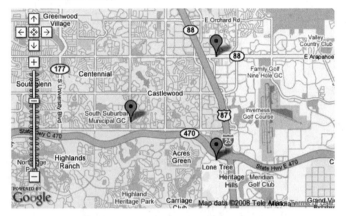

Discussion

Sometimes you just want to calculate a distance in memory, rather than in the context of database queries. To do that, you can call methods of the MultiGeocoder class directly:

```
$ ruby script/console
>> here = GeoKit::Geocoders::MultiGeocoder.
          geocode("9637 East County Line Road, Englewood, CO")
>> there = GeoKit::Geocoders::MultiGeocoder.
          geocode("9447 Park Meadows Dr, Lone Tree, CO")
>> here.distance_to(there)
=> 0.845315041284098
```

The MultiGeocoder will use the geocoding services you have configured. If one geocoding service fails to geocode an address, MultiGeocoder will try the next service, in the order you've configured them.

Tunnel Back to Your Application

By Christopher Haupt (http://www.buildingwebapps.com)
Christopher is a cofounder and chief technology officer at Collective Knowledge Works, Inc. He is a software architect, developer, and educator with more than twenty-five years of experience. These days he is focused on applying his experience in ways that can serve the wider development community.

Problem

You're developing the next great Facebook or other social network application, and you don't have the resources—time, spare servers, the ability to interrupt the existing application, and so on—to constantly redeploy your nonreleased app for testing. Instead, you want to set up a tunnel to your local development application so you don't have to redeploy to test changes.

Ingredients

- A publicly accessible server running the SSH daemon (sshd)
- An SSH client (ssh) on your development machine

Solution

Facebook and other social network platforms act as a kind of proxy for our applications. That is, they forward requests to the publicly accessible URL where our application lives. We want to arrange things so that the application running on our development box gets those requests. Here's the catch: our development machine may be behind a firewall or otherwise not accessible to the public Internet.

Good ol' Secure Shell (SSH) lets us set up a secure connection (a reverse tunnel) between our development machine and a publicly accessible server. Once the tunnel is open, we can point a social network service such as Facebook to the URL of our public server. Any request made to the public server will be transparently forwarded to our development machine. We could set that up using commands at the terminal, but it's tedious and repetitive. So, let's automate it!

First we need to make sure that the SSH daemon (sshd) is set up to allow our public server to act as a gateway. Let's start by logging in via SSH:

```
$ ssh admin@www.example.com
```

Next, we locate the sshd_config file (it's /etc/sshd_config on my OS). Within that file, we need to make sure a few important variables are set. Now, be *very careful* here! If you mess up something in this file and restart the sshd process, you'll likely get locked out of your server. So, proceed with caution, and double-check each variable:

- GatewayPorts needs to be set to clientspecified for recent versions of OpenSSH (4.0 and newer). On others, such as OpenSolaris' default install, it should be set to yes.

- AllowTcpForwarding needs to be set to yes.

- Depending on your configuration, you *may* need to update the KeepAlive variable or the TCPKeepAlive variable to yes. You can of course change this later if you find your connection drops out frequently. Alternatively, you can add these keep-alive settings to your local ~/.ssh/config file:

```
Host www.example.com
ServerAliveInterval 120
```

Once we're done editing the sshd_config file, we'll save it and restart the sshd process. (This is OS-specific, so check your documentation for the right way to do it on your system.)

Next, we turn our attention to our local Rails application. To automate setting up the reverse tunnel, we'll create a YML configuration file and a Rake task. Here's the configuration file:

TunnelingBackToYourApp/config/tunnel.yml

```
development:
  public_host_username: admin
  public_host: www.example.com
  public_port: 8868
  local_port: 3000

test:
  public_host_username: admin
  public_host: www.example.com
  public_port: 8868
  local_port: 3000
```

```
production:
  public_host_username: admin
  public_host: www.example.com
  public_port: 8868
  local_port: 3000
```

You can choose any public port you want; just be sure it isn't in use by another program. The local_port is the port on which you'll run your development Rails environment.

The Rake task just needs to load up the configuration for the current Rails environment and use it to start a secure connection:

TunnelingBackToYourApp/lib/tasks/tunnel.rake

```
namespace :tunnel do

  task :start => :environment do
    SSH_TUNNEL = YAML.load_file("#{RAILS_ROOT}/config/tunnel.yml")[RAILS_ENV]

    public_host_username = SSH_TUNNEL['public_host_username']
    public_host          = SSH_TUNNEL['public_host']
    public_port          = SSH_TUNNEL['public_port']
    local_port           = SSH_TUNNEL['local_port']

    puts "Starting tunnel #{public_host}:#{public_port} \
          to 0.0.0.0:#{local_port}"
    exec "ssh -nNT -g -R *:#{public_port}:0.0.0.0:#{local_port} \
                        #{public_host_username}@#{public_host}"
  end

end
```

OK, let's give it a whirl:

```
$ rake tunnel:start
```

This starts a tunnel in the foreground.

If we now run our Rails app on the correct local port (3000) and hit the public server's URL (http://www.example.com:8868, for example), we should see our app.

Once this works, we can then go ahead and set our Facebook application callback URL to http://www.example.com:8868/myapp, for example. Requests will happily flow to our development machine, and we won't need to deploy to test changes.

Finally, to kill the connection, press Ctrl+C in the terminal.

Discussion

Be sure to enable your Facebook (or other) application to receive traffic from the IPs of both your public servers *and* your development machine. If your development machine (or a router upstream) is supplied with dynamic IPs, you will have to update your setting whenever the IP number changes.

Each platform has different setup techniques for pointing the apps to your tunneled server, but all can use the convenience factor of pointing to a dev box for quick debugging/iterating on code work.

You can reduce the need for entering passwords by setting up SSH keys. Plenty of good resources on the 'net explain how to do this for your OS.

You can expand on externalizing this solution for a team by adding the concept of usernames to your YAML configuration and selecting the current username found in the development system's environment variables.

Part VII

Console Snacks

Write Console Methods

By P.J. Hyett and Chris Wanstrath (http://errtheblog.com)
By day, P.J. and Chris run the Rails consulting and training firm Err Free. By night, they maintain Err the Blog, a running commentary on both Ruby and Rails.

A lot of the irb tricks you develop or find on the Web are useful more than once. You know that obscure snippet that honks your computer's horn whenever a NoMethodError is raised is gonna come in handy for all sorts of fun, so you might as well keep it around.

So, where do we stockpile irb goodies? Well, as a courtesy, when irb starts up, it tries to load a file named .irbrc from your home directory. And, since script/console is just irb with a tuxedo T-shirt on, all of the irb hacks and customizations are always available. But we can do one better: we can write Rails-specific irb methods and use them across different Rails apps.

Say, for example, we routinely run arbitrary SQL from script/console the longhand way, like this:

```
$ ruby script/console
>> ActiveRecord::Base.connection.select_all 'show databases'
=> [{"Database"=>"activerecord_unittest"}, {"Database"=>"err_dev"} ... ]
```

Now let's save some typing by bottling this up in a method. To keep our Rails-specific console methods all together, we'll throw them in a file called .railsrc in our home directory. Here's our new method:

`console/.railsrc`

```
def sql(query)
  ActiveRecord::Base.connection.select_all(query)
end
```

Then, we just load up the .railsrc file from within our .irbrc file,[1] which in turn gets loaded when script/console is run. So in .irbrc, we have this:

`console/.irbrc`

```
if ENV['RAILS_ENV']
  load File.dirname(__FILE__) + '/.railsrc'
end
```

---

1. On Windows, .irbrc should be kept in C:\Documents and Settings\YourWindowsUsername. The HOME environment variable should then be set to that directory's path.

Now we can get at those hard-to-reach places with ease using the sql method:

```
$ ruby script/console
>> sql 'show databases'
=> [{"Database"=>"activerecord_unittest"}, {"Database"=>"err_dev"} ... ]
```

The console is your friend, and it's also extensible, so extend it!

Log to the Console

By P.J. Hyett and Chris Wanstrath (http://errtheblog.com)

When you're playing around in script/console, it's sometimes helpful to know which database queries are actually being run. No big deal—all we need to do is tell Active Record that instead of using Rails' default logger, it should use a custom logger pointed at STDOUT (your terminal).

These two lines do the trick:

```
ActiveRecord::Base.logger = Logger.new(STDOUT)
ActiveRecord::Base.clear_active_connections!
```

We'll stick 'em in our .railsrc[1] file and add a couple methods to turn logging on and off:

console/.railsrc

```
def loud_logger
  set_logger_to Logger.new(STDOUT)
end

def quiet_logger
  set_logger_to nil
end

def set_logger_to(logger)
  ActiveRecord::Base.logger = logger
  ActiveRecord::Base.clear_active_connections!
end
```

Then, when we want to sneak a peek at the SQL that Active Record is running, we call loud_logger from within script/console:

```
$ ruby script/console
>> User.find(:first)
=> #<User id: 1 ...>
>> loud_logger
=> {}
>> User.find(:first)
  User Load (0.000613)    SELECT * FROM users LIMIT 1
=> #<User id: 1 ...>
>> quiet_logger
=> {}
>> User.find(:first)
=> #<User id: 1 ...>
```

---

1. This is the file we created in Snack Recipe 37, *Write Console Methods*, on page 221.

That works great if we're interested only in seeing the SQL. But let's say we're pretending to be a casual web surfer by issuing faux requests to Rails using the app console helper:

```
$ ruby script/console
>> app.get '/people'
=> 200
```

During that request, a bunch of stuff happened behind the scenes and got stuck in development.log. So, let's go a step further and turn on systemwide logging in the console.[2]

We'll just chuck the following two lines in our .railsrc file to make the console logger get set up before Rails does its thing:

```
require 'logger'
Object.const_set(:RAILS_DEFAULT_LOGGER, Logger.new(STDOUT))
```

Now everything Rails would normally log to development.log is instead logged to our terminal while we're in the console:

```
$ ruby script/console
>> app.get '/people'
Processing PeopleController#index...
  Session ID: BAh7BiIKZmxhc2hJQz...
  Parameters: {"action"=>"index", "controller"=>"people"}
  Person Load (0.000630)   SELECT * FROM `people`
Rendering template within layouts/people
Rendering people/index
Completed in 0.00949 (105 reqs/sec) | Rendering: 0.00180 (18%) |
DB: 0.00063 (6%) | 200 OK [http://www.example.com/people]
=> 200
```

When we're playing in the console, there's really no need to go digging through the log files.

---

2. Thanks to Tim Lucas for this trick: http://toolmantim.com/article/2007/2/6/system_wide_script_console_logging.

Play in the Sandbox

By P.J. Hyett and Chris Wanstrath (http://errtheblog.com)

The console is great for playing around with your models and controllers. It's not nearly as much fun, though, if you have to worry about goofing something up.

No worries. The --sandbox switch has our back. What it does, surprisingly, is sandbox your data for the duration of your script/console session. Here, let's try to wreck a sand castle:

```
$ ruby script/console --sandbox
Loading development environment in sandbox
Any modifications you make will be rolled back on exit
>> Castle.destroy 1
=> #<Castle id: 1, ...>
>> Castle.find(1)
ActiveRecord::RecordNotFound: Couldn't find Castle with ID=1
>> exit
```

Uh-oh. Thankfully, the sandbox automatically pushes the Undo button at the end—it runs everything within a database transaction. So, any rows we modify or delete for the duration of the script/console session will be returned to their original state on exit. Let's check:

```
$ ruby script/console
Loading development environment
>> Castle.find(1)
=> #<Castle id: 1, ...>
```

Whew!

Tracking down a hard-to-isolate bug with your before_destroy callback? Toying with the idea of mass-updating data? Examining a copy of production data on your staging database? The --sandbox switch is the way to go. To play it safe, you may want to get into the habit of always running in sandbox mode when poking around your production environment. Then, when you really *need* to change production data, you can switch back to the live console.

Access Helpers

By P.J. Hyett and Chris Wanstrath (http://errtheblog.com)

By now you've discovered that the console isn't just our friend; it's also a power tool. It slices, it dices, and it even knows how to call view helpers. The appropriately named helper object can be used to play with any of Rails' default helper methods, like this:

```
$ ruby script/console
>> helper.pluralize(3, 'blind mouse')
=> "3 blind mice"
>> helper.submit_tag('Do it!')
=> "<input name=\"commit\" type=\"submit\" value=\"Do it!\" />"
>> helper.visual_effect :blindUp, :post
=> "new Effect.BlindUp(\"post\",{});"
```

This is handy for messin' around with built-in view helpers, but in the old days it had one problem: the helper object didn't know about our app-specific helpers. But, hey, it's a new day. Now in Rails 2.0 the sky has opened.

If we want to call any helper method defined in our ApplicationHelper, the methods are right there:

```
$ ruby script/console
>> helper.some_method_from_application_helper
=> true
```

We run into problems, though, when trying to use the helper object to access our other helpers. They're not included by default. But we can fix that. If we want to call any of the methods in our PeopleHelper, for example, we just give the helper object some, er, help:

```
>> helper :people
=> #<Object:0x18ab44c ...>
>> helper.some_method_from_people_helper
=> true
```

Just like that, we can call any of our app-specific view helpers through the helper object. Rinse and repeat for any other helper modules you want to access.

Shortcut the Console

Once you get addicted, you'll never want to leave the console. Creating little console shortcuts can boost your productivity and make you look cool when demoing at conferences. Here's a fun one.

Let's say our fingers are worn out from typing Order.find(:first) in the console. Instead, we want to type order(:first). In other words, order(*args) should simply be an alias for Order.find(*args).

Now, we want that to work for *all* models in our current application, generically. It sounds difficult, but it's actually quite easy with a bit of metaprogramming. We'll toss this code into our .railsrc file:[1]

`console/.railsrc`

```
def define_model_find_shortcuts
  model_files = Dir.glob("app/models/**/*.rb")
  table_names = model_files.map { |f| File.basename(f).split('.')[0..-2].join }
  table_names.each do |table_name|
    Object.instance_eval do
      define_method(table_name) do |*args|
        table_name.camelize.constantize.send(:find, *args)
      end
    end
  end
end
```

Using instance_eval, we define a shortcut method for every model in our app, which then simply passes the buck on to the real find method. We define the shortcuts on the Object class so that script/console can call the methods directly, as if they were built right into the console.

Then we need to make sure our define_model_find_shortcuts method is run when we fire up the console, but *after* all the Rails helpers have been loaded. It turns out irb has a neat configuration option for this:

`console/.railsrc`

```
IRB.conf[:IRB_RC] = Proc.new { define_model_find_shortcuts }
```

The IRB.conf(:IRB_RC) configuration value takes a Proc object, which irb will dutifully run whenever the context is changed. Some time after Rails loads, the context changes, and our shortcuts get defined.

---

1. This is the file we created in Snack Recipe 37, *Write Console Methods*, on page 221.

Now in the console we can call the shortcuts with any standard Active Record find options:

```
$ ruby script/console
>> order(:first)
=> #<Order id: 1 ...>
>> order(1)
=> #<Order id: 1 ...>
>> order(:all)
=> [#<Order id: 1 ...>]
```

Part VIII

Asynchronous-Processing Recipes

Send Lightweight Messages

You need a lightweight, persistent queue server so you can quickly push messages on a queue during a Rails request and then let an out-of-band process consume the messages on its own time.

- The memcache-client gem:

    ```
    $ gem install memcache-client
    ```

- The starling gem:

    ```
    $ gem install starling
    ```

Starling[1] is a powerful yet simple queue server that enables reliable distributed queuing with minimal overhead. It uses the memcached wire protocol, which means any language that speaks memcached can take advantage of Starling's queue facilities. Starling was built to drive Twitter's back end and is in production across Twitter's cluster. It's super simple to use, so let's get cookin'.

Let's say we're building an online jukebox that lets artists upload MP3 files for their albums. We happen to be using the attachment_fu plug-in to get the uploaded MP3 files stored on our server (Recipe 18, *Upload Images with Thumbnails*, on page 93 shows how to do this with album covers). We also want to upload the MP3s to our Amazon S3 account. That way we can fall back to the S3 file if our local file disappears.

However, we do not want to upload an artist's MP3 file to S3 synchronously while the artist waits for a response. Instead, we'll just pop a message on a queue and respond before the artist notices. Then we'll write a small client program (a Rake task) to work off the messages on the queue on its own time.

---

1. https://rubyforge.org/projects/starling/

Let's start by firing up the starling server as a daemonized process. It creates a few artifacts: a PID file and persistent queue logs. Instead of taking the default locations for those, we'll pass in a few options to create the PID file and queue logs relative to our current Rails application directory.

```
$ mkdir tmp/starling
$ starling -d -P tmp/pids/starling.pid -q tmp/starling
```

Then, over in our Rails application, we'll create an initializer file to set up a connection to the starling server when our Rails application starts. We'll stick with the default host and port (configurable via options to the starling command):

Starling/config/initializers/starling.rb
```
require 'memcache'
STARLING = MemCache.new('127.0.0.1:22122')
```

Now it's time to start putting messages on a queue. We want that to happen after the MP3 has been uploaded and saved in our application. Somehow we need to hook into that process. Thankfully, attachment_fu has an after_attachment_saved callback method that does the trick.

Next, we'll define the after_attachment_saved method in our Song class. When this method is called, we'll use the starling server connection to put a message on a queue:

Starling/app/models/song.rb
```
def after_attachment_saved
  STARLING.set('s3_uploads',
               {:file_name   => self.full_filename,
                :public_path => self.public_filename})
end
```

The set method takes a queue name and a message. In our case, we'll use a queue named s3_uploads and a message that's a lightweight hash. The hash contains two key/value pairs: the full path to the MP3 file on our server and the relative path we want to use in the S3 URL. The attachment_fu plug-in automatically assigns those attributes in our Song class. We just turn around and assign them to keys in the message hash. The messages you use will depend on the needs of your application. In this case, the client that ultimately consumes our messages requires these two pieces of information to upload the file to S3.

Next, we'll write a client program to consume the messages on the s3_uploads queue. For our example, we'll just use a Rake task that runs continuously:

Starling/lib/tasks/starling.rake
```
namespace :starling do

  task :consume do
    require 'memcache'
    require 's3_uploader'

    sleep_time = 0
    starling = MemCache.new('127.0.0.1:22122')

    loop do
      message = starling.get('s3_uploads')
      if message
        s3 = S3Uploader.new(message[:file_name], message[:public_path])
        begin
          s3.upload
          print s3.url
          sleep_time = 0
        rescue Exception
          print 'X'
          starling.set('s3_uploads', message)
          sleep_time = 30
        end
      else # no work
        print '.'
        sleep_time = 5
      end
      $stdout.flush
      sleep sleep_time
    end
  end
end
```

The consume task first connects to the starling server. Then it attempts to get messages from the s3_uploads queue in a loop. If there's no message waiting, it just sleeps for five seconds and tries again. If a message is available, we peel out the :file_name and :public_path values from the hash and delegate all the heavy lifting to the S3Uploader class. (Don't worry about what it does; it's in the book's code bundle if you're interested.) However, if an error occurs while trying to upload the MP3 file, we requeue the original message and sleep for thirty seconds to allow S3 extra time before attempting to process more messages.

Time for some action! We'll upload a couple of MP3 files and then run the starling:consume task. It consumes all the messages waiting in the s3_uploads queue and carries on waiting for another:

```
$ rake starling:consume
http://s3.amazonaws.com:80/jukebox/song-1.mp3
http://s3.amazonaws.com:80/jukebox/song-2.mp3
...
```

Then if we upload another MP3 file and there's a problem, the consumer waits thirty seconds before trying again. We'll see something like this:

```
$ rake starling:consume
...Xhttp://s3.amazonaws.com:80/jukebox/song-3.mp3...
```

What could be easier? With very little code or configuration, we're able to send and receive lightweight messages between processes. The messages are stored in Starling's queue log (on disk), so it's fairly fault tolerant.

Discussion

You could use this same technique to offload any number of tasks that may take too long during a Rails request: parsing MP3 info, invalidating caches, reindexing your search engine, running analytics or stats when certain information changes, and so on.

Also See

If you're doing anything more than simple message passing, see Recipe 43, *Off-Load Long-Running Tasks to BackgrounDRb*, on the next page. (Or mix these recipes together to create a BackgrounDRb task that consumes messages.) If your asynchronous workflow includes different states of processing, see Recipe 44, *Process Asynchronous, State-Based Workflows*, on page 245. You'll also likely want to use Monit to monitor your starling server process. See Recipe 80, *Monitor (and Repair) Processes with Monit*, on page 413 for examples you can use as a starting point.

Off-Load Long-Running Tasks to BackgrounDRb

By Gregg Pollack and Hemant Kumar (http://www.railsenvy.com,http://gnufied.org)
Gregg lives in Orlando, Florida, where he runs the Orlando Ruby Users Group, writes on his blog Rails Envy, and is always hunting for more Rails projects for his company Patched Software. Hemant is the current maintainer of the BackgrounDRb library.

Problem

You have an action that starts a long-running task—say, about thirty seconds. The task is something that the user wants to wait for, but you don't want to tie up the entire Rails process for one request/response cycle and risk the user inching his mouse toward the dreaded Refresh button.

Instead, you would like to off-load the task to a background process, respond to the original web request immediately, and continually give the user updates on the status of the task via their browser.

Ingredients

- The BackgrounDRb plug-in:[1]

  ```
  $ script/plugin install http://svn.devjavu.com/backgroundrb/trunk/
  ```

  This recipe was originally prepared with BackgrounDRb 1.0. It uses the packet library, which is currently dependent on fork(). Unfortunately, that means BackgrounDRb 1.0 won't work properly on Windows platforms.

- The packet gem:

  ```
  $ gem install packet
  ```

- The chronic gem:

  ```
  $ gem install chronic
  ```

---

1. http://backgroundrb.rubyforge.org/

Solution

Let's say our application is a virtual mall for boutique shops. Customers buy stuff throughout the day, and shop owners need to charge their customers in batch to optimize the payment process.

On a good sales day it might take a few seconds to run all the charges through the system, and the conventional web request/response cycle gets really clunky. To add insult to injury, every time a shop owner clicks the button to run the charges, we have one less Rails process available for other work. So, we need a way to run the billing code in a separate process and then periodically update the status in the browser.

All this talk of background tasks sounds like a lot of work, but it's surprisingly straightforward with BackgrounDRb. The BackgrounDRb server is just a process that has access to our Rails environment. We queue up work through a MiddleMan object living in our Rails application, and the MiddleMan delegates the work to workers, leaving our Rails process free to take new web requests. And just like any good middle man, we can ask it for an update on worker status.

After installing the BackgrounDRb plug-in, we'll configure it by running this Rake task:

```
$ rake backgroundrb:setup
```

This gives us three files and a directory:

- The config/backgroundrb.yml file contains the basic configuration required to run the BackgrounDRb server:
  ```
  ---
  :backgroundrb:
    :port: 11006
    :ip: 0.0.0.0
  ```
  The BackgrounDRb server will listen on the specified port and ip. By default, all workers will be loaded in the development environment, which can be changed using this:
  ```
  ---
  :backgroundrb:
    :environment: production
  ```
- The script/backgroundrb script starts, stops, and restarts the BackgrounDRb server process.
- The test/bdrb_test_helper.rb is a helper file for testing our workers.
- The lib/workers directory houses the worker code.

Let's go ahead and create a worker to handle our long-running billing chores:

```
$ script/generate worker billing
```

This generates a skeleton lib/workers/billing_worker.rb file:

```
class BillingWorker < BackgrounDRb::MetaWorker
  set_worker_name :billing_worker

  def create(args = nil)
  end
end
```

Next, we'll add code inside the create method. To get the hang of things, let's start with some logging and a delay:

```
class BillingWorker < BackgrounDRb::MetaWorker
  set_worker_name :billing_worker

  def create(args=nil)
    args.each do |customer_id|
      logger.info "Billing customer #{customer_id}..."
      sleep(3)
    end
    logger.info "All Done"
    exit
  end
end
```

Now that we've created a worker, we'll start the BackgrounDRb server:

```
$ script/backgroundrb start
```

Then we'll jump straight into the console and start our worker:

```
$ ruby script/console
>> key = MiddleMan.new_worker(:worker => :billing_worker,
                              :job_key => "abc123",
                              :data => [1, 2, 3])
=> "abc123"
```

This creates a BillingWorker in a new process and invokes the create method, passing in our array of customer IDs (the array we used for the :data option). Because we have three customers with a three-second delay between each, this method should run for nine seconds. But we don't have to wait: the new_worker method returns as soon as the worker has started and hands us back the job key for future reference.

Now if we peek in the log/backgroundrb.log file, we'll see this:

```
Billing customer 1...
Billing customer 2...
Billing customer 3...
All Done
```

This is all hunky-dory, but it's currently a one-way street through the MiddleMan, and well, the work isn't very interesting. So, we'll revise our worker to actually bill each customer and keep track of the status along the way:[2]

`BackgroundDrb/lib/workers/billing_worker.rb`

```ruby
class BillingWorker < BackgroundDRb::MetaWorker
  set_worker_name :billing_worker
  set_no_auto_load(true)

  def create(args=nil)
    register_status(:percent_complete => 0)
    args.each_with_index do |customer_id, index|
      c = Customer.find(customer_id)
      c.bill!
      percent_complete = ((index + 1) * 100) / args.length
      logger.info "Billing is #{percent_complete}% complete..."
      register_status(:percent_complete => percent_complete)
    end
    exit
  end

end
```

We have access to our Customer model from inside the worker, which means we can neatly hide the billing logic behind the bill! method. As each customer is billed, we use the register_status method to accumulate how far along the worker is by way of the :percent_complete status variable.

We've also slipped in a call to the set_no_auto_load method. By default each of the workers found in the lib/workers directory will be started in a separate process when the BackgrounDRb server starts. We don't need to do this automatically, so we've disabled autoloading.

That takes care of the worker. Next we need to plug all this into our Rails application.

Let's assume we have a form that lists all the customers who haven't been billed yet and includes a checkbox next to each one indicating whether we want to bill them. When we post the form, we want to call the MiddleMan.new_worker method and toss all the customer IDs that need billing to our worker.

---

2. If you change the source of one of your workers, you'll need to stop and start your BackgrounDRb server to see the changes.

Rather than clutter the controller with BackgrounDRb details, we'll encapsulate how to start the billing job and get its status in methods of our Shop model. Here's the full model:

BackgrounDrb/app/models/shop.rb

```ruby
class Shop < ActiveRecord::Base
  has_many :customers
  validates_presence_of :name, :login, :password

  def unpaid_customers
    customers.find(:all, :conditions => "last_billed_at is null")
  end

  def start_billing(customers_to_charge)
    MiddleMan.new_worker(:worker  => :billing_worker,
                         :job_key => self.id,
                         :data    => customers_to_charge)
  end

  def self.billing_status(job_key)
    status = MiddleMan.ask_status(:worker  => :billing_worker,
                                  :job_key => job_key)
    status[:percent_complete]
  end

end
```

The start_billing method simply creates a BillingWorker, just like we did in the console previously. We're using the Shop model object's ID as the job key. The billing_status method gets the status status and returns the percent complete.

Then over in the create action of our ChargesController, we'll roll up all the customers to charge and start the billing:

BackgrounDrb/app/controllers/charges_controller.rb

```ruby
def create
  customers_to_charge = []
  params[:charge_customer].each do |customer_id, charge|
    customers_to_charge << customer_id if charge == "yes"
  end

  session[:bill_job_key] = @current_shop.start_billing(customers_to_charge)

  redirect_to :action => 'check_bill_status'
end
```

Just like in the console, we get the job key back as soon as the worker has started. In this case, we stash it away in the session. Then we immediately redirect to the check_bill_status action and use the job key to ask our worker for a status by calling the billing_status method:

`BackgroundDrb/app/controllers/charges_controller.rb`

```ruby
def check_bill_status
  @percent_complete = Shop.billing_status(session[:bill_job_key])

  if request.xhr?
    if @percent_complete == 100
      render :update do |page|
        flash[:notice] = "Billing is complete!"
        session[:bill_job_key] = nil
        page.redirect_to :action => "index"
      end
    else
      render :update do |page|
        page[:billingStatus].setStyle :width => "#{@percent_complete * 2}px"
        page[:billingStatus].replace_html "#{@percent_complete}%"
      end
    end
  end
end
```

At this point, the action falls right through to a template that shows no progress. However, it starts a periodic remote call to the check_bill_status method to poll for a status every three seconds:

`BackgroundDrb/app/views/charges/check_bill_status.html.erb`

```erb
<h1>Billing in Progress</h1>

<div id="billingStatus" class="progress">
</div>

<%= periodically_call_remote :url => "check_bill_status", :frequency => 3 %>
```

Each time the check_bill_status action is called, it asks the Shop for its billing status and uses an RJS update block to update the billingStatus progress bar. When the billing is complete, we clear out the job key and use RJS to issue a full redirect to the list of pending charges.

Now let's say we also want to send receipt e-mails to our customers. Unlike the billing task, we basically just want to fire off a request to a specific worker method without waiting for the result.

To do that, we can use the ask_work method to run a mail_receipts method in our worker:

```
MiddleMan.ask_work(:worker          => :billing_worker,
                   :worker_method => :mail_receipts,
                   :data            => customer_ids)
```

However, on a really busy day, we might have multiple shop owners all sending e-mails at the same time. And if the worker is already busy when a new task arrives, the work won't get queued. Pretty soon customers start phoning up asking what happened to their receipt. Instead, we want our mail_receipts tasks to pile up and get worked off one after the other reliably.

The solution is simple: we'll configure the built-in thread pool with a worker size of 1 and use the thread_pool.defer method:

```
class BillingWorker < BackgrounDRb::MetaWorker
  set_worker_name :billing_worker
  pool_size 1

  def create(args=nil)
    ...
  end

  def mail_receipts(customer_ids)
    thread_pool.defer(customer_ids) do |customer_ids|
      customer_ids.each do |customer_id|
        CustomerMailer.deliver_receipt(customer_id)
      end
    end
  end
end
```

Now no matter how many e-mail jobs we send to the worker, they'll all be queued in a thread pool. And since the thread pool has a size of 1, only one of the tasks will run at a time. Similarly, if we wanted concurrent processing of tasks, we could increase the size of the thread pool using the pool_size method and process tasks concurrently.

Last, but by no means least, we might have background tasks that we want to run on an automated schedule. The general solution is to use cron, but managing cron jobs and checking their status can be cumbersome. Thankfully, BackgrounDRb has a built-in scheduler, too. In the backgroundrb.yml file, we can configure certain worker methods to be invoked on a periodic basis (and check it in to version control, of course).

For example:

```
---
:backgroundrb:
  :port: 11006
  :ip: 0.0.0.0

:schedules:
  :billing_worker:
    :check_incoming_email:
      :trigger_args: */30 * * * *
    :generate_reports:
      :trigger_args: 0 30 5 * * *
      :data: "Summary Report"
```

This configuration schedules the check_incoming_email method of the BillingWorker to execute every thirty seconds and the generate_reports to execute at 5:30 in the morning. The data specified with the :data option is passed to the method as an argument. If you use the scheduler this way, it's important to remember that you should not disable the autoloading of worker classes.

The result is a fairly straightforward way to fire up separate processes to handle long-running tasks *and* continuously reporting their status to the user.

Discussion

As of version 1.0, BackgrounDRb is no longer implemented via Ruby's DRb library. And unlike other techniques of network programming that use threads, BackgrounDRb uses I/O multiplexing to make use of non-blocking socket I/O and stays largely thread-free. It does that using the packet library (http://code.google.com/p/packet/), which is an event-driven network programming library.

The basic idea is to have a reactor loop monitoring a socket, and when an event occurs on the socket, a callback method is invoked. BackgrounDRb is basically a process that watches for incoming events from Rails and invokes workers to execute Rails code out of band. There are other powerful BackgrounDRb clustering and network programming capabilities available in workers.

Also See

See Recipe 80, *Monitor (and Repair) Processes with Monit*, on page 413 for an example of how to configure Monit to monitor the BackgrounDRb daemon process.

Process Asynchronous, State-Based Workflows

By Jonathan Dahl (http://slantwisedesign.com)
Jonathan is a founding partner at Slantwise Design, a web application development shop in Minnesota. Besides twenty-odd Rails projects, Jonathan has done extensive work with video transcoding and has just released Zencoder, a distributed video-processing system built with Ruby (http://zencoder.tv).

Problem

Your application needs to execute a time-consuming process such as video transcoding or large PDF generation. The process will take more than a few seconds, so you can't do it synchronously within the life cycle of an HTTP request. But you want the processing to begin immediately, so you can't just trigger it with a nightly or hourly cron job. And here's the kicker: you also want to track the status of the job as it transitions from one state to the next.

Ingredients

- The acts_as_state_machine plug-in:

  ```
  $ script/plugin install ↩
      http://elitists.textdriven.com/svn/plugins/acts_as_state_machine/trunk
  ```

- The simple-daemon gem:

  ```
  $ gem install simple-daemon
  ```

Solution

Let's take the example of PDF generation. Requests for PDF updates come in, and we need to get them stamped as soon as possible. On a particularly busy day when PDFs get queued up, we also need to track their status.

This seems like a fairly difficult task, but with a few off-the-shelf ingredients we'll be up and running in no time. We'll use a simple Ruby daemon (simple-daemon) to poll our database looking for new PDF generation jobs and the acts_as_state_machine plug-in to manage the workflow states.

First, we need a model that represents the work to be done, so let's start by creating a Pdf model and migration:

```
$ script/generate model pdf title:string state:string ↩
    version:integer priority:integer processing_error_message:string
$ rake db:migrate
```

Of particular note are the state and version columns:

- The state column will be used by acts_as_state_machine to track what's currently happening with a PDF.

- The version column is a special Active Record column used for optimistic locking. It ensures that if two processes access the same row and try to save competing edits, the second edit will fail with an ActiveRecord::StaleObjectError exception. We'll handle that shortly.

Next, in our Pdf model we set up acts_as_state_machine to transition between states when certain events are fired (see Recipe 16, *Create Multistep Wizards*, on page 81 for a state machine refresher):

AsyncWorkflow/app/models/pdf.rb

```ruby
class Pdf < ActiveRecord::Base

  acts_as_state_machine :initial => :pending

  state :pending
  state :processing
  state :complete
  state :error

  event :start_pdf_generation do
    transitions :from => :pending, :to => :processing
  end

  event :finish_pdf_generation do
    transitions :from => :processing, :to => :complete
  end

  event :processing_error do
    transitions :from => :processing, :to => :error
  end

  def self.find_for_pdf_generation
    find(:first,
        :conditions => "state = 'pending'",
        :order => "priority, created_at")
  end
```

```ruby
  def generate_pdf
    logger.info("Generating #{title} PDF...")
    # Insert your long-running code here to generate PDFs.
  end
end
```

A Pdf starts in the pending state. When a start_pdf_generation event occurs, for example, the Pdf transitions to the processing state. In this way, it goes from pending through to complete provided there are no errors. We've also written a custom find_for_pdf_generation method to fetch all the pending PDFs, ordered by priority.

Next, we need a side dish of code to drive our PDF state machine. Because it's not a model, we'll just put it in the lib directory:

`AsyncWorkflow/lib/generate_pdf.rb`

```ruby
require File.dirname(__FILE__) + '/../app/models/pdf.rb'

class GeneratePdf

  def self.run
    begin
      pdf = Pdf.find_for_pdf_generation
      raise ActiveRecord::RecordNotFound if pdf.nil?

      pdf.start_pdf_generation!
      pdf.generate_pdf
      pdf.finish_pdf_generation!

    rescue ActiveRecord::StaleObjectError
      # do nothing
    rescue ActiveRecord::RecordNotFound
      sleep 10
    rescue
      return unless pdf
      pdf.processing_error!
      pdf.update_attributes(:processing_error_message => "unknown error: #{$!}")
    end
  end
end
```

The single method in this class, run, first tries to pick a PDF off the pile using the find_for_pdf_generation method we wrote to return the next-highest-priority PDF. If a PDF is pending, the run method marks the PDF as being in-process by triggering the start_pdf_generation event. Then it carries on with the real work of generating the PDF. Finally, the finish_pdf_generation event is triggered, and our PDF transitions to the complete state.

However, if there are no pending PDFs, the run method sleeps for ten seconds and then checks again. If a StaleObjectError is raised—where two processes tried to save competing changes to the same PDF record—the second process will fail silently and move on to the next PDF. Finally, if an unknown exception is encountered, the PDF is moved to the error state, and the exception message is saved in the processing_error_message column.

The last piece of the puzzle is the daemon process that calls our run method in a loop. It's a script we'll run from the command line, so it goes in the scripts/pdf_generator file:

AsyncWorkflow/script/pdf_generator

```ruby
#!/usr/bin/env ruby

RAILS_ENV = ARGV[1] || 'development'

require File.dirname(__FILE__) + '/../config/environment.rb'

class PdfGeneratorDaemon < SimpleDaemon::Base

  SimpleDaemon::WORKING_DIRECTORY = "#{RAILS_ROOT}/log"

  def self.start
    loop do
      GeneratePdf.run
    end
  end

  def self.stop
    puts "Stopping PDF Generator..."
  end
end

PdfGeneratorDaemon.daemonize
```

This script uses the SimpleDaemon::Base class to manage a PID file. When the daemon starts, the log/pdf_generator.pid file is created, and the process ID of the daemon process is slipped inside. When the daemon is stopped, the PID is read from the log/pdf_generator.pid, and the corresponding process is stopped.

Before we run all this, we need to add two requirements that we'll throw in a Rails initializer file:

AsyncWorkflow/config/initializers/generate_pdf.rb

```ruby
require 'simple-daemon'
require 'generate_pdf'
```

OK, now let's fire up the daemon in development mode:

```
$ ruby script/pdf_generator start development
Daemon started.
```

Then we'll throw a PDF into the database using the console:

```
$ ruby script/console
>> p = Pdf.create(:title => "Advanced Rails Recipes", :priority => 1)
>> p.state
=> "pending"
```

Behind the scenes, the PDF gets picked up and processed:

```
>> p.reload
>> p.state
=> "complete"
```

When we're all done, it's polite to give the daemon a rest:

```
$ ruby script/pdf_generator stop development
```

Finally, to put all this into production, we'll add two custom tasks to our Capistrano recipe in the config/deploy.rb file:

```
task :start_pdf_generator :roles => :app do
  run "ruby #{current_path}/script/pdf_generator start production"
end

task :stop_pdf_generator :roles => :app do
  run "ruby #{current_path}/script/pdf_generator stop production"
end

after(:deploy) { stop_pdf_generator; start_pdf_generator }
```

These tasks run automatically after the standard deployment chores are done. Now sit back, relax, and let the hamsters do all the work....

Discussion

Workflows often include multiple states (or stages) with various events leading to each state. The rules can get fairly complex quickly, and acts_as_state_machine really shines in these scenarios. In this case, we used it as an effective way to model a simple workflow with a daemon processing it asynchronously. If you have multiple servers running your main application, you can run a processing daemon on each server. The downside (if you'd call this a downside) is that your processor is tightly bundled to your Rails application. It integrates at the model level, using the Pdf model in this case to find and process jobs.

Another approach to asynchronous processing—and there are many—is to integrate with a message queue as described in Recipe 42, *Send Lightweight Messages*, on page 233. Whenever a new PDF is available for processing, your Rails application would put a message on a queue that identifies the PDF, the location of the file, and the instructions for processing. Then your processing scripts would poll the queue looking for new jobs. When they find one, they would do their processing and then respond to your Rails application synchronously through REST, for example. Amazon's Simple Queuing Service (SQS) is also worth considering.

You should consider at least two additional improvements:

- Check for lost jobs. If a job enters the processing state but doesn't finish, it will be lost in limbo. Add a processed_at column to the Pdf model, and set the state machine to populate processed_at with the current time when the document enters the processing state. You'll also need to change the find_for_pdf_generation method to look for jobs with a state of processing that were marked as processed_at more than *N* minutes or hours ago.

- Monitor the daemon process with Monit, as described in Recipe 80, *Monitor (and Repair) Processes with Monit*, on page 413.

Part IX

E-mail Recipes

Validate E-mail Addresses

By Michael Slater (http://www.buildingwebapps.com)
Michael is president of Collective Knowledge Works, Inc., which publishes the BuildingWe-
bApps.com portal for Ruby on Rails developers. He has worked as a freelance web developer, director of digital imaging research at Adobe Systems, cofounder and chairman
of software start-up Fotiva, editor and publisher of the Microprocessor Report newsletter,
hardware engineering consultant, and engineer at Hewlett-Packard.

Problem

When people create an account for your application, they enter their
e-mail address. You use that address to send them account activation
links, order receipts, and so on. Sometimes people mistype their e-mail
address, and they never receive your e-mails. (Instead, you get an e-
mail from them complaining they never received thus and such.) So,
you need to verify their e-mail address before it gets stored in your
database.

Solution

We could require that people enter their e-mail address twice in hopes
of catching mistakes, but that seems clunky. Or we could send them
an e-mail with an activation link that provides the only true validation.
Wait, that won't work! We don't have a valid address where we can send
it. What we really need to do is validate the e-mail address when the
user enters it.

There are two parts to this solution: checking that what they enter
looks like an e-mail address *and* checking that the domain name is
valid. Let's tackle the tricky part first.

The only way to check the domain name is to actually go out over the
network and ask the domain whether it handles e-mail. We'll do that in
our Account model with the help of the Ruby standard resolv library:

`ValidateEmail/app/models/account.rb`

```ruby
require 'resolv'

class Account < ActiveRecord::Base

  EMAIL_PATTERN = /(\S+)@(\S+)/
  SERVER_TIMEOUT = 3 # seconds
```

```ruby
def valid_domain?(email)
  domain = email.match(EMAIL_PATTERN)[2]

  dns = Resolv::DNS.new

  Timeout::timeout(SERVER_TIMEOUT) do
    # Check the MX records
    mx_records =
      dns.getresources(domain, Resolv::DNS::Resource::IN::MX)

    mx_records.sort_by {|mx| mx.preference}.each do |mx|
      a_records = dns.getresources(mx.exchange.to_s,
                                   Resolv::DNS::Resource::IN::A)
      return true if a_records.any?
    end

    # Try a straight A record
    a_records = dns.getresources(domain, Resolv::DNS::Resource::IN::A)
    a_records.any?
  end
rescue Timeout::Error, Errno::ECONNREFUSED
  false
end
end
```

After teasing out the domain name from the rest of the e-mail address using a regular expression, we use the resolv library to look for mail exchanger (MX) records at the domain. If it finds mail records, they just contain a domain name, so the inner check verifies that the name corresponds to a valid domain. If we find an MX record with a name that matches an A record, then that's the best shot we have at being able to send e-mail to that domain. However, a server doesn't need an MX record to receive an e-mail. So if no MX records were found or had valid domain names, we fall back to checking for an A record. And if doing all this takes too long because a DNS server times out, we treat the e-mail as being invalid.

Then we combine this with simple formatting validation in our Account model, and we have everything we need:

`ValidateEmail/app/models/account.rb`

```ruby
validates_format_of :email, :with => EMAIL_PATTERN

def validate
  unless errors.on(:email)
    unless valid_domain?(email)
      errors.add(:email, 'domain name appears to be incorrect')
    end
  end
end
```

Only if the e-mail matches a loose format do we then go ahead and try to run the network tests with the valid_domain? method. And if everything shakes out, then we wind up with what we believe to be a valid e-mail address in our database.

This is a good step forward: it protects against typos. However, it doesn't validate that there's a working SMTP server living at the other end. We could try to ping the SMTP server through port 25, but modern spam prevention techniques implemented by many servers make this difficult and potentially very slow.

Discussion

A lot of people try using a fancy, strict regular expression they found on the Web to check the e-mail format. While certainly a challenging exercise in regex mojo, these days valid e-mail addresses can have all kinds of weird and wacky characters. I've had better luck using the really basic regular expression shown in this recipe. Your mileage may vary, as they say.

It's possible to take this a step further by sending the SMTP server referenced in the MX record a RCPT TO: command. In theory, this would check that the username is valid as well as the domain name. However, it takes additional time, and mail servers don't always respond reliably.

Also See

You might also want to look at the Email Veracity plug-in,[1] which runs similar validations. We chose to implement our own recipe from scratch to demonstrate the concepts.

---

1. http://rails.savvica.com/2007/11/6/email-veracity-plugin

Receive E-mail Reliably via POP or IMAP

By Luke Francl (http://railspikes.com)
Luke is a Ruby on Rails developer for Slantwise Design, a Minneapolis-based Rails consultancy. He is a contributor to the MMS2R project and an active member of the Ruby Users of Minnesota. Luke has presented on Ruby and Rails at conferences worldwide. Luke comes to Rails from the Java world and still thinks foreign key constraints belong in the database.

Problem

You need to process incoming e-mail with your Rails application, but you want to make sure you can handle large volumes of e-mail (or a e-mail bomb) without breaking a sweat. You'd rather not configure and run your own mail server.

Ingredients

- An e-mail account that you can access via POP3 or IMAP. If you have a choice, IMAP is better because you can move messages that can't be processed to a folder (call it "bogus" if you want) for later investigation.

- The Fetcher plug-in:

  ```
  $ script/plugin install ↩
      svn://rubyforge.org/var/svn/slantwise/fetcher/trunk
  ```

  The fetcher includes code to download e-mail from POP3 and IMAP servers and includes backports from Ruby 1.9 to support secure POP and the PLAIN authentication type for IMAP. It also contains utility code to generate long-running daemon processes, using the Daemon::Base library.[1]

- Optionally, the MMS2R gem:[2]

  ```
  $ gem install MMS2R
  ```

  This is a time-saver for dealing with multipart MIME messages that have attachments. It's targeted at MMS messages but works for all e-mail with attachments.

---

1. http://snippets.dzone.com/posts/show/2265
2. http://mms2r.rubyforge.org

> **Solution**

Imagine we're at the helm of a popular website that lets people e-mail recipes (and a picture of what came out of the oven) to our application, and all the recipes get displayed on a page that updates every few minutes.

The most frequently given solution is to create a procmail rule something like this:

```
:0 c
* ^To:.*@example.com
| /your/rails/app && ruby script/runner "MailProcessor.receive(STDIN.read)"
```

This rule says to take all e-mail sent to any address at example.com and send it to a class called MailProcessor. This approach has two drawbacks for our situation:

- It will fork a Rails process for each e-mail we receive. We hope to get a lot of e-mail, and this approach may overwhelm our server.

- It requires that we run an MTA such as sendmail or postfix, perhaps even with special mail delivery rules, which (as anyone who has tried to configure one knows) is a task best avoided if possible.

Instead, we're going to use a third-party mail server via POP3 or IMAP and let them sweat the details. Using POP3 or IMAP to access our e-mail requires a little more code than the procmail route, but in the end we'll have a better solution.

First, we need an ActionMailer::Base subclass to handle the e-mail when it comes in:

> ReceivingEmail/app/models/mail_processor.rb

```ruby
class MailProcessor < ActionMailer::Base

  def receive(mail)
    # Your e-mail handling code goes here
    puts "Received a message with the subject '#{mail.subject}'"
  end

end
```

Then we need a way to fetch e-mail from the mail server and deliver it into our MailProcessor model. And, of course, we want it to run continuously so that we get e-mail in a timely manner. The fetcher plug-in handles all that for us.

Next, we generate a fetcher daemon to fetch the mail:

```
$ script/generate fetcher mail
```

In this case, we'll end up with a fetcher called MailFetcherDaemon in script/mail_fetcher. We also get a config/mail.yml configuration file that we will update with the e-mail accounts we will use in different Rails environments:

> ReceivingEmail/config/mail.yml

```
development:
  type: pop
  server: mail.example.com
  username: recipes@example.com
  password: yum

test:
  type: pop
  server: localhost
  username: username
  password: password

production:
  type: pop
  server: localhost
  username: username
  password: password
```

We have several configuration options here, including the following:

- type: POP or IMAP.
- server: The IP address or domain name of the server.
- port: The port to connect to (defaults to the standard ports: 110 for POP3 or 143 for IMAP).
- ssl: Set to any value to use SSL encryption.
- authentication: The authentication scheme to use (IMAP only). Supports LOGIN, CRAM-MD5, and PASSWORD (defaults to PLAIN).
- use_login: Set to any value to use the LOGIN command instead of AUTHENTICATE (IMAP only). Some servers, such as Gmail, do not support AUTHENTICATE.
- processed_folder: The name of a folder to move mail to after it has been processed (IMAP only). If not specified, mail is deleted.
- error_folder: The name of a folder to move mail to if it causes an error during processing (IMAP only). Defaults to "bogus."
- sleep_time: The number of seconds for the generated daemon to sleep between fetches (defaults to 60 seconds).

Then we'll edit the generated fetcher daemon to use our MailProcessor class as the receiver of e-mail:

ReceivingEmail/script/mail_fetcher

```
def self.start
  puts "Starting MailFetcherDaemon"
  @fetcher = Fetcher.create({:receiver => MailProcessor}.merge(@config))

  loop do
    @fetcher.fetch
    sleep(@sleep_time)
  end
end
```

The Fetcher.create factory method creates a Fetcher::Imap or Fetcher::Pop instance (depending on your configuration settings) with the MailProcessor as the receiver. When the Fetcher#fetch method is called, the e-mail from the configured mail server is downloaded. Then each message is fed to MailProcessor#receive in turn and deleted from the mail account. Between fetches, the daemon sleeps for the configured sleep time or a default of sixty seconds.

All that's left is to start the daemon with the proper Rails environment (it defaults to development):

```
$ RAILS_ENV=production script/mail_fetcher start
```

Remember, by default the fetcher deletes e-mail after processing it, so it's probably unwise to test it on your personal e-mail account. Also, in the case of problems or a server restart, the daemon won't start up automatically.[3]

Having started the daemon, it keeps running until we call stop:

```
$ RAILS_ENV=production script/mail_fetcher stop
```

Now we can receive incoming e-mail from our existing POP3 or IMAP account without worrying about the overhead.

Discussion

This solution required some extra code to keep the fetcher running continuously. Why not just use cron for this? Using cron would probably work fine in most cases. In fact, you could use the fetcher plug-in to fetch mail every minute with cron.

---

3. A good way to resolve this is to use Monit as described in Recipe 80, *Monitor (and Repair) Processes with Monit*, on page 413.

For example:

```
* * * * * script/runner 'Fetcher.create({:receiver => MailProcessor,
  :type => "pop", :server => "mail.example.com",
  :authentication => "PLAIN", :username => "username",
  :password => "password" }).fetch'
```

A drawback to this approach is that if the e-mail takes more than a minute to process, another cron job will start up and process the same e-mail twice. Unexpected results may occur! The daemon will always run for as long as it takes to process the current e-mail in the mailbox and then sleep for :sleep_time seconds. This ensures there's only one process accessing the same e-mail box at a time (assuming you don't start up two daemons!)

As an alternative to using the fetcher plug-in, you could roll your own solution using Ruby's built-in support for POP3 (net/pop) and IMAP (net/imap). For example, Benjamin Curtis[4] uses the following script to create Bug model objects in his bug tracker while iterating over a list of e-mails found in an IMAP inbox:

```
require 'rubygems'
require 'lockfile'
require 'net/imap'

Lockfile('lock', :retries => 0) do
  require File.dirname(__FILE__) + '/../config/boot'
  require File.dirname(__FILE__) + '/../config/environment'

  imap = Net::IMAP.new('imap_server_name')
  imap.authenticate('LOGIN', 'imap_login', 'imap_password')

  imap.select('INBOX')
  imap.search(["ALL"]).each do |message_id|
    email = imap.fetch(message_id, 'RFC822')[0].attr['RFC822']
    parsed_mail = TMail::Mail.parse(email)

    unless parsed_mail.to.nil? # Spam
      Bug.create(:tmail => parsed_mail)
    end
    imap.store(message_id, "+FLAGS", [:Deleted])
  end

  imap.expunge
  imap.logout
  imap.disconnect
end
```

---

4. http://www.bencurtis.com/

Typically this script would be run from cron or daemonized, and it's possible that a run of the script could take long enough to bump into the next invocation of the script. So, the script uses the lockfile gem to make sure that only one instance is running at any time.

To keep the details of bug creation out of the IMAP script, you'd create a method in your Bug model that contains the logic for creating a new record given a parsed e-mail (a Mail::TMail object). Here's an example:

```
class Bug < ActiveRecord::Base
  belongs_to :user

  def tmail=(tmail_obj)
    self.user = User.find_or_create_by_email(tmail_obj.from.first)
    self.summmary = tmail_obj.subject
    self.description = tmail_obj.body
  end
end
```

Send E-mail via Gmail

By Daniel Fischer (http://www.danielfischer.com/)
Daniel is your friendly Los Angeles technology geek. He runs the technology and design blog "Got Fisch." He spends his days rocking code at the world-renowned development shop CitrusByte.

Setting up a mail server and making sure e-mails sent from your app reach their destination is a hassle. It's one of those jobs worth delegating to someone who delivers the mail through rain, sleet, *and* snow. You know, someone like Gmail.

Off-loading your e-mail to Gmail takes a couple nonintuitive steps. First, you need to sign up for a free account with Google Apps[1] for your domain.

Gmail requires some funky security tunneling to authenticate (TLS). The Ruby net/smtp library doesn't support TLS, so you'll need to grab Marc Chung's plug-in:[2]

```
$ cd vendor/plugins
$ svn export ←
    https://openrain.com/opensource/public/rails/plugins/action_mailer_tls ←
    action_mailer_tls
```

Finally, configure ActionMailer by creating an smtp_gmail.rb file inside your config/initializers directory with the following:

```
require "smtp_tls"

ActionMailer::Base.smtp_settings = {
  :address        => "smtp.gmail.com",
  :port           => 587,
  :user_name      => "your-gmail-username@your-domain.com",
  :password       => "your-gmail-password",
  :authentication => :plain
}
```

There's one catch (you knew there would be): the free version of Google Apps allows you to send only up to 500 e-mails per day for each domain e-mail address.

---

1. http://www.google.com/a/
2. The standard script/plugin install incantation doesn't work.

Keep E-mail Addresses Up-to-Date

By Mike Mangino (http://www.elevatedrails.com)
Mike is the founder of Elevated Rails. He lives in Chicago with his wife, Jen, and their two Samoyeds.

Problem

E-mail, for better or worse, remains the primary way to communicate with your application's users: sending password resets, account confirmations, order receipts, and so on. Unfortunately, e-mail addresses become invalid at a rate of around 15 to 20 percent a year. How do you keep the e-mail addresses for your users up-to-date?

Solution

The key to keeping valid e-mail addresses is proactive maintenance. If you regularly correspond with users, detecting bounces can be simple and painless. Indeed, the first edition of *Rails Recipes* [Fow06] contains a recipe on handling e-mail bounces. However, some e-mail servers don't provide bounced messages in a format suitable for that recipe.

We will tackle how to handle bounced e-mail in two steps: detecting bounces and notifying e-mail owners of the problem (and how to fix it).

First, the easiest way to detect bounces is to use a consistent reply-to and from address in all the e-mail we send from our application. Addresses such as no-reply@example.com or bounces@example.com tend to work well. If we receive an e-mail at one of these addresses, it's a strong indication of a bounce (but not always guaranteed).

Then, once we've received a bounced e-mail, we need to associate it with a user. There are two simple methods we can use, depending upon how much control we have over our e-mail environment.

If we have complete freedom in the e-mail addresses we can use, it's easiest to use a unique e-mail address per recipient. For example, if all e-mail sent to the user with ID 37 is sent with a from address and a reply-to of no-reply-37@example.com, then we can easily match it up with the right user. To do that, we'll create a setup_for_user helper method in our mailer model, which we'll call UserMailer.

`EmailBounces/app/models/user_mailer.rb`

```ruby
class UserMailer < ActionMailer::Base

  def new_comment(user, comment)
    setup_for_user(user)
    @subject += " A new comment has been left for you!"
    @body[:comment] = comment
  end

  def setup_for_user(user)
    recipients  user.email
    from  "No Reply <bounces-#{user.id}@example.com>"
    @subject = "[APP_NAME] "
    @body[:user] = user
  end

  def receive(email)
    Bounce.create_for(email)
  end

end
```

This just makes sure we're consistently including the user's ID in the from address. The mailer also includes a receive method. In this recipe, we'll simply handle bounced e-mails in the receive. Recipe 46, *Receive E-mail Reliably via POP or IMAP*, on page 257 describes how this method gets called when an e-mail arrives at your mail account.

If we don't have that sort of flexibility in our e-mail environment, we can instead encode user information in a custom e-mail header. Most e-mail servers will give back the entire bounced e-mail, including headers. All we'd need to do to support that is change the setup_for_user method to set an X-User-ID header, for example:

`EmailBounces/app/models/user_mailer.rb`

```ruby
def setup_for_user(user)
  recipients  user.email
  from  "No Reply <bounces@example.com>"
  @subject = "[APP_NAME] "
  headers["X-User-ID"] = user.id
  @body[:user] = user
end
```

Next, we'll create a bounces database table to record bounced e-mails, where each bounce belongs to a user. We'll do that by generating the Bounce model and applying its migration:

```
$ script/generate model bounce text:body user_id:integer
$ rake db:migrate
```

Then we'll add a create_for method to the Bounce model to parse incoming (defunct) e-mails:

EmailBounces/app/models/bounce.rb

```ruby
class Bounce < ActiveRecord::Base
  belongs_to :user

  def self.create_for(email)
    body = email.to_s

    return unless body.match(/MAILER-DAEMON/i)

    email.to.each do |recipient|
      address = recipient.split(/@/)[0]
      if address and match = address.match(/bounces-(\d+)/)
        process_match(match, email)
      end
    end

    if match = email.to_s.match(/X-User-ID:\s+(\d+)/mi)
      process_match(match, email)
    end
  end
end
```

The create_for method first looks for the MAILER-DAEMON string to make sure the e-mail is a bounce. If it isn't found, processing stops. Next, it looks at both the recipients and the headers for strings we used in our UserMailer to try to find a user ID associated with this e-mail. If it finds an e-mail address and a user ID, then the pair is handed off to the process_match method. We'll add that method and a helper to the Bounce class, too:

EmailBounces/app/models/bounce.rb

```ruby
def self.process_match(match, email)
  user_id = match[1]
  user = User.find(user_id)

  cleanup_old_bounces(user)
  bounce = create!(:user => user, :body => email.to_s)
  user.email_bounced(bounce)
end

def self.cleanup_old_bounces(user)
  old = user.bounces.find(:all,:conditions => ["created_at < ?", 21.days.ago])
  old.each(&:destroy)
  user.bounces.reload
end
```

This code creates a new Bounce record associated with the user and purges old bounces to keep things tidy. (Saving off the contents of the message takes a little extra space, but it also makes bounce debugging possible.)

Once the bounce has been processed and recorded, we call the email_bounced method on the User model to signal a bounce condition. Let's assume that e-mail is a crucial component to our app, and we want the user to correct the e-mail address as quickly as possible. (How you respond to e-mail bounces will depend greatly upon your application's needs.) To do that, we'll set an email_validated_at flag indicating that the user must update or verify their address. Here's the final User class:

EmailBounces/app/models/user.rb

```ruby
class User < ActiveRecord::Base
  has_many :bounces

  MAX_BOUNCES = 1

  def email_bounced(bounce)
    if bounces.size > MAX_BOUNCES
      update_attribute(:email_validated_at, nil)
    end
  end

  def should_email?
    email_validated_at?
  end

end
```

Then, over in our ApplicationController, we'll use two before_filter methods to make sure a user is logged in *and* has a validated e-mail address on file:

EmailBounces/app/controllers/application.rb

```ruby
before_filter :login_required
before_filter :require_valid_email

def login_required
  @user = User.find(session[:user_id])
  redirect_to new_session_path and return false if @user.nil?
end

def require_valid_email
  unless @user.should_email?
    render :action=> "users/validate_email"
    return false
  end
end
```

Finally, we'll skip this before_filter for actions a user might use to change and/or reconfirm their e-mail address:

```
skip_before_filter :require_valid_email,
                   :only => [:edit, :verify, :update]
```

With bounce detection in place and an easy way for users to take corrective measures, our application is now in a good position to keep e-mail addresses up-to-date.

Discussion

Because e-mail occasionally bounces because of misconfigured servers, you may not want to disable an account on the first bounce. It often makes sense to send a verification e-mail 24 to 48 hours after the first bounce. If that e-mail bounces, it's probably safe to mark the address as bouncing. If that e-mail doesn't bounce, it makes sense to clear the bounce history. You can adjust the MAX_BOUNCES constant used in this recipe to control how many bounces are necessary to disable an account. If you have other methods of communicating with your users, such as RSS or SMS, you may want to use these channels to notify them of e-mail bounces, as well.

Bounce messages come from the SMTP server that you use to send e-mail. Be sure to test with your production SMTP server, because implementations vary between vendors.

If you use IDs in your bounce detection that are easy to guess, a malicious user could potentially shut down another user's account. This could be a real problem for auction- or finance-related applications. There is more than one solution to prevent this. First, instead of using the ID column, use a UUID or other long and fairly random ID. You could also record each message sent and use a unique ID per message. This is more secure and can give you better traceability but may not be worth the trouble, especially if you send a large number of messages.

Part X

Testing Recipes

Maintain Fixtures Without Frustration

Test fixtures have become a millstone around your neck, dragging you down every time you try to be a good little tester. You spend hours getting all the fixture records knitted together with IDs, only to have it all come crumbling down with the slightest change to test data. If only you didn't have to remember all those numbers, life would be a little sweeter (and you'd actually get some tests written).

Let's start with a little recap of just how quickly text fixtures can go bad. Suppose we have a has_and_belongs_to_many relationship between users and tags. To populate the tags_users join table of our test database, we painstakingly created the following tags_users.yml fixture file:

```
fred_caveman:
  user_id: 1
  tag_id: 1

fred_programmer:
  user_id: 1
  tag_id: 3

barney_caveman:
  user_id: 2
  tag_id: 1

barney_juggler:
  user_id: 2
  tag_id: 2
```

Tying these relationships together with primary keys really hurts and leads to brittle fixture files. It also makes the fixture files hard to decipher, too: what exactly are Barney's tags? It's pretty much all bad news. So, let's clean this mess up using the new (foxy) fixtures in Rails 2.0.

First, we'll delete the tags_users.yml fixture file altogether. We don't need it because we already have a tags.yml file, and each tag record has a label:

```
programmer:
  name: Programmer

juggler:
  name: Juggler

caveman:
  name: Caveman
```

Then we'll update the users.yml fixture file and tag each user using the labels from our tags.yml file:

```
fred:
  name: Fred Flintstone
  email: fred@flintstones.com
  tags: caveman, programmer
barney:
  name: Barney Rubble
  email: barney@rubbles.com
  tags: caveman, juggler
```

Now that's more like it! Rather than using IDs, we can just use the tags association because the fixture knows that our User model declares a has_and_belongs_to_many association to our Tag model.

In fact, we don't need to type *any* IDs into our fixture files—they're generated for us by hashing the fixture record label. All we need to remember is the label. And if we really need the ID for a label, for example when patching up old fixtures, we can turn it inside out using ERb in our fixture file:

```
tag_id: <%= Fixtures.identify(:caveman) %>
```

Or we can track down IDs from Rake:

```
$ rake db:fixtures:identify LABEL=caveman
```

Now let's use fixture labels to clean up another association in our app: an event has_many users through registrations, and vice versa. That is, we have a join model called Registration that points to both an Event and a User.

In this case, because a Registration isn't a pure join table, we'll need a registrations.yml fixture file for the registrations table. In the old days, the fixture file would be littered with foreign keys, like this:

```
fred_for_rails:
  event_id: 1
  user_id: 1
  price: 10.00
  paid_at: <%= 1.day.ago.to_s(:db) %>

barney_for_ruby:
  event_id: 2
  user_id: 2
  price: 20.00
  paid_at:
```

But we'll make that a lot more readable with foxy fixtures:

events/test/fixtures/registrations.yml

```
DEFAULTS: &DEFAULTS
  price: 10.00
  paid_at: <%= 1.day.ago.to_s(:db) %>

fred_for_rails:
  user: fred
  event: railsconf
  <<: *DEFAULTS

barney_for_ruby:
  user: barney
  event: rubyconf
  <<: *DEFAULTS
```

The fixture knows about the belong_to associations in our Registration model, so we can replace event_id with event, for example. While we're at it, refactoring all the duplicated fixture keys into a set of defaults that each record references makes the fixture even easier to maintain. Any fixture labeled DEFAULTS is ignored, and YAML takes care of the rest.

If you're writing test fixtures, using this new style goes a long way toward keeping everything in sync and flexible.

Discussion

Yes, foxy fixtures also support polymorphic associations. For example, suppose we have an Address model that can belong to an Event, a User, or any other model that's *addressable*, like so:

```
class Addressable
  belongs_to :addressable, :polymorphic => true
end
```

Instead of using the ID and the type in the fixture file, we can just use the polymorphic target label and type. Here's an example:

```
rails_in_denver:
  address: 10345 Park Meadows Drive
  city: Denver
  state: CO
  addressable: rails_studio (Event)

fred_in_denver:
  address: 123 Main Street
  city: Denver
  state: CO
  addressable: fred (User)
```

Describe Behavior from the Outside In with RSpec

By David Chelimsky (http://blog.davidchelimsky.net/)
David is the lead developer of RSpec and also leads software development at Articulated Man, Inc., in Chicago, Illinois. Prior to joining Articulated Man, David developed and taught courses in object-oriented design, test-driven development, and refactoring with Object Mentor, Inc. In addition to exploring Ruby, Rails, and behavior-driven development, David likes to play guitar and is learning to speak Portuguese.

Problem

You've heard a little bit about behavior-driven development and RSpec. You want to see what it's all about, but you don't know how to get started.

Ingredients

- The RSpec[1] plug-in:

    ```
    $ script/plugin install ↩
        http://rspec.rubyforge.org/svn/tags/CURRENT/rspec
    ```

- The RSpec rspec_on_rails plug-in:

    ```
    $ script/plugin install ↩
        http://rspec.rubyforge.org/svn/tags/CURRENT/rspec_on_rails
    ```

RSpec maintains a CURRENT tag, which will always get you the latest release.

Solution

RSpec supports *behavior-driven development*, which is basically test-driven development with more natural, behavior-centric language. That is a mouthful, but it's really quite simple. In BDD we write *executable examples* of how an object should behave and then write the code that makes that object behave correctly. We aim to make each example concise and focused on a single facet of behavior of the object being *described*.[2] Let's dive right in.

---

1. http://rspec.rubyforge.org
2. In BDD, we say we are describing the behavior of an object rather than testing it.

First we need to bootstrap RSpec into our Rails application:

```
$ script/generate rspec
      create  spec
      create  spec/spec_helper.rb
      create  spec/spec.opts
      create  spec/rcov.opts
      create  script/spec_server
      create  script/spec
      create  stories
      create  stories/all.rb
      create  stories/helper.rb
```

RSpec is under constant development, so you may see slightly different output depending on which version you are using. The important pieces for this recipe are the script/spec script, the spec directory, and the spec/spec_helper.rb file.

Then to make sure everything is happy, let's run the examples using the script/spec command, which is installed with the rspec_on_rails plug-in:

```
$ ruby script/spec spec

Finished in 0.00995 seconds

0 examples, 0 failures
```

Great! Now it's time to start writing some executable examples. We're going to work from the outside in: describe the behavior we want, and then write the code that satisfies the examples. What we want is a list of names and e-mail addresses for people. So, let's start from scratch by writing this example in spec/views/people/index.html.erb_spec.rb:

```
require File.join(File.dirname(__FILE__), "..", "..", "spec_helper.rb")

describe "/people/index.html.erb" do

  it "should list all the good people in an unordered list" do
    render '/people/index.html.erb'

    response.should have_tag("ul") do
      with_tag("li") do
        with_tag("div", "First Person")
        with_tag("div", "first@person.com")
      end
      with_tag("li") do
        with_tag("div", "Second Person")
        with_tag("div", "second@person.com")
      end
    end
  end
end
```

There's quite a bit going on here. Let's take it step by step.

First, the describe method creates an object that's similar to a test case. The it method creates an object that's similar to a test method.

The render method does just what it says: it renders the view template. RSpec uses a custom controller to render views based solely on their paths, which is why we need to supply the full path relative to app/views.

The meat of the example is where we express expectations[3] about the HTML that should be rendered by the view. Expectations are intended to be easy to read. So, we're saying that the response should have a ul tag, and inside that tag we should find other tags that list the people. By way of comparison, we could describe the same behavior using the assert_select method that comes with Rails, like so:

```
assert_select("ul") do
  assert_select("li") do
    assert_select("div", "First Person")
    assert_select("div", "first@person.com")
  end
  assert_select("li") do
    assert_select("div", "Second Person")
    assert_select("div", "second@person.com")
  end
end
```

So now with the example written, let's go ahead and run the examples again, this time with the spec task that comes with the plug-in:

```
$ rake spec
```

Hmm, we get an ActionController::MissingTemplate error. To resolve that error, we need to create the template app/views/people/index.html.erb. Let's leave it blank for now and run the examples again. This time we'll use the following:

```
$ rake spec
```

```
Expected at least 1 element matching "ul", found 0.
```

---

3. In BDD, we refer to *expectations* instead of *assertions*.

Clearly, we need some structure in our template. So, let's add the following to app/views/people/index.html.erb:

```
<ul>
<% for person in @people -%>
  <li>
    <div><%= h person.full_name %></div>
    <div><%= h person.email %></div>
  </li>
<% end -%>
</ul>
```

This time when we run the examples, we get "You have a nil object when you didn't expect it!" from our @people instance variable. Well, of course! There are no people. We have a view example and a view template, but there are absolutely no models or controllers.

Let's supply our view with the data that it needs, but let's do it without building out the other pieces. The view wants an array of @people, so let's just simulate one:

RSpec/spec/views/people/index.html.erb_spec.rb
```
require File.join(File.dirname(__FILE__), "..", "..", "spec_helper.rb")

describe "/people/index.html.erb" do

  it "should list all the good people in an unordered list" do
    assigns[:people] = [
      stub("person1", :full_name => "First Person",
                      :email => "first@person.com"),
      stub("person2", :full_name => "Second Person",
                      :email => "second@person.com")
    ]

    render '/people/index.html.erb'

    response.should have_tag("ul") do
      with_tag("li") do
        with_tag("div", "First Person")
        with_tag("div", "first@person.com")
      end
      with_tag("li") do
        with_tag("div", "Second Person")
        with_tag("div", "second@person.com")
      end
    end
  end
end
```

The assigns method lets us specify instance variables that will be available to the view. In this case, there will be a @people instance variable containing an array of two stub objects.[4] Each stub object returns stub (fake) values for full_name and email.

Now let's come full circle by running the examples again:

```
$ rake spec
.

Finished in 0.081351 seconds

1 example, 0 failures
```

As a bonus, let's list all our expectations:

```
$ ruby script/spec spec --format specdoc

/people/index.html.erb
- should list all the good people in an unordered list

Finished in 0.113134 seconds

1 example, 0 failures
```

And while we're at it, let's also generate a nice HTML report:

```
$ ruby script/spec spec --format html:rspec_report.html
```

All the things we expect our object to do are listed in the rspec_report.html file.

That's all there is to it—we've described our first bit of Rails behavior using RSpec. We started with a failing executable example, added the code to make it pass, and did so without relying on the existence of any controllers or models in our app.

In addition, without even thinking about it, we've discovered exactly what our controller will need to provide for the view (a collection of people) and that each person will need to have first_name and last_name attributes. Imagine how powerful that can be when you're dealing with a complex model. This is what *outside in* is all about: we start with the outermost layers and let them guide us all the way down to the low-level components of our applications.

---

4. RSpec comes with a built-in mocking and stubbing framework. If you are already familiar with either FlexMock or Mocha, you can use those instead.

Discussion

We went through that example pretty quickly, but there are a few interesting things that happened that we should talk about.

RSpec supports a philosophy that you should be able to describe each component in isolation from each other. For this to work effectively, you should include some level of integration testing[5] in your process. If you don't, it's possible to get all of the objects working correctly in isolation and then watch things fall apart when you fire up your application.

If you're experienced with TDD or BDD, you probably recognized that starting with so much of the example was a bigger step than we normally take in practice. Doing TDD/BDD with discipline, we would start with a much more granular step: perhaps a single line stating an expectation that some specific text is rendered. Then we follow the errors until the example passes and then add more detail to the example, follow the errors, get it to pass, rinse, and repeat, until the passing example expresses the detail that we saw earlier.

Did you notice that we wrote the code in the view before the stubs? Did that strike you as backward? Well, it is backward from how a lot of people use stubs, but think about this: we started by expressing our desired outcome, the list of people. That desired outcome led us to write the code that we expect to produce that outcome. It was only then, after we wrote that code and could see it, that we knew exactly what stubs to write. In the same way that the example expressed expectations of the view, the view code expressed expectations of its environment, which we then satisfied with the stubs.

Another thing you might have noticed is that the have_tag expectation is very specific. It will fail unless the particular tags are present with the correct nesting structure. This much detail tends to make the examples quite brittle, meaning that the example needs to change every time the HTML design changes.

Generally, the approach I take is to put in only the detail that has relevant business value. For example, a form won't work correctly if the input elements are not nested inside the form element. For that reason, I'll usually be specific about the structure of a form. Another case might be that there is JavaScript and/or CSS that will fall apart

---

5. RSpec 1.1.0 and newer support integration testing with the Story Runner, including a wrapper for Rails integration tests.

if things aren't structured in a specific way. Again, depending on the business value of that JavaScript or CSS, I might include that detail.

RSpec does express some opinions. In this example, the fact that we could render a view with no underlying controller and model is quite frightening to some who aren't experienced with this style of testing. Rails' functional tests express a different opinion—that you should run all the pieces in each of your tests to make sure they all work together. If you prefer that approach, you *can* achieve this with RSpec using RSpec's controller examples in integration mode.

Test First with Shoulda

Problem

You've heard about behavior-driven development (BDD) and you want to give it an honest try, but you want to start with a low-ceremony testing library that plays nicely with all your existing Test::Unit tests.

Ingredients

• The Shoulda plug-in:

```
$ svn export https://svn.thoughtbot.com/plugins/shoulda/tags/rel-<version> ↩
  vendor/plugins/shoulda
```

Solution

The Shoulda plug-in[1] is a thin layer of BDD-style syntax on top of Test::Unit that allows us to seamlessly mix it in with our existing Test::Unit tests and tools. Plus, we get a handy set of Rails-specific macros to help keep our test code concise.

In the BDD style, we'll start by expressing the behavior we want our code to have *before* writing the code. And we do this in small, incremental steps. So, let's say we need a model that represents an event, you know, like a party. We start by creating a regular Rails unit test:

events/test/unit/event_test.rb

```
class EventTest < ActiveSupport::TestCase
end
```

Now it's time to really think about events. What are they? Well, for starters an event should have a number of required attributes, and the name attribute should always be unique. We'll express that with Shoulda's validation helpers inside our unit test file:

events/test/unit/event_test.rb

```
class EventTest < ActiveSupport::TestCase
  should_require_attributes :name, :description, :image_location,
                            :starts_at, :location, :capacity

  should_require_unique_attributes :name
end
```

---

1. http://thoughtbot.com/projects/shoulda

Next, let's add some more expectations. The price should be a positive number, of course:

`events/test/unit/event_test.rb`

```
should_only_allow_numeric_values_for :price

should_not_allow_values_for :price, -1.0,
  :message => /must be greater than or equal to 0/
```

Oh, and real people attend events, so an event should have a many-to-many relationship with attendees:

`events/test/unit/event_test.rb`

```
should_have_many :attendees, :through => :registrations
```

Hey, that's a lot of thinking, and we haven't even written the code to make our expectations pass. Now, before writing the code, a card-carrying BDDer would first run all the tests and watch them fail. Better yet, they would have done it stepwise: written one assertion, watched it fail, and then written the code. Unfortunately, that makes for some fairly tedious reading material.

Let's go ahead and create the Event model with all the validations and associations we need:

`events/app/models/event.rb`

```
class Event < ActiveRecord::Base

  validates_presence_of    :name, :description, :image_location,
                           :starts_at, :location, :capacity
  validates_uniqueness_of :name

  validates_numericality_of :price, :greater_than_or_equal_to => 0.0

  has_many :registrations
  has_many :attendees, :through => :registrations,
                       :source => :user
end
```

We'll also need to create some event and registration test data. We'll do that in test fixture files:

`events/test/fixtures/events.yml`

```
railsconf:
  name: RailsConf
  description: The annual Rails conference..
  image_location: /images/railsconf.png
  starts_at: <%= 30.days.from_now.to_s(:db) %>
  location: Portland, OR
  capacity: 800
  price: 795
```

```
events/test/fixtures/registrations.yml
fred_for_rails:
  user: fred
  event: railsconf
```

Then we'll run the unit test using any of the standard tools and celebrate a small victory of programming!

You might consider breaking this test-code cycle down into snappier feedback loops. Personally, I like a steady diet of programmer treats, so I would have done this in two quick steps: one for the validations and one for the associations.

Moving onward, an event should be free when its price is $0. Now, we're talking about Event objects, so we'll need one to test against. We'll likely need that Event object for other tests, as well. So, we'll use a context block to keep everything together:

```
events/test/unit/event_test.rb
context "An event" do

  setup do
    @event = events(:railsconf)
  end

  should "be free when the price is $0" do
    @event.price = 0
    assert_equal true, @event.free?
  end

  should "not be free when the price isn't $0" do
    @event.price = 1.0
    assert_equal false, @event.free?
  end

end
```

The context block is just a name for the enclosing scenario, if you will. In this context, we're dealing with an Event object that we initialize in the setup block. The should block is a way of creating a test with a meaningful name. In fact, should blocks just create regular Test::Unit test methods behind the scenes. Inside the should blocks we can use any Test::Unit assertions, common assertions that come with Shoulda or custom assertions we write.

Now to make it pass, we'll add some code to the Event model:

events/app/models/event.rb

```ruby
def free?
  self.price == 0
end
```

One fairly unique feature of Shoulda is nested contexts. Say, for example, we're thinking through the behavior of event capacity. We'll need a couple of tests that require an event arranged a certain way. To do that, we'll just create a new context block within the one we already have and define a setup block that tweaks the existing @event object slightly. Here's the full test:

events/test/unit/event_test.rb

```ruby
context "An event" do

  setup do
    @event = events(:railsconf)
  end

  context "with excess capacity" do

    setup do
      @event.capacity = 2
      @event.registrations = [registrations(:fred_for_rails)]
    end

    should "have spaces remaining" do
      assert_equal 1, @event.spaces_remaining
    end

    should "not be sold out" do
      assert_equal false, @event.sold_out?
    end
  end
end
```

What we end up with here is something fairly readable: an event with excess capacity should not be sold out. We're also able to share the cumulative setup blocks, which helps remove duplication in our tests. The setup blocks for the contexts are run in order and before each should block. First the @event object is initialized, then its capacity and registrations are assigned, and finally the should block is run.

We can also mix Shoulda tests in with our existing functional tests and use Shoulda macros to keep the code concise. Here's how we'd express what a show action should do, for example:

events/test/functional/events_controller_test.rb

```
context "showing an event" do
  setup { get :show, :id => events(:railsconf) }

  should_assign_to :event
  should_respond_with :success
  should_render_template :show
  should_not_set_the_flash
end
```

Shoulda, coulda, woulda. Now you can!

Discussion

There's also a stripped-down version of the Should gem[2] for non-Rails projects, which includes just context and should blocks.

Also See

test/spec[3] is another lightweight BDD library that maps many of the standard Test::Unit assertions to a "should-like" syntax.

---

2. http://shoulda.rubyforge.org
3. http://chneukirchen.org/repos/testspec/

Write Domain-Specific RSpec Matchers

By Josh Stephenson (http://elctech.com)
Josh is a web developer specializing in Ruby on Rails and agile development at ELC Technologies. His penchant for clean code and test-driven development leads him to look for elegant solutions to complex problems.

Problem

You're using RSpec to describe your application's behavior from the outside in, and you're enjoying the expressive syntax. However, sometimes you have domain-specific expectations that don't map naturally to any of the stock matchers. After all, RSpec doesn't know about your domain. You want to write your own expectation matchers to make your tests more readable and maintainable over time.

Ingredients

- The RSpec[1] plug-in:

```
$ script/plugin install ↩
    http://rspec.rubyforge.org/svn/tags/CURRENT/rspec
```

- The RSpec rspec_on_rails plug-in:

```
$ script/plugin install ↩
    http://rspec.rubyforge.org/svn/tags/CURRENT/rspec_on_rails
```

RSpec maintains a CURRENT tag, which will always get you the latest release.

Solution

Custom RSpec expectation matchers are very easy to write and yet not often utilized. Let's say, for example, we're working with an application that pairs users based on their zodiac signs, and we're not satisfied with expectations that look like this:

```
@josh.likes?(@alicia).should be_true
```

---

1. http://rspec.rubyforge.org

Instead, we want something a tad more expressive, like this:

```
@josh.should like(@alicia)
```

To start building that custom matcher, we need to get RSpec ready. In the spec/spec_helper.rb file, we'll add the following to the top of the file below the other require lines:

RSpecMatcher/spec/spec_helper.rb

```
require 'spec/zodiac_match_maker'
```

Then inside the Spec::Runner.configure block, we'll add the following:

RSpecMatcher/spec/spec_helper.rb

```
config.include(ZodiacMatchMaker)
```

Next, we'll write the ZodiacMatchMaker class. It goes in the spec/zodiac_match_maker.rb file. All custom expectation matchers have this basic structure:

RSpecMatcher/spec/zodiac_match_maker.rb

```
module ZodiacMatchMaker
  class Like
    def initialize(expected)
      @expected = expected
    end

    def matches?(target)
    end

    def failure_message
    end

    def negative_failure_message
    end
  end
end
```

First, we'll fill in the matches? method. This is where we hide that ugliness from our original expectation:

RSpecMatcher/spec/zodiac_match_maker.rb

```
def matches?(target)
  @target = target
  @target.likes?(@expected)
end
```

The @target in this case will be a User object, and the @expected is another User looking for a compatible date.

Then we'll fill in the failure_message and negative_failure_message methods. The only difference is the negative_failure_message is used when you specify that a user should like another user and sadly it ends up not being true.

RSpecMatcher/spec/zodiac_match_maker.rb

```
def failure_message
  "expected #{@target.inspect} to like  #{@expected.inspect} but doesn't!"
end

def negative_failure_message
  "expected #{@target.inspect} not to like #{@expected.inspect} but does!"
end
```

Lastly, we'll write a method inside the ZodiacMatchMaker module that gives our specs access to an initialized Like class:

RSpecMatcher/spec/zodiac_match_maker.rb

```
def like(sign)
  Like.new(sign)
end
```

Now over in our specs, we'll use the like method we just wrote, like this:

```
@josh.should like(@alicia)
```

Going a step further, let's now say we want to support an even more expressive syntax:

```
@josh.should like_virgos
@josh.should_not like_leos
```

To pull this off, we're going to take a page right out of the RSpec playbook and use method_missing. Back in the spec/zodiac_match_maker.rb file, we'll add the following new module:

RSpecMatcher/spec/zodiac_match_maker.rb

```
module ZodiacMatchMakerExtension
  def method_missing(sym, *args, &block) # :nodoc:
    zodiac_signs = User.find_distinct_signs.map(&:pluralize)
    sym.to_s.scan(/like_(#{zodiac_signs.join('|')})/) do
      mock_user = mock_model(User, :sign => $1.singularize)
      return ZodiacMatchMaker::Like.new(mock_user)
    end
    super
  end
end
```

The first argument to method_missing corresponds to the name of the method called. In our example it's either like_virgos or like_leos. We use a regular expression to scan the method name to see whether it's something we recognize. We're assuming the User class has a find_distinct_signs method that finds an array of signs. If we find a match, we create a mock User with the zodiac sign we matched in the method name and initialize a new Like object with the mock User. Equally important, we need to call super if the method name doesn't match any of our signs.

Finally, we'll include this new module in the spec/spec_helper.rb file. Here's the order in which our two modules are included:

RSpecMatcher/spec/spec_helper.rb

```
config.include(ZodiacMatchMaker)
config.include(ZodiacMatchMakerExtension)
```

Now all our specs can use any of the following expectations:

```
@josh.should like(@alicia)
@josh.should_not like(@sandy)

@josh.should like_virgos
@josh.should_not like_leos
```

Better yet, we can change how the custom expectations work without having to change all of our specs.

Custom expectation matchers make the practice of behavior-driven development more fun and the syntax even more readable.

Write Custom Testing Tasks

Not all tests are created equal. Some run fast, some slow. Most can be run while you're on an airplane, but some may need a network connection. Of course, all of them should pass all the time.

But when you're working on code that has fast, localized tests, you don't want the slow, networked tests to get in your way. Instead, you want to organize automated tests around what they need and how frequently they're run.

Let's say we have a performance-critical algorithm in our application. It must run within a second, or users start shopping around for a new site (and we end up shopping around for a new job). The trouble is, this algorithm is fairly sensitive to changes.

We'll start by writing a test that uses the Benchmark module to time how long the algorithm takes to run. If we introduce a change that slows it down too much, the test will let out a yelp. Here's what it looks like:

`TestTasks/test/performance/perf_test.rb`

```
require File.dirname(__FILE__) + '/../test_helper'
require 'benchmark'

class PerfTest < Test::Unit::TestCase
  def test_performance_critical_code
    time = Benchmark.realtime do
      # run code that should not
      # take more than 1.0 seconds
    end

    assert time <= 1.0
  end
end
```

Now, we could have put this file in the test/unit directory, but we want our unit tests to run as fast as possible. So, we put the performance test file in the test/performance directory to keep it away from all the other tests.

Next, we'll create the following Rake task in a file called testing.rake in the lib/tasks directory:

TestTasks/lib/tasks/testing.rake

```
namespace :test do
  Rake::TestTask.new(:performance => "db:test:prepare") do |t|
    t.libs << "test"
    t.pattern = 'test/performance/**/*_test.rb'
    t.verbose = true
  end
  Rake::Task['test:performance'].comment =
    "Run the performance tests in test/performance"
end
```

This task is similar to how the default Rails testing tasks are created. The only difference is the name of the target and the directory. It gathers up all the test files in the test/performance directory and runs them in batch. Now we can quickly run all the unit tests in isolation. And whenever we're messing around with that performance-critical algorithm, we'll explicitly run the performance tests using this:

```
$ rake test:performance
```

We can create as many of these testing buckets as we need. For example, we might also have a suite of tests for the code we use to validate e-mail addresses. Checking the e-mail domain name requires a good network connection. So, we might define a test:network task that runs all the network-related tests in the test/network directory, for example.

Discussion

Of course, you want to run all your tests at least once per day to detect small problems before they compound into bigger messes. Creating custom Rake tasks makes it easy to run logical groups of tests on an automated schedule based on when you need feedback. Here's an example build schedule:

- Unit and functional tests run every five minutes.
- Integration tests run every hour.
- Network tests run every four hours.
- Performance tests run at 2 a.m. daily.

If you're not already testing your code on a recurring schedule, check out CruiseControl.rb[1] to get started in minutes.

---

1. http://cruisecontrolrb.thoughtworks.com/

Test JavaScript with Selenium

By Marty Haught, Andrew Kappen, Chris Bernard, Greg Hansen (http://www.logicleaf.com/)
Marty, Andrew, Chris, and Greg all work together at LogicLeaf, an agile software consulting company. To support their projects, they've developed several streamlined testing processes, including a simpler way to integrate Selenium into the daily development cycle.

Problem

Your application uses Ajax for a creamy, smooth user experience. Unfortunately, debugging JavaScript can be a royal pain, so you'd rather put some tests in place that will catch JavaScript bugs before they fall through the cracks.

Ingredients

- The Selenium on Rails plug-in:

  ```
  $ script/plugin install↩
    http://svn.openqa.org/svn/selenium-on-rails/selenium-on-rails
  ```

- Windows users should also install the win32-open3 gem:

  ```
  $ gem install win32-open3
  ```

Solution

Let's say our application has a login link that when clicked shows a login form in an otherwise empty div. There are many ways to pull off this sort of dynamic page manipulation, but they all rely on JavaScript to do the heavy lifting. Here's what the view looks like:

`TestingJSWithSelenium/app/views/users/index.html.erb`

```erb
<div id="intro">
  <p id="intro_text">
    Do you want to see this page?
    Just click <%= link_to_function "login", "$('login_form').toggle();" %>.
  </p>
</div>

<div id="login_form" style="display: none;">
  <% form_tag :action => 'login' do -%>
    <p>
      User Id: <%= text_field_tag :user_id %>
    </p>
```

```
  <p>
    Password: <%= password_field_tag :password %>
  </p>
  <p>
    <%= submit_tag 'Submit' %>
  </p>
  <% end -%>
</div>
```

This is all fairly ordinary stuff. The interesting part is figuring out how to test it, and the implementation suggests a few things we need to verify:

- Rendering the page displays a login link but no login form.

- Clicking the login link displays the login form.

- Logging in displays the correct dynamic content on the resulting page.

We can handle two of these with a good batch of assert_select calls in a functional test:

TestingJSWithSelenium/test/functional/users_controller_test.rb

```ruby
def test_index
  get :index
  assert_response :success
  assert_template 'index'
  assert_select "div#intro p#intro_text a[href='#']", 'login'
  assert_select "div#login_form", 1
  # no form inputs in the div yet
  assert_select "div#form_area input[name='user_id']", 0
end

def test_login
  post :login, :user_id => 'Joe', :password => 'password'
  assert_response :success
  assert_template 'home'
  assert_select "h1.heading", "Thank you for logging in, Joe!"
end
```

The test_index method covers the first requirement nicely: when the page is rendered, it has a login link, but no login form is visible. If the login_form div were mistakenly commented out, for example, this test would fail. And the third requirement is covered, too: after a login, we see the username on the resulting page.

That leaves us with the second requirement: testing the execution of the JavaScript that displays the login form. To do that, we really need an execution environment for JavaScript code.

Selenium[1] gives us such an environment. It embeds a JavaScript-based test engine within a running browser. And, as a nice bonus, it lets us do cross-browser testing. That said, Selenium is a general-purpose web testing tool and needs a little coaxing to integrate into a Rails application. The selenium-on-rails plug-in makes it seamless.

Let's start by generating a stub Selenium test file:

```
$ script/generate selenium login_test.rsel
```

Specifying the .rsel extension lets us write the test using a thin Ruby wrapper for the client-side JavaScript functions[2] that Selenium uses to manipulate the browser. We like Ruby.

Then we'll fill in the file with a mix of assertions and commands to the browser:

TestingJSWithSelenium/test/selenium/login_test.rsel

```
open '/users'
assert_text "css=div#intro p#intro_text a[href='#']", "login"
assert_element_present "css=div#login_form"

click "link=login"
# wait for any form text input to appear
wait_for_element_present "css=div#login_form input"
assert_element_present "css=div#login_form input[type='text'][name='user_id']"
assert_element_present "css=div#login_form
  input[type='password'][name='password']"

type "css=div#login_form input[type='text'][name='user_id']", "Joe"
type "css=div#login_form input[type='password'][name='password']", "pass"
click "css=div#login_form input[type='submit']"
wait_for_page_to_load 3000

assert_text "css=h1.heading", "Thank you for logging in, Joe!"
```

The login_test.rsel file looks similar to the functional test we looked at earlier, but we're speaking the RSelenese lingo[3] here. And this time we can run our JavaScript code. The tests clicks the login link, and we wait for any input fields to appear in the login_form div. Then we go ahead and test the actual login process by typing a user_id and password and clicking the submit button.

---

1. http://OpenQA.org
2. http://release.openqa.org/Selenium-core/0.8.0/reference.html
3. You can find the RSelenese documentation at vendor/plugins/Selenium-on-rails/doc/index.html.

By default the click method is asynchronous, so we have to call wait_for_page_to_load. (RSelenese also dynamically adds xxx_and_wait commands for each action, so we could just call click_and_wait in a one-liner.) Finally, we check for the expected dynamic content on the resulting page.

Now let's see how it all comes together by running the test in the browser. Selenium looks for a config.yml file in the selenium-on-rails plugin directory to tell it which browser(s) to run. Simply copy the config.yml.example file, and edit it for your environment. Then we'll start our Rails application in test mode:

```
$ ruby script/server -e test
```

Then to run the Selenium tests in our configured browsers, we use this:

```
$ rake test:acceptance
```

Each browser will launch in turn and show the tests in a table at the top and our application in the lower portion. Then you'll see invisible fingers run through our test script, and the tests should light up green.

That's cool, but when a test passes the first time, it makes us doubt that it did anything. So, it's time to break some JavaScript and see what happens. In index.html.erb, remove the code that generates the password field and submit button. The functional test still passes, but the Selenium test fails. Even better, the Selenium test catches the missing submit button when it attempts to click it, even though we neglected to proactively check for its existence in the test. By implicitly checking the existence of a form control when manipulating it, we can remove the brittle assertion on the view's structure and just simulate the desired interactions.

Now we have a test that fully validates our custom JavaScript in a concise syntax. We've found that testing workflow across several pages is made much easier by Selenium and lends itself to writing a testing language that naturally expresses what a user is really doing instead of focusing on low-level functions of the HTML inner workings. Better yet, this allows us to rewrite the implementation without forcing us to also rewrite our functional and integration tests.

Discussion

If you're a Mac OS X user, one handy configuration setting is start_server. If it is true, then running rake test:acceptance will start your Rails application in test mode before running the Selenium test suite. Currently this setting is not reliable under Windows, and you must manually launch the application in test mode before starting the acceptance tests.

The selenium-on-rails plug-in also lets you manually run specific tests from within the browser. Just launch your Rails application in test mode, and browse to http://localhost:3000/selenium. The Selenium IDE Firefox plug-in is also worth trying. It lets you (or a nonprogrammer friend) record a test interactively and export it in a format usable by the selenium-on-rails plug-in. See the Selenium website for more details.

Running Selenium tests generally takes a while longer than functional or integration tests. Because of the slow feedback loop, Selenium is not really a good choice for test-driven development. For the same reason, you may not want to rely on Selenium as your only (or primary) testing layer. For best results, and a restful night's sleep, run a nightly Selenium smoke test.

One current drawback to the selenium-on-rails plug-in is that it requires that you do not have any open browser windows. If you launch the rake:test:acceptance task with an open Firefox window, for example, an error pops up asking you to close the window. And even when you do, the tests may not run completely. We hope this issue will be addressed in a future version of the plug-in.

Mock Models with FlexMock

By Matthew Bass (http://matthewbass.com)
Matthew is an independent software developer who has been enjoying the freedom
of Ruby for many years now. He is a speaker, agile evangelist, and Mac addict. He co-
organizes the Ruby Meetup in his hometown of Raleigh, North Carolina.

Problem

Your functional tests always seem to be breaking, and for the wrong
reasons. It is usually because someone changed an implementation
detail down in a model. You need to reduce the dependencies your controllers have on the rest of the system, but how do you do it without
adding a bunch of special testing hooks?

Ingredients

- The FlexMock gem:[1]

    ```
    $ gem install flexmock
    ```

Solution

Let's say we have a model with a wee bit of validation:

MockingCornerCases/app/models/gadget.rb

```
class Gadget < ActiveRecord::Base
  validates_presence_of :name, :price
end
```

We also have a typical controller action for creating a gadget, something
like this:

MockingCornerCases/app/controllers/gadgets_controller.rb

```
def create
  @gadget = Gadget.new(params[:gadget])

  if @gadget.save
    flash[:notice] = "Gadget was successfully created."
    redirect_to @gadget
  else
    flash[:error] = "Whoops, gadget couldn't be created."
    render :action => "new"
  end
end
```

---

1. http://onestepback.org/software/flexmock/

Being good little programmers, we also have a functional test for the action:

MockingCornerCases/test/functional/gadgets_controller_test.rb

```ruby
def test_should_create_gadget
  assert_difference('Gadget.count') do
    post :create, :gadget => { :name => "Chronometer", :price => 6 }
  end
  assert_not_nil assigns(:gadget)
  assert_not_nil flash[:notice]
  assert_redirected_to gadget_path(assigns(:gadget))
end
```

However, we're verifying only that the action does the right thing if the gadget can be saved. We don't have a test for what happens if the gadget cannot be saved. Worse yet, running rcov tells us that we're pretty bad about testing corner cases like this in general.

Now, to test the failure case, we could pass an empty hash to the create action. Since our model is validating the presence of the name and price attributes, the save would fail. But that would make our test a tad brittle. If we were to remove the gadget validations in the future, our failure test case would fail.

The real problem here is our functional test is too tightly coupled to the presence of validations in our Gadget model. Instead, our functional test should be verifying one thing and one thing only—that if the gadget fails to save, the controller handles that failure correctly.

So, let's simulate a failure by introducing a mock object into the mix. First, we require FlexMock's Test::Unit helper inside our test/test_helper.rb file:

MockingCornerCases/test/test_helper.rb

```ruby
require "flexmock/test_unit"
```

Next, we'll mock the save method on new instances of our Gadget class. The save method should return false so it triggers our failure condition:

MockingCornerCases/test/functional/gadgets_controller_test.rb

```ruby
def test_create_invalid_gadget_fails
  flexmock(Gadget).new_instances.should_receive(:save).
                  once.and_return(false)
  post :create, :gadget => { }
  assert_not_nil assigns(:gadget)
  assert_response :success
  assert_template 'new'
  assert_not_nil flash[:error]
end
```

This test won't break if we change validations on the Gadget model. In fact, the save fails regardless of the parameters we post to the create action. And that's exactly what we want. We aren't concerned with the internals of the Gadget model or whether the save method is actually working. We have unit tests for that. In our functional test, we're concerned only with how our controller responds when save returns false. The use of a mock lets us precisely control our gadgets so they behave in a predictable way.

This is all well and good, but after writing failure tests for several controllers, we begin smelling duplication:

- Try to save the model.

- If the save succeeds, populate the flash, and redirect.

- If the save fails, populate the flash, and fall through to the default render.

Duplication in tests is just as bad (if not worse) as duplication in production code. So, we'll clean this up with some metaprogramming that builds failure tests on the fly. We'll put this in the test_helper.rb file, too:

MockingCornerCases/test/test_helper.rb
```ruby
def self.test_create_invalid_fails(options={})
  if options[:model]
    model = options[:model]
  else name.demodulize.to_s =~ /^(.*)ControllerTest$/
    model = $1.singularize.constantize rescue nil
  end

  define_method("test_create_invalid_fails") do
    flexmock(model).new_instances.should_receive(:save).
                    once.and_return(false)
    post :create
    assert_not_nil assigns(model.to_s.underscore)
    assert_response :success
    assert_template 'new'
    assert_not_nil flash[:error]
  end
end
```

The test_create_invalid_fails class method turns around and dynamically creates a test_create_invalid_fails instance method. This method does exactly what we did before, but in a generic way. It takes a model name as an optional parameter. If no model name is given, we try to glean the model class name from the functional test name.

Now in our functional test, we will just call the test_create_invalid_fails method. Here is the final version covering both paths in the create action:

MockingCornerCases/test/functional/gadgets_controller_test.rb

```ruby
require File.dirname(__FILE__) + '/../test_helper'

class GadgetsControllerTest < ActionController::TestCase

  test_create_invalid_fails

  def test_should_create_gadget
    assert_difference('Gadget.count') do
      post :create, :gadget => { :name => "Chronometer", :price => 6 }
    end
    assert_not_nil assigns(:gadget)
    assert_not_nil flash[:notice]
    assert_redirected_to gadget_path(assigns(:gadget))
  end
end
```

We could do the same thing with the happy path, replacing our test_should_create_gadget test with a one-liner.

This declarative style can be quite useful for testing a large system with many controllers that do similar things. RESTful controllers, in general, are ideal candidates for this sort of metaprogramming.

Discussion

We barely scratched the surface of what FlexMock can do. It has an extensive (and yet extremely usable) mocking API, so be sure to check out the excellent documentation for all your mocking needs.

Track Test Coverage with rcov

Writing tests is all well and good, but how do you know when your application is sufficiently tested? And if you're learning to write automated tests, where do you start? Well, if your bug-tracking system is empty and your phone isn't ringing at 2 a.m., that's a good start. But when the phone does ring, it's usually too late. You'd like to get some insight into how well your code is tested *before* it's rolled into production.

- The rcov gem:
  ```
  $ gem install rcov
  ```
- The rails_rcov plug-in (optional):
  ```
  $ script/plugin install http://svn.codahale.com/rails_rcov
  ```

There are many different metrics for tracking the efficiency of our tests. One of the easiest metrics to collect is code coverage. Simply put, it tells us which parts of our code get exercised by our tests.

Test coverage is a no-brainer to measure because rcov automates the entire process. We just run our tests—or put them on an automated run cycle—and rcov tallies up statistics. We'll get to the *how* in a moment. First, a peek at the HTML output:

C0 code coverage information

Generated on Wed Dec 12 18:07:56 -0700 2007 with rcov 0.8.1.2

Name	Total lines	Lines of code	Total coverage		Code coverage	
TOTAL	322	227	88.2%		83.3%	
app/helpers/application_helper.rb	25	18	68.0%		55.6%	
app/controllers/registrations_controller.rb	13	11	76.9%		72.7%	
app/controllers/application.rb	33	19	84.8%		73.7%	
app/controllers/events_controller.rb	86	60	86.0%		80.0%	
app/controllers/users_controller.rb	37	32	83.8%		81.2%	
app/models/user.rb	70	48	94.3%		91.7%	
app/models/event.rb	45	30	100.0%		100.0%	
app/models/tag.rb	5	3	100.0%		100.0%	
app/models/registration.rb	6	4	100.0%		100.0%	
app/helpers/events_helper.rb	2	2	100.0%		100.0%	

This is telling. Our RegistrationsController has only about 77% test coverage, and it plays a central role in our business. That's unfortunate but fairly easy to correct. To see which lines are untested, we just click the filename:

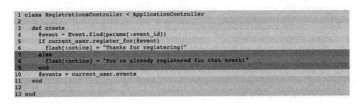

Whoops! We tested the blue-sky scenario but forgot about the edge case. It's embarrassing, but it's exactly the kind of quick feedback we need to guide our testing efforts. Plus, it just feels good to write a new test that pushes the coverage bar to 100%.

That's a taste of the treat; now for the ingredients. All we need is a Rake task that calls the rcov command-line utility and remembers all our options. We'll stick that in the lib/tasks/rcov.rake file,[1] for example:

events/lib/tasks/rcov.rake

```
namespace :test do

  desc 'Tracks test coverage with rcov'
  task :coverage do
    rm_f "coverage"
    rm_f "coverage.data"

    unless PLATFORM['i386-mswin32']
      rcov = "rcov --sort coverage --rails --aggregate coverage.data " +
             "--text-summary -Ilib -T -x gems/*,rcov*"
    else
      rcov = "rcov.cmd --sort coverage --rails --aggregate coverage.data " +
             "--text-summary -Ilib -T"
    end

    system("#{rcov} --no-html test/unit/*_test.rb")
    system("#{rcov} --no-html test/functional/*_test.rb")
    system("#{rcov} --html test/integration/*_test.rb")

    unless PLATFORM['i386-mswin32']
      system("open coverage/index.html") if PLATFORM['darwin']
    else
      system("\"C:/Program Files/Mozilla Firefox/firefox.exe\" " +
             "coverage/index.html")
    end
  end
end
```

---

1. Thanks to Chris Noble for working out the Windows-specific bits.

Then we're just one command away from running all our tests, generating the aggregated HTML report, and popping it open in our default browser:

```
$ rake test:coverage
```

We also get a textual summary for the unit, functional, and integration tests as they're being run. Either way, the reports can be quickly scanned for warning signs.

Discussion

We have to say this (otherwise the testing gurus come out of the woodwork): code coverage is an inexpensive metric to collect, but it should *not* be the only yardstick by which we evaluate our tests. All rcov does is check whether a line of code was executed, not that it's the correct code. Having gotten that out of the way, using rcov is a lot better than throwing arbitrary tests at your application and hoping it's time well spent.

So, is it 100% code coverage or bust? Well, that's a worthy goal but sometimes not practical. In some cases, rcov can't accurately measure one-liners, for example. Chad Fowler's rule is "Everything green except when rcov is too dumb to understand that my code is covered." The goal isn't 100% coverage but rather to make sure you don't have any large swathes of code that aren't touched at all. If you do, that's a good indication that you're probably missing an important test that could teach you something about the feature under development...or expose a potentially embarrassing bug.

Also See

If you're the sort who doesn't mind adding yet another plug-in, the rcov_rails plug-in gives you Rake tasks out of the box. For every test:xxx task in your Rails application, the rails_rcov plug-in adds two more: test:xxx:rcov and test:xxx:clobber_rcov. For example, to track the coverage of unit tests and then remove the unit test coverage reports, use this:

```
$ rake test:units:rcov
$ rake test:units:clobber_rcov
```

Automatically Validate HTML

By Peter Marklund (http://marklunds.com)
Peter has extensive experience in object orientation, web development, relational databases, and testing, and he has been doing web development with Java and Tcl since 2000. In late 2004, he was introduced to Ruby on Rails and has since helped develop an online community and a CRM system with Rails. Peter is currently working as a Ruby on Rails developer and teacher in Stockholm and is helping organize events for the local Rails community.

Problem

You want to make sure your site renders consistently (and correctly) across all modern browsers. A good start is to validate your markup so that it complies with the W3C standards, doesn't have loop holes in HTML escaping, and doesn't contain broken links, form POSTs, or redirects. But how do you automatically validate all that in an application that dynamically generates HTML?

Ingredients

- The HTML Test plug-in:

  ```
  $ script/plugin install http://htmltest.googlecode.com/svn/trunk/html_test
  ```

- The RailsTidy plug-in[1] is optional, but it's a useful complement to the W3C validator since it generates warnings about empty tags, for example. RailsTidy depends on the HTML Tidy library as well as its Ruby API.

Solution

The HTML Test plug-in gives us a handful of assertion methods that we can use in functional and integration tests. Let's jump right in with a test that asks the W3C whether our index template passes muster:

```
def test_index
  get :index
  assert_response :success
  assert_template 'index'
  assert_validates
```

---

1. http://www.cosinux.org/~dam/projects/rails-tidy/doc/

The assert_validates method simply calls two underlying assertions: assert_w3c and assert_tidy. (You'll just call assert_w3c if you aren't using Tidy.) Those assertions are run after the request is processed, and they're useful if we're looking only to validate a subset of our pages. The last generated W3C error report is written to /tmp/w3c_last_response.html for debugging fun.

Let's raise the bar by validating *all* pages that are requested by our functional and integration tests in one fell swoop. We also want to make sure that URLs in links, forms, and redirects resolve. Instead of using assert_validates directly in test methods, we just add this to our test_helper.rb file:

```
ApplicationController.validate_all = true
ApplicationController.validators = [:tidy, :w3c]
ApplicationController.check_urls = true
ApplicationController.check_redirects = true
```

Then, when we run our functional or integration tests, the HTML validity is automatically tested. That's pretty handy, but it comes at a price. By default the HTML Test plug-in uses the online W3C validator.[2] This can significantly slow our tests down (plus we like to run tests while on airplanes).

A better solution is to install the W3C validator locally.[3] Then we point the assertions to our local install by adding this to our test_helper.rb file, for example:

```
Html::Test::Validator.w3c_url = "http://localhost/cgi-bin/check"
```

Now let's say we want to restrict HTML validation to a subset of our controllers or actions. For example, suppose we don't want to run it on the admin side of our application. To do that, in test_helper.rb we'll override the should_validate? method to turn off validation under /admin:

```
module Html
  module Test
    class ValidateFilter
      def should_validate?
        response.headers['Status'] =~ /200/ &&
        params[:controller] !~ /^admin/
      end
    end
  end
end
```

---

2. http://validator.w3.org
3. See http://validator.w3.org/docs/install.html for installation instructions for your operating system.

In a similar fashion, we could override the skip_url? method to skip checking whether a URL in a link, form, or redirect resolves.

Finally, here's a trick for finding unquoted data in your templates: add characters such as "&" and "<" to your fixture data. That way, HTML validation will fail if unquoted fixture data is included in a template. Of course, this assumes that the template is covered by a controller or integration test.

Discussion

Tidy can sometimes be a bit too picky. If it barks about things you don't care about, you can tell Tidy to ignore them:

```
Html::Test::Validator.tidy_ignore_list =
  [/<table> lacks "summary" attribute/]
```

Also See

You might want to look into a couple of alternative Rails plug-ins for your validation needs:

- Assert Valid Markup[4] caches the results and hits the validator only when the generated HTML response changes.

- The RaiLint plug-in[5] can validate all HTML, CSS, and JavaScript assuming you have Java, the JavaScript Lint validator, and a few other things installed locally.

If you have problems installing the W3C validator locally, you can use the xmllint command-line validator instead. The xmllint validator is part of the libxml2 library that you can download from http://xmlsoft.org. The W3C validator is favored over xmllint because it's more authoritative, and it also produces easier-to-debug error reports with references to line numbers in your document.

---

4. http://redgreenblu.com/svn/projects/assert_valid_markup/README
5. http://rubyforge.org/projects/railint/

Mock with a Safety Net

By Kevin Clark (http://glu.ttono.us)
Kevin is a Ruby hacker. He was a founder of SanDiego.rb and an author of Heckle. He is currently building tools and infrastructure in Ruby at Powerset in San Francisco.

Problem

You're writing tests for bits of code that are going to hit an external service (or three), and you're using mocks and stubs with Mocha[1] or FlexMock[2] to return canned data. But let's face it, everyone forgets to set up a mock on occasion. So, you need to make sure remote calls aren't made on accident while the tests run.

Solution

Let's say we're using the AWS::S3 library[3] to store and fetch files from Amazon's S3 service. In our application we're making calls to the AWS:: S3::S3Object class to query S3. During testing, we don't want to make *any* requests to the S3 service. Instead, all calls to S3Object should let us know by raising an exception.

Rails gives us a clever way to solve this with its test/mocks directories. In testing, the test/mocks/test directory is added to the front of $LOAD_PATH. This means that if we create a file called s3.rb in test/mocks/test and then require 's3' in our application, the s3.rb file in test/mocks/test will be loaded instead of the "real" file.

Suppose we have require 'aws/s3' in our environment.rb file to load the legit S3 library. We need to mimic that path structure in our test/mocks/test directory. We'll create an s3.rb in the test/mocks/test/aws directory.

---

1. http://mocha.rubyforge.org/
2. http://onestepback.org/software/flexmock/
3. http://amazon.rubyforge.org/

Here's what it does:

```ruby
module AWS
  module S3
    class S3Object
      def self.method_missing(action, *args)
        raise "You forgot to stub #{action}!"
      end
    end
  end
end
```

This file is the only version of the S3Object class that gets loaded during testing. And since we haven't defined any methods in this version, all calls to it will end up going to the method_missing method. It just raises an exception, and that's exactly what we want!

Next, we'll write a test that directly (or indirectly) tries to use S3Object:

```ruby
def test_s3_call_will_raise_exception
  picture = AWS::S3::S3Object.find 'headshot.jpg', 'photos'
end
```

Then if we run the test, we get the expected exception:

```
1) Error: test_s3_call_will_raise_exception(S3Test):
RuntimeError: You forgot to stub find!
...
test/unit/s3_test.rb:7:in `test_s3_call_will_raise_exception'
```

Now we know exactly where we're missing a stub, and we have a failing test that should pass when the stub is in place.

Discussion

Providing an alternate implementation of an entire class is often too heavy-handed, so you'll want to be more surgical about which methods of a class raise an exception when you forget to mock. In those cases, instead of using the method_missing trick, you probably want to require the original class in your mock version, open the class, and redefine specific methods.

The other thing to note about this example is that we implemented method_missing on the S3Object class by defining self.method_missing. In many cases, you want to make sure methods on an *instance* aren't called rather than on the class. In those cases, you shouldn't define method_missing on self.

Drive a Feature Top-Down with Integration Tests

By Nathaniel Talbott (http://terralien.com/)
Nathaniel got started with Ruby right after the original Pickaxe book was published, and he cut his teeth by writing what eventually became the test/unit framework that ships with Ruby. An attendee and speaker at every RubyConf and a long-time organizer of the Raleigh-area Ruby Brigade, he's an active and enthusiastic member of the Ruby community. These days he runs Terralien, a startup-focused custom development shop, and Spreedly, soon to achieve total subscription management world domination.

Problem

The last time you started implementing a "simple" feature you thought would take about an hour, it ended up turning into an all-day affair. You're older and wiser now. Instead of throwing caution to the wind, you want to use tests to drive your next trivial feature because, well, you know you should.

Solution

The key to quickly turning out a simple, tested feature is in keeping our eye on the ball and not getting distracted. A great way to do that is to drive the feature interface-first, because it forces us to write only the code that directly contributes to the end-user experience. That's where integration tests come in: they're great for driving a feature from an interface-first perspective, especially if we apply a few tactics to keep them simple and clean.

Let's say we've written the next great web application and we want to invite a bunch of folks to try it. It's time for us to write an invitation system *and* make it to lunch on time.

The very first thing we want to do when we implement our invitation system is to drive a spike through one feature. *Spiking* is a technique in which we very quickly touch every aspect of a feature before going back and worrying about edge cases. For invitations, that means we'll start by just getting an invite created.

Here's a first pass:

```
class InvitationsTest < ActionController::IntegrationTest

  def test_should_allow_creating_invitations
    get '/admin/invitations'
    assert_select %(input[type=text][name='invitation[email]'])

    post '/admin/invitations', :invitation => {:email => 'joe@example.com'}
    invitation = Invitation.find_by_email('joe@example.com')
    assert_match(%r{#{invitation.code}},
                 ActionMailer::Base.deliveries.last.body)
  end

end
```

Note two things here. First, integration tests have full access to your application's routing, so they can leverage named routes. At first blush this seems like a good idea: if we decide to change our routes, our tests will still function, right? Well, our goal is to test-drive the interface as quickly as possible, and routes are a big part of that interface. So, instead of creating a route, or even referring to a nonexistent one, we'll just use a string.

Second, assert_select is crazy-powerful, but don't let all the wacky things you can do with it distract you from the simplicity of just checking to see whether an element is on the page. As we rapidly build out this feature, we just want to make sure our form is there.

We don't care so much where it's at on the page or exactly how many elements it includes. And simple selects have the nice side benefit of making our tests less vulnerable to future changes in markup.

With the test in place, we then get the thrill of writing code to make it pass. Now it's time to ameliorate: add little niceties, test edge cases, and polish the code, all while continuously running the tests. After shining up that test and test-driving a few more features, we might end up with something like this:

IntegrationTest/test/integration/invitations_test.rb

```
class InvitationsTest < ActionController::IntegrationTest
  fixtures :users, :invitations

  def setup
    ActionMailer::Base.deliveries.clear
  end
```

```
def test_should_allow_creating_invitations
  new_session_as 'alex' do
    get '/admin/invitations'
    assert_select %(form[action=/admin/invitations][method=post]) do
      assert_select %(input[type=text][name='invitation[email]'])
    end

    assert_difference 'Invitation.count', 1 do
      assert_difference "ActionMailer::Base.deliveries.size", 1 do
        post '/admin/invitations',
             :invitation => {:email => 'joe@example.com'}
        assert_redirected_to '/admin/invitations'
        assert_match(/sent/i, session['flash'][:notice])
        assert_not_nil(invitation =
          Invitation.find_by_email('joe@example.com'))
        assert_match(%r{https://spreedly.dev/signup/#{invitation.code}},
                     ActionMailer::Base.deliveries.last.body)
      end
    end
  end
end

def test_should_list_outstanding_invitations
  new_session_as 'alex' do
    get '/admin/invitations'
    assert_select 'li', :text => /bob@example\.com/ do
      resend_url = "/admin/invitations/#{invitations(:bob).id}/resend"
      assert_select %(a[href=#{resend_url}])
    end
  end
end

def test_should_allow_resending
  new_session_as 'alex' do
    assert_difference "ActionMailer::Base.deliveries.size", 1 do
      post "/admin/invitations/#{invitations(:bob).id}/resend"
      assert_redirected_to '/admin/invitations'
    end
  end
end
```

This second version of test_should_allow_creating_invitations is still pretty simple, but it reports better if something is wrong, and it checks a few more corners. Here's the best part: we were able to make these adjustments with confidence, since we know the simple first test we spiked out will at least tell us whether we broke the core of the feature. If we tweak something and e-mails stop being delivered, then we have immediate feedback that we need to double-check what we just did.

Notice that our integration tests have no compunction about hitting the database (they use assert_difference to make sure the record was created). Purists might turn their nose up at this, but there's nothing worse than dogma to distract us when we're trying to whip something up. That purity is inconsequential to our goal: flushing out a feature quickly and simply. Be pragmatic!

Discussion

The key to good outcomes from any design process (and that's certainly what this is) is aggressive iteration. Each time we "turn the crank"—writing a test, implementing it, trying to run it, tweaking anything that doesn't work, and getting it to pass—we learn something. It works best if during or after each revolution you take a minute to sit back and ask yourself some questions like "Is there a better way to do this?" and "Was that overly painful? Why?" You can then apply the answers to make the next turn of the crank that much more effective.

Of course, integration tests aren't just good for doing test-first feature development. They're also great for turning exploratory testing sessions (manually using your application while looking for holes) into automated test runs and for banging out a quick test to demonstrate a regression and make sure it never happens again. Finally, integration tests are definitely not the only form of testing you can or should do. There are still plenty of times when you'll need to dive down deeper and unit test a model, for example.

Also See

See Recipe 56, *Track Test Coverage with rcov*, on page 307 for how to run rcov to see how well your tests exercise your code.

Part XI

Performance and Scalability Recipes

Cache Data Easily

By Mark Bates (http://www.markbates.com)
Mark is currently the director of architecture for Helium (http://helium.com). He spends his days fighting the establishment and wishing he'll be called up as the next front man for Van Halen. In addition to knowing the true meaning of Arbor Day, Mark also knows who let the dogs out, where the beef is, and who shot J.R.

Problem

You need a cheap and easy way to speed up slow parts of your application by keeping the results of calculations, renderings, or database calls around for subsequent requests.

Ingredients

- Rails 2.1 or higher

- Optionally, the memcached daemon.[1] On a Mac we install it like this:

  ```
  $ sudo port install memcached
  ```

  There is also a port for memcached on Windows.[2]

Solution

Rails 2.1 gives us four cache storage mechanisms right out of the gate—memory, file, DRb, and memcached—with minimal configuration in the environment file:

```
ActionController::Base.cache_store = :memory_store
ActionController::Base.cache_store = :file_store, "/path/to/cache/directory"
ActionController::Base.cache_store = :drb_store, "druby://localhost:9192"
ActionController::Base.cache_store = :mem_cache_store, "localhost"
```

Action and fragment caching now both transparently use the currently configured cache store. Nothing has changed in how you use them—simply in how you configure them. This is certainly good news, but (as they say) there's more! It turns out you can cache anything you want.

---

1. http://www.danga.com/memcached
2. http://jehiah.cz/projects/memcached-win32/

For our example, let's imagine we have a little online store with a marketing mind of its own. It can tally up all the books, T-shirts, and coffee mugs you've already purchased, and it can recommend other goodies you might like. The trouble is, the database query to do that is sort of expensive, despite our best optimization efforts. We need a cache.

The cache store API is really easy to use—it's basically like a hash. The best way to see how it works is in the console:

```
$ ruby script/console
>> products = Product.related_products("fred")
=> [#<Product id: 17, ...]

>> ActionController::Base.cache_store.write("fred", products)
=> [#<Product id: 17, ...]

>> ActionController::Base.cache_store.read("fred")
=> [#<Product id: 17, ...]

>> ActionController::Base.cache_store.delete("fred")
=> [#<Product id: 17, ...]

>> products = Product.related_products("barney")
>> ActionController::Base.cache_store.fetch("barney") { products }
=> [#<Product id: 21, ...]
```

The write method takes a key and value, and the read and delete methods take just the key. Finally, the fetch method does dual duty to perform "just-in-time" caching. When it doesn't find your key in the cache, it'll run the block, save its results into the cache, and give them back to you.

Let's go ahead and put this to use in our ProductsController and introduce a couple handy new things while we're at it:

```
def show
  @product = Product.find(params[:id])

  user_id = session[:user_id]
  @related_products = cache(['related_products', user_id],
                            :expires_in => 15.minutes) do
    Product.related_products(user_id)
  end

end
```

In a controller or view, you can simply use the cache convenience method. It wraps fetch but performs the caching only if caching is enabled. We've passed in an array for the key, which will get expanded into a namespaced key of controller/related_products/fred, for example. We've also used the :expires_in option[3] to invalidate this cache entry fifteen minutes from now.

So, here's what happens: the first time a particular user views a product, the heavyweight database query is run to haul in her related products. Each subsequent time the user views a product, we get a cache hit on the related products for a significant performance boost. If a particular user doesn't show a product within fifteen minutes, her related products are automatically kicked out of the cache.

To test this in development, you'll need to enable caching by updating your development.rb environment file as follows:

```
config.action_controller.perform_caching = true
```

Restart your app, and you're off to the races!

Discussion

memcached is by far the preferred store for this kind of stuff. The other options are there, but if you have the opportunity to use memcached, it's just about always the right answer. The nice thing about this new cache store API is it's all transparent. By default it's using the memory_store cache store, which is a great option in your development environment. In production, however, you can switch to using the memcached store by adding the following to your production.rb environment file:

CheapEasyCaching/config/environments/production.rb

```
config.cache_store = :mem_cache_store, 'localhost'
```

Then on your production box you'll need to fire up the memcached daemon:

```
$ memcached -vv
```

If you'd prefer not to use the currently configured cache store, you can instead instantiate your own store:

```
ActiveSupport::Cache.lookup_store(:drb_store, "druby://localhost:9192")
```

Using this method makes it very easy to segregate your caches either to use different types of cache stores for particular situations or to better namespace them.

---

3. The :expires_in option works only with the memcached store, as of this writing.

We could have buried the caching calls back in the related_products method of our Product model. But when you cache at the model layer, you don't have an easy way of sidestepping the cache to get fresh data. The caching mechanism built into Rails is intended to be used in controllers or views.

Also See

If you need a caching solution with a few more bells and whistles (or you're not using Rails 2.1 yet), see Recipe 63, *Cache Up with the Big Guys*, on page 337.

Look Up Constant Data Efficiently

By Patrick Reagan (http://www.viget.com)
Patrick is a recovering PHP user who finally realized the immense power that Rails brings to the web development space. As the development director for Viget Labs, he's been helping lead the charge in adopting Rails as the framework of choice when building applications for their start-up clients. This recipe is based on an initial implementation by Dave Thomas.

Problem

Your application has constants stored in the database: states, countries, planets, statuses, and so on. You want to list the constants in a form selection, for example, but you don't want to fetch the constants from the database every time the form is displayed. Instead, you want to load the constant data *once* at the start of your application.

Solution

Let's start with the example where a person needs to select their home state as part of their profile. We'll assume we have an empty Person model and a bare-bones migration file that looks like this:

`ConstantCaches/db/migrate/001_create_people.rb`

```ruby
class CreatePeople < ActiveRecord::Migration

  def self.up
    create_table :people do |t|
      t.string :name
      t.string :email
      t.string :state
    end
  end

  def self.down
    drop_table :people
  end
end
```

On the profile form we want to show full state names in the selection, but when a person saves their profile, we want the people.state column to contain the state's abbreviation.

First we'll create a migration file to create the states table where we'll store the state names and abbreviations. When the migration is applied, we'll go ahead and populate the table with all 50 states.

ConstantCaches/db/migrate/002_create_states.rb

```ruby
class CreateStates < ActiveRecord::Migration

  def self.up
    create_table :states do |t|
      t.string :name
      t.string :abbreviation
    end

    State.create([
      {:name => 'Alaska',   :abbreviation => 'AK'},
      {:name => 'Alabama',  :abbreviation => 'AL'},
      {:name => 'Arkansas', :abbreviation => 'AR'},
      {:name => 'Arizona',  :abbreviation => 'AZ'},
      # ... more states ...
      {:name => 'Wyoming',  :abbreviation => 'WY'}
    ])
  end

  def self.down
    drop_table :states
  end
end
```

Once we have those constants tucked away in the database, we need to read them into our application's memory...exactly once. You might be surprised to learn that Ruby (with some help from Rails) makes that easy to do. When you define a class in Ruby, it's executable code. That means you can have arbitrary code run *while* a class is being defined. And in production mode Rails doesn't reload classes, so they'll be defined one time.

Next, we need a class to trigger creating the cache. It seems reasonable to have a State model class for our states table. While the State class is being defined, we can call any method on the State class object. In this case, we'll call find to read all the states from the database into a NAMES_ABBREVIATIONS constant. Here's what that looks like:

ConstantCaches/app/models/state.rb

```ruby
class State < ActiveRecord::Base

  NAMES_ABBREVIATIONS = self.find(:all, :order => :name).map do |s|
    [s.name, s.abbreviation]
  end
end
```

Remember, we want to display the state names but store a state abbreviation in the person's record. In other words, we don't need to carry around all the attributes of each State model object. Instead, we use the map method to turn each model into an array containing just the name and abbreviation and store everything in the NAMES_ABBREVIATIONS constant.

Let us drop into the console to see how the constant state data gets packaged:

```
$ ruby script/console
>> State::NAMES_ABBREVIATIONS
=> [["Alabama", "AL"], ["Alaska", "AK"], ["Arizona", "AZ"],
    ["Arkansas", "AR"], ... ["Wyoming", "WY"]]
```

It's just an array of arrays. Now we have a really simple, but effective, "compile-time" cache. From anywhere in our application we can reference State::NAMES_ABBREVIATIONS and get all the state names and abbreviations without hitting the database.

Next, we'll write a form to capture a person's home state:

```
ConstantCaches/app/views/people/_form.rhtml
<% form_for(@person) do |f| -%>
  <p>
    <strong>Name</strong>:
    <%= f.text_field :name %>
  </p>
  <p>
    <strong>Email</strong>:
    <%= f.text_field :email %>
  </p>
  <p>
    <strong>State</strong>:
    <%= f.select(:state, State::NAMES_ABBREVIATIONS) %>
  </p>
  <p>
    <%= f.submit 'Save' %>
  </p>
<% end -%>
```

The select form helper will happily use the array of arrays contained in our State::NAMES_ABBREVIATIONS. The first element of each array (the state name) is used as the text displayed for the option, and the second element (the state abbreviation) is used as the value that gets sent to the server when the form is submitted.

Here's the HTML that gets generated:

```html
<select id="person_state" name="person[state]">
  <option value="AL">Alabama</option>
  <option value="AK">Alaska</option>
  <option value="AZ">Arizona</option>
  <option value="AR">Arkansas</option>
  . . .
  <option value="WY">Wyoming</option>
</select>
```

Now let's look at another situation where constant caches come to the rescue. Say, for example, the user accounts in our application can have an associated status: pending, active, or disabled. Here's the migration for our Status model:

ConstantCaches/db/migrate/004_create_statuses.rb

```ruby
class CreateStatuses < ActiveRecord::Migration

  def self.up
    create_table :statuses do |t|
      t.string :name
    end

    add_column :accounts, :status_id, :integer

    Status.create([
      {:name => 'Pending'},
      {:name => 'Active'},
      {:name => 'Disabled'}
    ])
  end

  def self.down
    remove_column :accounts, :status_id
    drop_table :statuses
  end

end
```

These statuses are relatively static, and it's useful to be able to quickly refer to each of the statuses by an intuitive identifier. For example, we could have a Status model that maps these constants to their corresponding IDs in the database:

```ruby
class Status < ActiveRecord::Base
  ACTIVE   = 1
  PENDING  = 2
  DISABLED = 3
end
```

But of course that's brittle and won't automatically adapt to changes. So instead, we'll use a bit of metaprogramming to dynamically add constants for all the statuses in the database. We'll do that in an initializer file:

ConstantCaches/config/initializers/constant_cache.rb

```
module ConstantCache
  module ClassMethods
    def caches_constants
      find(:all).each do |instance|
        const = instance.name.gsub(/\s+/, '_').upcase
        if const_defined?(const)
          raise RuntimeError,
              "Constant #{self.to_s}::#{const} has already been defined"
        else
          const_set(const, instance)
        end
      end
    end
  end
end
```

```
ActiveRecord::Base.send(:extend, ConstantCache::ClassMethods)
```

The caches_constants is added to ActiveRecord::Base (through the call to send at the end) and is available to all Active Record classes in our application. It finds all the statuses in the database and uses the const_set class method to turn each status into a constant scoped to the class. It's just as if we manually added PENDING = find_by_name('Pending'), for example, to the Status class definition. As a little icing, it replaces whitespace with underscores and raises an exception when there is an already defined constant.

Now we will change our Status model to use the caches_constants declaration:

ConstantCaches/app/models/status.rb

```
class Status < ActiveRecord::Base
  caches_constants
end
```

Then, over in the console, we'll look at the newly created constants and assign them directly to the :status attribute of an Account model:

```
$ ruby script/console
>> Status::PENDING
=> #<Status id: 1, name: "Pending">
>> Status::DISABLED
=> #<Status id: 3, name: "Disabled">
```

```
>> a = Account.create!(:username => 'preagan', :status => Status::PENDING)
=> #<Account id: 1, username: "preagan", status_id: 1>
>> a.status
=> #<Status id: 1, name: "Pending">
```

Now, instead of performing multiple (unnecessary) find calls each time we want to grab a state or a status, we load them once when the application starts.

Discussion

Bear in mind that you won't see the benefits of caching unless you're running the application in production mode. In development mode, your application's code is reloaded on every request. To test the caching in development, you need to make the following change (and remember to change it back!) in your config/environments/development.rb file:

```
config.cache_classes = true
```

Profile in the Browser

By Aaron Batalion (http://blog.batalion.com)

Aaron likes long walks in the park and developing web applications. He is an early adopter who picked up Ruby on Rails in 2005 while working at Blockbuster, where he led the architectural effort to build an online subscription portal, from online experience through fulfillment. Later, as an architect for Revolution Health, he led the organizational shift from Java and other technologies to a Rails platform and has enjoyed stretching Rails to its enterprise limits ever since. He has authored and coauthored several plug-ins, many of which are available on RubyForge.

Problem

As more and more users flock to your application, performance will be increasingly important. You may have tried profiling certain pages by writing integration tests that are wrapped in timing code. But your Rails app behaves differently when it's nestled in its production environment. So, you really need to profile your application *in production* to answer questions such as these:

- Is that Amazon API call that you mocked out in development taking 80% of the request time in production?

- Do you have an Active Record finder that was speedy with a small dataset but needs some love with bigger datasets?

- Is your caching solution paying off as expected?

Ingredients

- The ruby-prof profiler gem:

```
$ gem install ruby-prof
```

Solution

You might be surprised to learn that we can fairly easily get profiling information for any web request right in our browser!

First, we need a good profiler library, and RubyProf[1] doesn't disappoint. It can generate thread/method level reports that outline hotspots in our application. The trick, though, is getting RubyProf to profile a controller action and then append the profile report to the action's response.

---

1. http://ruby-prof.rubyforge.org

To do that, we'll use an around_filter to wrap an action with some profiling code. Here's a really simple around_filter that just brackets a call to any action:

```ruby
around_filter do |controller, action|
  logger.debug "before #{controller.action_name}"
  action.call
  logger.debug "after #{controller.action_name}"
end
```

Next, we'll mix this together with RubyProf in our ApplicationController:

BrowserProfiling/app/controllers/application.rb

```ruby
class ApplicationController < ActionController::Base
  around_filter do |controller, action|
    if controller.params.key?("browser_profile!")
      require 'ruby-prof'

      # Profile only the action
      profile_results = RubyProf.profile { action.call }

      # Use RubyProf's built in HTML printer to format the results
      printer = RubyProf::GraphHtmlPrinter.new(profile_results)

      # Append the results to the HTML response
      controller.response.body << printer.print("", 0)
    else
      action.call
    end
  end
end
```

Hey, we have ourselves an in-browser profiler for any request! If any incoming request has a browser_profile! parameter, we'll still call the requested action but under the watchful eye of RubyProf. Then we tack the profile report onto the end of the response.

Now if we type in the following URL, for example, we see the inline report:

http://localhost:3000/recipes?browser_profile!

Listing recipes

Name	Ingredients			
Rock 'n Roll	Seared red snapper, avocado, cucumber crisp	Show	Edit	Destroy
Volcano Roll	Diver scallops, salmon, cream cheese, avocado	Show	Edit	Destroy

New recipe

Profile Report

Thread ID	Total Time
24353540	0.057467

Thread 24353540

%Total	%Self	Total	Self	Wait	Child	Calls	Name
100.00%	0.00%	0.06	0.00	0.00	0.06	0	**ActionController::Base#process**
		0.06	0.00	0.00	0.06	1/1	ActionController::SessionManagement#process_without_browser_profiling
		0.06	0.00	0.00	0.06		ActionController::Base#process
100.00%	0.07%	0.06	0.00	0.00	0.06	1	**ActionController::SessionManagement#process_without_browser_profiling**
		0.06	0.00	0.00	0.06	1/1	ActionController::Filters::InstanceMethods#process_without_session_management_support
		0.00	0.00	0.00	0.00	1/1	ActionController::Components::InstanceMethods#set_session_options
		0.06	0.00	0.00	0.06	1/1	ActionController::SessionManagement#process_without_browser_profiling

There's just one small problem. Our around_filter is not guaranteed to be the first and last filter in the filter chain. That means some other before_filter or after_filter could be to blame for our performance problems, and we'd never know it. That is, we wouldn't know it until we rearranged our code slightly.

Instead of using an around_filter to wrap the action, we'll wrap the entire request *process*. It involves basically the same code. This time we'll add it to ActionController::Base in an initializer file:

BrowserProfiling/config/initializers/core_extensions.rb

```ruby
module ActionController
  class Base
    def process_with_browser_profiling(request, response,
                                       method = :perform_action,
                                       *arguments)

      if request.parameters.key?('browser_profile!')
        require 'ruby-prof'

        # Profile only the action
        profile_results = RubyProf.profile {
          response = process_without_browser_profiling(request, response,
                                                       method, *arguments)
        }

        # Use RubyProf's built in HTML printer to format the results
        printer = RubyProf::GraphHtmlPrinter.new(profile_results)

        # Append the results to the HTML response
        response.body << printer.print("", 0)

        # Reset the content length (for Rails 2.0)
        response.send("set_content_length!")

        response
      else
        process_without_browser_profiling(request, response,
                                          method, *arguments)
      end
    end
    alias_method_chain :process, :browser_profiling
  end
end
```

The key to making this work is the alias_method_chain at the bottom. When a request comes into our app, the process method is invoked to handle it. But we want to do that with profiling enabled.

So, alias_method_chain says that whenever the profile method is called, our profile_with_browser_profiling method should be called instead. Then, to invoke the original process method in our profiling block (or if the request shouldn't be profiled), we call process_without_browser_profiling.

Having this profiler just a URL parameter away in your application makes it really handy to pinpoint where in production bottlenecks are.

Also See

While this recipe works for most scenarios, it doesn't support POST operations or redirects. To do that, you'd need to append the profiling results to a file instead of the HTML response. For a more full-featured profiler based on this recipe, check out the BrowserProfiler plug-in:[2]

```
$ script/plugin install svn://rubyforge.org/var/svn/browser-prof
```

If you dig having inline reports, you might also like the BrowserLogger plug-in,[3] which appends the current request's log to the end of a response. You'll never tail a log file again!

---

2. http://rubyforge.org/projects/browser-prof/
3. http://rubyforge.org/projects/browser-logger/

Cache Up with the Big Guys

By P.J. Hyett and Chris Wanstrath (http://errtheblog.com)
By day, P.J. and Chris run the Rails consulting and training firm, Err Free. By night, they maintain Err the Blog, a running commentary on both Ruby and Rails.

Problem

You've received massive funding. You've hit the front page of Digg-Crunch. New users are flowing like champagne at your launch party. But despite using standard Rails template caching, your app is slowing, slowing, slowing down.

All that beautifully concise Active Record code spread throughout your app is now becoming a serious bottleneck as your tables (and bandwidth bills) start growing by the millions. Wouldn't it be great to change that clever code slightly into something simple and watch (most of) your problems disappear?

Ingredients

- The memcached daemon.[1] On a Mac we install it like this:

  ```
  $ sudo port install memcached
  ```

  There is also a port of memcached for Windows.[2]

- The memcache-client gem:

  ```
  $ gem install memcache-client
  ```

- The cache_fu plug-in:

  ```
  $ script/plugin install svn://errtheblog.com/svn/plugins/cache_fu
  ```

---

1. http://www.danga.com/memcached
2. http://jehiah.cz/projects/memcached-win32/

At some point, even the cleanest, most-efficient code can't handle massive loads—not because it's slow but commonly because a resource it depends on is slow. For web apps, it's usually the database. That's where the gentle developers of LiveJournal come in. They wrote an awesome library called memcached, of which they have this to say:[3]

"memcached is a high-performance, distributed memory object caching system, generic in nature, but intended for use in speeding up dynamic web applications by alleviating database load."

Sounds great, right? It may not cook your chicken rotisserie style in ten minutes, but it has saved sites like Gamespot, Facebook, Wikipedia, and Digg from an early demise. And developers in the Rails community are working toward making memcached one of the easiest ways to scale your app. So, let's get right to it, shall we?

First we'll start up the memcached daemon process:

```
$ rake memcached:start
```

Conceptually, memcached is just a distributed hash: it caches objects indexed by a key. The Rake task fires it up on a server and port combo specified in the config/memcached.yml file. Here's the default development configuration that was created when the cache_fu plug-in was installed:

```
development:
  servers: localhost:11211
```

Cool, now let's get to the goods with something simple. Say we have an action that fetches a user along with all of their groovy tags:

```
class UsersController < ApplicationController
  def show
    @user = User.find(params[:id], :include => :tags)

    respond_to do |format|
      format.html # show.html.erb
      format.xml  { render :xml => @user }
    end
  end
end
```

---

3. http://www.danga.com/memcached

It's very clean, but it's slowing down as our database and traffic grow. So, let's cache each user in the memcached daemon's memory. To do that, we'll just add acts_as_cached to our User model:

```
class User < ActiveRecord::Base
  acts_as_cached :include => :tags
end
```

Then we'll replace the find method in the show action with get_cache:

```
class UsersController < ApplicationController
  def show
    @user = User.get_cache(params[:id])

    respond_to do |format|
      format.html # show.html.erb
      format.xml  { render :xml => @user }
    end
  end
end
```

That's all there is to it, mostly. Pretty simple object caching. The get_cache method will try to fetch data uniquely identified by the User model and value of params(:id) from the cache. If nothing is found (a *cache miss*), it will call User.find with the params(:id) value and cache the result. In other words, the first time the show action is hit, a DB query is run. Here, let's have a look in the log:

```
User Load Including Associations (0.189375)  SELECT `users`.`id`...
==> Set User:694624473 to cache. (0.01550)
Completed in 4.63984 (0 reqs/sec) | Rendering: 0.00114 (0%) |
Memcache: 0.01745 | DB: 0.19800 (4%) | 200 OK
```

If something is found, it will just return it. That means when we hit the action a second time, there's no DB query:

```
==> Got User:694624473 from cache. (0.00983)
Rendering users/show
Completed in 0.02702 (37 reqs/sec) | Rendering: 0.00334 (12%) |
Memcache: 0.00983 | DB: 0.00281 (10%) | 200 OK
```

That's a good start! However, as our controllers become skinnier and our models fatter, we're going to end up with lots of custom finders. Say we have a page displaying the last fifty users who have signed up and we want to show them along with their crazy profile picture and maybe their tags. That's not a big deal, but this query involves three quite large tables.

For example, here's what our custom finder might look like:

```ruby
class User < ActiveRecord::Base
  def self.find_latest
    find :all, :order => 'users.id desc',
               :limit => 50,
               :include => [:picture, :tags]
  end
end
```

And here's our index action that uses it:

```ruby
class UsersController < ApplicationController
  def index
    @users = User.find_latest

    respond_to do |format|
      format.html # index.html.erb
      format.xml  { render :xml => @users }
    end
  end
end
```

Skinny controller, fat model? Check! Ordering by ID? Check! Loading pictures and tags in bulk? Check! Query takes two seconds to execute? Check! Wait, that last check is no good.

So instead of running that two-second query on every page load, let's just run it once every five minutes and cache the result. To do that, we'll change the acts_as_cached call slightly in our User model. Here's our revised model in its entirety:

CachingUp/app/models/user.rb

```ruby
class User < ActiveRecord::Base

  has_one :picture
  has_and_belongs_to_many :tags

  acts_as_cached :ttl => 5.minutes

  def self.find_latest
    find :all, :order => 'users.id desc',
               :limit => 50,
               :include => [:tags, :picture]
  end
end
```

The custom finder method in the model wasn't changed? That's right! The cache_fu plug-in offers a number of really sweet features, and one of our favorites is being able to pass a method name to the cached method and have the result cached.

Now over in our UsersController, we'll change the index action to use User.cached(:find_latest):

CachingUp/app/controllers/users_controller.rb
```ruby
class UsersController < ApplicationController
  def index
    @users = User.cached(:find_latest)

    respond_to do |format|
      format.html # index.html.erb
      format.xml  { render :xml => @users }
    end
  end
end
```

Calling cached(:find_latest) caches the result of the finder and puts it in the cache using the method name as the key.

This is the crux of caching. Databases are always the bottleneck in web applications, so you avoid that stress by putting as much of your data in memory as makes sense. The idea is that the data is retrieved from the database once, put into the cache, and returned from the cache on any subsequent requests until it has been invalidated.

Speaking of invalidation, how do we ensure our cache is fresh beyond setting an appropriate timeout? The way we have our User model set up now, the cache is expired every five minutes. Rails, conveniently, provides hooks into a model object's life cycle.

Next, we'll automate the cache expiry process by adding an after_save hook to call the expire_cache method provided by cache_fu:

```ruby
class User < ActiveRecord::Base
  acts_as_cached
  after_save :expire_cache
end
```

Now when a User object is updated, the user's record will be expired from the cache. When the next request comes in for that user, Rails will grab a fresh copy from the database and put the object right back in the cache where it belongs. This means we have strong cache integrity— we'll rarely get stale data.

However, if we think we have stale data and want to see our page generated straight from the database, we can write a before_filter to force a cache reset:

`CachingUp/app/controllers/application.rb`

```ruby
class ApplicationController < ActionController::Base
  before_filter :set_cache_override

private

  def set_cache_override
    returning true do
      ActsAsCached.skip_cache_gets =
        !!params[:skip_cache]
    end
  end

end
```

Setting skip_cache_gets tells cache_fu to treat every cache lookup as a cache miss. We can trigger it by hitting this:

http://localhost:3000/users?skip_cache=1

But be very careful with this! If you do this on the front door of a big site during peak hours, all those expensive queries get rerun. A safer alternative is to call User.reset_cache, which grabs data and sets it in the cache without expiring the key. While this is going on, every request gets the old cached data.

Hey, this site is getting faster! But there's one more wrinkle. Let's say we also have a page that lists all the recent forum posts, and next to each post we show the user's name and picture. Some users appear more than once. So, we need to load all the users who have posts on this page, but we don't want to cache users along with their forum posts. Otherwise, every time a user changed her picture, we'd have to clear the cache of every post she made.

Instead, we'll pass a list of user IDs into the get_cache method, like so:

```ruby
user_ids = @posts.map(&:user_id).uniq
@users   = User.get_cache(user_ids)
```

This grabs all the matching keys in parallel, filling in the cache misses as it goes. When all is said and done, @users is a hash keyed by the user ID, and the value is the corresponding User model. Then we can iterate through the hash data in our view to keep things speedy.

Finally, it's time to put all this caching goodness into production. First, we'll check the configuration of the production section of the config/memcached.yml file:

```
production:
  namespace: killer_app
  servers:
    - 192.185.254.121:11211
    - 192.185.254.138:11211
    - 192.185.254.160:11211
```

The namespace is important because it's the namespace all the keys live under, and setting it for our app lets us have different apps sharing the same memcached daemon. It's also important to use IP addresses for where the memcached daemons live to avoid DNS requests.

Then once we have the production environment configured, we'll fire up the memcached daemon on the production machines using this:

```
$ rake memcached:start
```

There's also a memcached_ctl script that comes with cache_fu for managing the daemon on multiple servers.

Using memcached isn't a silver bullet—there are a number of hardware and architectural considerations to keep in mind as your app grows. For example, if you can't keep up with the I/O requests, then you won't benefit from memcached. And in smaller apps it may actually make things slower. Focus on your app first, and then add cache_fu later when you have evidence that you really need it.

Discussion

You can cache anything: generated images, intense number crunching, HTML, and so on.

Using memcached adds at least one more moving part to your production environment. As reliable as memcached may be, it's wise to monitor the daemons across multiple servers using Monit. Recipe 80, *Monitor (and Repair) Processes with Monit*, on page 413 has some examples you can tailor for your environment.

Dynamically Update Cached Pages

By Mike Subelsky (http://www.subelsky.com/)
Mike is a former Navy cryptologic officer and cybersecurity analyst now working as a freelance software developer and Rails hacker. He lives and hacks in Baltimore, Maryland.

Problem

You want to use page caching but still dynamically customize a few page elements for each user. For example, in the header of every cached page you want to show a Log In link to users who haven't already logged in and show the user's name and a Log Out link if they are logged in.

Solution

Suppose at the top of every page in our application we make the logged-in user feel warm and fuzzy, like this:

The dynamic part is contained within a login span in our application layout file:

`DynamicCacheContent/app/views/layouts/application.html.erb`

```erb
<span id="login">
  <% if logged_in? -%>
  Welcome, <%= h user_name %>!
  (<%= link_to 'Log Out', logout_path %>)
  <% else -%>
    <%= link_to 'Log In', login_path %>
  <% end -%>
</span>
```

Now let's say the front page of our app gets a lot of action, so we enable page caching. The next request for the front page will cache it, and subsequent requests will bypass Rails completely—the web server merely serves the static page from our public directory. That results in lightning-fast page loads.

The only downside is that the static page is, well, static. So if Wally is already logged in and he's the first person to hit our front page, then everyone sees Wally's greeting. Worse yet, it appears as though everyone is logged in as Wally. That is, that happens unless we add a wee bit of JavaScript into the page. Then we can have our cake and eat it too!

Let's assume that when a user logs in, we put their user ID in the session. That's how our application remembers that the user has already logged in. But we need the cached *page* to remember, too. To do that, when the user logs in, we'll also create a cookie that contains the user's name. So in the controller that handles our login/logout functions, we'll have methods that look like this:

```ruby
def login
  user = User.authenticate(params[:login], params[:password])
  if user
    reset_session
    session[:user_id]   = user.id
    cookies[:user_name] = {:value => user.name}
    redirect_to home_url
  else
    flash[:error] = "Sorry, try again."
    render :action => 'new'
  end
end

def logout
  reset_session
  cookies.delete :user_name
  redirect_to home_url
end
```

Next, we need some JavaScript that looks for the user_name cookie and dynamically updates the personalized area. As we're already using the Prototype library for other features, we'll use it here for simplicity. We'll just chuck this in our application.js file:

DynamicCacheContent/public/javascripts/application.js

```javascript
var LoginCheck = Class.create({
  initialize: function(cookie_name) {
    var cookie_value = get_cookie(cookie_name);
    if (!cookie_value) {
      $('login').update("<a href=\"/login\">Log In</a>");
    } else {
      $('login').update("Welcome, " + cookie_value.escapeHTML() + "!" +
                        " (<a href=\"/logout\">Log Out</a>)");
    }
  }
});
```

```
function get_cookie(name) {
  var value = null;
  document.cookie.split('; ').each(function(cookie) {
    var name_value = cookie.split('=');
    if (name_value[0] == name) {
      value = name_value[1];
    }
  });
  return value;
}
```

If the user_name cookie is found in the browser, then we update the login element in our header to contain a Log Out link with the user's name. If no user_name cookie is found, we update the page to show the Log In link instead.

Finally, we'll call our JavaScript magic at the bottom of our application layout file, passing in the name of the cookie we're looking for:

DynamicCacheContent/app/views/layouts/application.html.erb

```
<script type="text/javascript">
  // <![CDATA[
  new LoginCheck('user_name');
  // ]]>
</script>
```

Now when the cached page is written to disk, the page includes the JavaScript call. When the page is loaded from disk, the JavaScript runs and dynamically updates the links on the page depending on whether the cookie was found.

To test this in development mode, remember to (temporarily) enable caching in your config/environments/development.rb file:

```
config.action_controller.perform_caching = true
```

Discussion

You could also use Prototype Ajax calls back to your server to perform more complex, dynamic page updates.

You'll likely want to name your cookie something unique, rather than just user_name.

Also See

If you need to cache pages that contain flash messages, check out the Cacheable Flash plug-in.[1]

---

1. http://www.pivotalblabs.com/articles/2007/08/08/cacheable-flash

Use DTrace for Profiling

By Scott Barron (http://rubyi.st)
Scott is currently a Rubyist working with EdgeCase, a hip company based in Columbus, Ohio. He is also the author of the (in)famous acts_as_state_machine plug-in. (Another release is due out Real Soon Now. He promises.)

Problem

You have a method in a running application (perhaps even in production) that you'd like to do some quick profiling on, without adding any special hooks to the code.

Ingredients

- Mac OS X Leopard or Solaris

  If you're on Mac OS X, you'll need to use the version of Ruby that's preinstalled with Leopard. If you're on Solaris, you'll need Ruby 1.8.6 built with the DTrace patch.

Solution

DTrace (http://www.sun.com/bigadmin/content/dtrace) is a very powerful tracing tool that can gather metrics on and examine running code from the OS kernel up through application code. It was originally developed for Sun's Solaris operating system, but it's now preinstalled with Mac OS X Leopard. Along with putting DTrace into Leopard, Apple also included a patched version of Ruby that has a useful set of DTrace probes built in. The best way to learn about DTrace is to see it in action, so let's give it a spin!

Suppose we're running the Depot application—you know, the one described in *Agile Web Development with Rails* [TH05]—and we want to get the method count and elapsed method times of the two code paths in the Cart#add_product method:

DTrace/depot/app/models/cart.rb

```ruby
def add_product(product)
  current_item = @items.find {|item| item.product == product}
  if current_item
    current_item.increment_quantity
```

```
    else
      current_item = CartItem.new(product)
      @items << current_item
    end
    current_item
end
```

The first thing we need to do is write a script for DTrace to tell it what we want to trace. The D language syntax[1] is a bit unconventional, so let's start with a simple example and break it down from the top:

DTrace/method-profile.d

```
ruby*:::function-entry
/copyinstr(arg0) == "Cart" && copyinstr(arg1) == "add_product"/
{
  self->profile_it = 1;
}
```

The first line here is what's called a *probe specification*. It's divided into four parts, separated by a colon. For our purposes, we need to worry only about the first and last parts. In this probe specification, the first part is ruby*. This tells DTrace to trace all processes on the system that define the Ruby probes (that is, all Ruby processes). The last part is function-entry. This means that we want to match the function-entry probe, which is one of the probes that has been built into Ruby. In this case, the function-entry probe fires every time a Ruby-level method is invoked.

A probe specification can be followed by an optional conditional to narrow down what we're looking for. In this case, we're interested only in watching for Cart#add_product methods. To do that, we check the arguments passed along through the function-entry probe. arg0 is the name of the class that defines the method, and arg1 is the method name. (The copyinstr function just copies the argument string into a scratch buffer so we can access it.) This probe will take action every time Cart#add_product is called and ignore all other methods.

Following the conditional is a block containing all of the things we want to do when the probe we've matched finally fires. In this case, we simply set a profile_it variable indicating that we want to start profiling things. We just picked this variable name arbitrarily; it's not built into DTrace. All the variables beginning with self-> are thread-local variables.

---

1. http://wikis.sun.com/display/DTrace/Documentation

Once we've entered Cart#add_product, we want to watch every method that runs. We'll add another probe for that:

```
ruby*:::function-entry
/self->profile_it == 1/
{
  self->depth++;
  self->function[self->depth] = timestamp;
}
```

This probe specification watches all methods using function-entry, but notice the conditional block. We take action only if our profile_it switch is on, meaning we're inside Cart#add_product. When this probe fires, we use the built-in timestamp variable to record the current time for later use in determining how long the method took to run. We also increment the depth variable (again, an arbitrary name) to keep track of where we are in the call graph.

Next, we need to tally up some metrics when a method returns while we're tracing Cart#add_product. We'll add a third probe to do the actual bookkeeping (notice the conditional):

```
ruby*:::function-return
/self->profile_it == 1/
{
  /* Measure how long the method took. */
  this->elapsed = timestamp - self->function[self->depth];
  self->function[self->depth] = 0;

  /* Save the method name.  Example: "CartItem::initialize". */
  this->name = strjoin(strjoin(copyinstr(arg0), "::"), copyinstr(arg1));

  /* Count the number of times this method was called */
  @method_count[this->name] = count();

  /* Count the total number of methods called */
  @method_count["total"] = count();

  /* Sum the total amount of time this method has used */
  @method_time[this->name] = sum(this->elapsed);

  self->depth--;
}
```

The conditional block has some new syntax that's worth highlighting. All the variables beginning with this-> are clause-local variables, so they're scoped within the conditional block. For example, when we construct this->name in the function-return probe, we don't need to keep it around forever. By using a clause local variable, its storage will be reused each time.

Also, when you see a variable beginning with an at sign (@), it's called an *aggregation*. You can think of it being like a hash: it has a key and a value. DTrace stores the results of aggregating functions, such as count() and sum(), in aggregations. For example, calling count() increments the value in the aggregation every time it's called.

When Cart#add_product finally returns, we're no longer interested in tracing anything. We'll write another probe to turn our variable switch off:

DTrace/method-profile.d

```
ruby*:::function-return
/copyinstr(arg0) == "Cart" && copyinstr(arg1) == "add_product"/
{
  self->profile_it = 0;
}
```

Finally, we'll write an END probe that uses the aggregations to dump out the report:

DTrace/method-profile.d

```
dtrace:::END
{
  printf("\nMethod Count,\n");
  printf("  %-64s %8s\n", "NAME", "TOTAL");
  printa("  %-64s %@8d\n", @method_count);

  normalize(@method_time, 1000);
  printf("\nElapsed times(us),\n");
  printf("  %-64s %8s\n", "NAME", "TOTAL");
  printa("  %-64s %@8d\n", @method_time);
}
```

OK, now let's put this to use profiling our application. Looking back at the Cart#add_product method, we have two paths to execute: first, if the item is already in the cart, the code just increments its count; second, if the item has not been added to the cart, then a new CartItem object is created and stored.

Let's start with an empty cart and run a trace when we add an item to it. Fire up the Depot application, and start the first trace using this:

```
$ sudo dtrace -s method-profile.d
```

When the DTrace script is ready, you'll see this output:

```
Tracing... Hit Ctrl-C to stop.
```

Now over in our browser, we'll add an item to the cart. When we're done, we hit Ctrl+C in the DTrace console and look at the output. It should look similar to this:

DTrace/empty-cart-output.txt

```
Method Count,
    NAME                                                        TOTAL
    Array::<<                                                       1
    Array::each                                                    1
    CartItem::initialize                                           1
    Class::new                                                     1
    Object::find                                                   1
    total                                                         5

Elapsed times(us),
    NAME                                                        TOTAL
    Array::each                                                   26
    Array::<<                                                     26
    CartItem::initialize                                          59
    Class::new                                                   456
    Object::find                                                2023
```

One path down, one to go. Start up the tracer again:

```
$ sudo dtrace -s method-profile.d
```

If we now add the same item to the cart again and hit Ctrl+C, we should get output looking something like this:

DTrace/same-cartitem-output.txt

```
Method Count,
    NAME                                                        TOTAL
    ActiveRecord::Base::==                                          1
    ActiveRecord::Base::new_record?                                1
    CartItem::increment_quantity                                   1
    Fixnum::+                                                      1
    Fixnum::==                                                     1
    Object::class                                                  1
    Object::equal?                                                 1
    Object::find                                                   1
    Object::instance_of?                                           1
    Hash::[]                                                        2
    Product::id                                                    2
    String::to_i                                                    2
    total                                                         15

Elapsed times(us),
```

```
NAME                                                    TOTAL
Fixnum::==                                                 23
Fixnum::+                                                  23
Object::equal?                                             25
Object::instance_of?                                      26
ActiveRecord::Base::new_record?                           28
Object::class                                             33
Hash::[]                                                   56
String::to_i                                               84
CartItem::increment_quantity                             215
Product::id                                             1630
ActiveRecord::Base::==                                  4677
Object::find                                            5003
```

The calculations here are very simple, and the time is a cumulative time. That is, the reported time for a method is the sum of the time that method took for all of the times it executed, including all the methods it called. You could take this a step further by building a call graph of the methods. This would give you a better idea of not only exactly how long a specific instance of a method took but where in the code the method was being called.

We have used DTrace to examine a single method of our application, without changing any application code. We could even use DTrace in our production environment, provided we're running on Mac OS X or Solaris.

Discussion

When you're tracing, even during development, it's probably best to be running in production mode and warm the app up a little by hitting the areas you want to trace before you trace them. This will get any of the Rails magic class loading out of the way so it doesn't interfere with the measurements.

In the test output you'll notice that the total method count is three times as large when adding the same item to the cart and takes about two-and-a-half times as long. Granted, in this case we're talking 3,000 microseconds, which is .003 seconds. You can extrapolate this example to a scenario with a larger dataset or more complex code to see how DTrace would help pinpoint otherwise elusive problem spots.

The difference can be explained by looking at the reported methods executed. The first time around, there is nothing in the cart, so the find loop is very fast, and only a CartItem object must be created. The second time around, there's an item already in the cart, so the find loop must do a little more work. We can see this by methods like Object::equal?, Object::instance_of?, and ActiveRecord::Base::new_record? being reported, amongst others. After that, we can see that CartItem::increment_quantity is finally called.

Also See

If you're on Mac OS X and want to run your trace in a GUI or easily take a look at your events compared to memory, disk, and other diagnostics, check out Instruments,[2] which is part of Xcode.

---

2. http://www.apple.com/macosx/developertools/instruments.html

Part XII

Security Recipes

Constrain Access to Sensitive Data

If you can read only one recipe in this book, make it this one! The steps are trivial but oh-so easy to forget. And the cost of forgetting—well, you don't want to find out.

Take, for example, this innocent-looking model:

```ruby
class User < ActiveRecord::Base
end
```

Imagine this model wraps a users table that has a number of boolean columns, including is_admin and gets_free_orders. Of course, we'd never put those attributes on the account creation form with checkboxes next to them. Otherwise, anyone could make themselves special and never pay for another order. However, as this model stands, ordinary people don't need no stinkin' form to rule our system!

That's right, anyone with a 'net connection and a little time on their hands (indeed, the devil's workshop) can simply post values for any columns in our users table directly via our create action. After all, most create actions start off doing this:

```ruby
@user = User.new(params[:user])
```

This assigns all the user's POST parameters to the User model in bulk. Thankfully, there's an easy fix. You can protect sensitive attributes from bulk assignment by using attr_accessible in your model. It takes the names of the attributes that can safely be assigned in bulk.[1] In this case, we just need to add the following to our User model:

events/app/models/user.rb

```ruby
attr_accessible :name, :email, :password
```

This one-liner means that only those attributes are eligible for bulk assignment. For example, to upgrade a user to an administrator, we would need to explicitly assign a value in code, like so:

```ruby
@user.is_admin = true
@user.save
```

---

1. The attr_protected method does the reverse and in doing so leaves the door open if you add new columns. It's generally better to use positive access control with attr_accessible.

Don't put this recipe down just yet! We have one more security hole to plug up in this application. Take a gander at this innocent-looking action:

```
def index
  @users = User.find(:all)

  respond_to do |format|
    format.html # index.html.erb
    format.xml  { render :xml => @users }
  end
end
```

Of course, we'd never show any sensitive user information on the HTML page, even if it's viewable by admins only. But as this action stands, prying eyes don't need no stinkin' HTML page to compromise our data! Instead, they can simply access this action with the xml format and read the secret data in raw XML form.

Again, the fix is easy. You can (and should!) override the to_xml method in your models to serialize only publicly consumable attributes as XML. In this case, we'll spit out only the id, name, and email attributes from our User model:

events/app/models/user.rb

```
def to_xml(options = {})
  default_only = [:id, :name, :email]
  options[:only] = (options[:only] || []) + default_only
  super(options)
end
```

Do yourself a big favor. Spend a couple minutes looking through your models and your tables (yes, *especially* if your app is already in production). Add attr_accessible and override to_xml where appropriate. You don't have to tell anybody you did....

Encrypt Sensitive Data

By Val Aleksenko (http://hungrymachine.com/)

Val is a partner at Hungry Machine, a full-service web development group specializing in the design and deployment of Ruby on Rails applications, and he has deep experience in the Facebook application platform. He has more than seventeen years of software development experience, with focus on Rails since 2005, and is an author/coauthor of many Rails plug-ins addressing shortcomings in the enterprise area.

Problem

You're handling sensitive data in your application, and you're required (by HIPPA[1] regulations, for example) to store the sensitive data encrypted in your database. You need an easy and yet secure way for the rest of your application to access this data through Active Record models.

Ingredients

- The acts_as_secure plug-in:
  ```
  $ script/plugin install ↩
  svn://rubyforge.org/var/svn/acts-as-secure/trunk/vendor/plugins/acts_as_secure
  ```
- The ezcrypto gem:
  ```
  $ gem install ezcrypto
  ```

Solution

Let's suppose we need to protect sensitive medical patient records—you know, those forms you fill out when you visit the doctor, and then someone punches the information into a computer while you wait.

Now, we could roll our own solution using Active Record callbacks, but acts_as_secure is a tidy little plug-in that uses callbacks to take care of that for us. All we need to do is mark our models with acts_as_secure and use a :binary type to identify database columns that need to be encrypted.

Before we get on to encrypting data, it's important to recognize that the acts_as_secure plug-in doesn't actually encrypt anything. Instead, it lets us plug in any external crypto provider that offers encrypt and decrypt methods. For our example, we'll use the ezcrypto gem (an easy-to-use wrapper around Ruby's OpenSSL library) to encrypt the data

---

1. http://www.hhs.gov/ocr/hipaa/

using the AES 128 CBC encryption algorithm. The acts_as_secure plug-in then calls the crypto providers at the appropriate times. It supports a master key encryption approach for all records, as well as individual encryption keys for specific records.

Let's start by protecting the patient's address and Social Security number with a master key. First we need a migration for the patient records, which in this case has two binary columns:

EncryptData/db/migrate/001_create_secret_patients.rb

```ruby
class CreateSecretPatients < ActiveRecord::Migration
  def self.up
    create_table :secret_patients do |t|
      t.string :name
      t.binary :address
      t.binary :ssn
    end
  end

  def self.down
    drop_table :secret_patients
  end
end
```

Next, we need to create a class that has encrypt and decrypt methods. We'll call it MasterCryptoProvider and put it in the lib directory. There's not much to it; the ezcrypto gem does all the important stuff:

EncryptData/lib/master_crypto_provider.rb

```ruby
require 'ezcrypto'

class MasterCryptoProvider

  CONFIG = YAML.load_file(RAILS_ROOT +
            '/config/crypto.yml')[ENV['RAILS_ENV']].symbolize_keys

  class << self
    def encrypt(field)
      key.encrypt field
    end

    def decrypt(field)
      key.decrypt field
    end

    def key
      EzCrypto::Key.with_password CONFIG[:master_key], CONFIG[:salt]
    end
  end
end
```

Here's what the crypto.yml file looks like:

EncryptData/config/crypto.yml

```
development:
  master_key: YOUR_SECRET_MASTER_KEY
  salt: YOUR_SALT

test:
  master_key: YOUR_SECRET_MASTER_KEY
  salt: YOUR_SALT

production:
  master_key: YOUR_SECRET_MASTER_KEY
  salt: YOUR_SALT
```

Then we'll secure all the SecretPatient records by stamping the model with acts_as_secure and plugging in our crypto provider:

EncryptData/app/models/secret_patient.rb

```
class SecretPatient < ActiveRecord::Base
  acts_as_secure :crypto_provider => MasterCryptoProvider
end
```

Now if we jump into the console, we see no difference between encrypted and unencrypted attributes:

```
$ ruby script/console
>> SecretPatient.create(:name => 'John Doe', :address => 'Somewhere Secret',
                        :ssn => '012-345-6789')
=> #<SecretPatient id: 1, name: "John Doe", address: "Somewhere Secret",
                   ssn: "012-345-6789">

>> SecretPatient.find :first
=> #<SecretPatient id: 1, name: "John Doe", address: "Somewhere Secret",
                   ssn: "012-345-6789">
```

But if we peek in the database, the address and ssn column values have been encrypted:

```
mysql> select * from secret_patients;
+----+----------+----------------------+------------------+
| id | name     | address              | ssn              |
+----+----------+----------------------+------------------+
|  1 | John Doe | ?)????"???G????x      | ?z??/?"/4Z?       |
|    |          |      s2?????#A?       |    ????k??5?v??Ec |
+----+----------+----------------------+------------------+
```

This is exactly what we want, but this comes with a few limitations. Because the address and ssn fields are stored encrypted, using an Active Record find operation against either of them is very limited. In general, you won't be able to search across encrypted fields. This usually isn't an issue, though, because protected data is often referential.

Now let's ratchet things up a bit. Suppose we also need to encrypt certain records with individual encryption keys. That is, we need a more secure approach than using one master key. For our example, we'll assume we need to store a patient's DNA sequence. Here's a new migration file for patients who need extra encryption measures:

EncryptData/db/migrate/002_create_uber_secret_patients.rb

```
class CreateUberSecretPatients < ActiveRecord::Migration
  def self.up
    create_table :uber_secret_patients do |t|
      t.string :name
      t.binary :address
      t.binary :ssn
      t.binary :dna_sequence
    end
  end

  def self.down
    drop_table :uber_secret_patients
  end
end
```

In this case, we don't need to specify a crypto provider on our model, just that it acts_as_secure:

EncryptData/app/models/uber_secret_patient.rb

```
class UberSecretPatient < ActiveRecord::Base
  acts_as_secure
end
```

However, any access to an UberSecretPatient record must be wrapped in a crypto provider call. To do that, we need a crypto provider that uses an individual key rather than a master key. We'll write a simple IndividualCryptoProvider class that again uses the ezcrypto gem to perform the actual encryption/decryption:

EncryptData/lib/individual_crypto_provider.rb

```
require 'ezcrypto'

class IndividualCryptoProvider

  CONFIG = YAML.load_file(RAILS_ROOT +
            '/config/crypto.yml')[ENV['RAILS_ENV']].symbolize_keys

  def initialize(password)
    @password = password
  end
```

```
  def encrypt(field)
    key.encrypt field
  end

  def decrypt(field)
    key.decrypt field
  end

  def key
    EzCrypto::Key.with_password @password, CONFIG[:salt]
  end
end
```

The only real difference here is the addition of the initialize method, which takes a key. Back over in the console, first we'll create a new provider with an individual key:

```
>> secret = "extra super uber secret key"

>> crypto_provider = IndividualCryptoProvider.new(secret)
=> #<IndividualCryptoProvider:0x3777a48 ...>
```

Then we must wrap standard Active Record operations such as create and find in a with_crypto_provider block:

```
>> UberSecretPatient.with_crypto_provider(crypto_provider) {
     UberSecretPatient.create(:name => "John Doe",
                              :address => "Somewhere Secret",
                              :ssn => "012-345-6789",
                              :dna_sequence => "ACAAGATGCCATTGTCCCC...")
   }

>> UberSecretPatient.with_crypto_provider(crypto_provider) {
     UberSecretPatient.find(:first).dna_sequence
   }
=> "ACAAGATGCCATTGTCCCC..."
```

When we access the records this way, the address, ssn, and dna_sequence column values are decrypted on the fly. If we try to access a record with an incorrect key, we get an exception:

```
>> secret = "bogus"
>> crypto_provider = IndividualCryptoProvider.new(secret)

>> UberSecretPatient.with_crypto_provider(crypto_provider) {
     UberSecretPatient.find(:first).dna_sequence
   }
RuntimeError: Failed to decode the field. Incorrect key?
```

The exception occurs because the binary fields are marshaled into YAML format before encryption. Then, when we use an incorrect key, the decrypt method returns a string that cannot be unmarshaled properly.

The benefit of encrypting data this way is that it's all handled transparently. Our application can continue accessing the data through our Active Record models, and with the exception of queries on encrypted fields, we can add encryption without impacting a lot of code.

Discussion

In this example, we stored the master key directly in a YAML file. You could also have the YAML file hold a key for unlocking a record in the database that contains the actual key. This would prevent secure data from being compromised if either the code or the DB is stolen, but not both. Alternatively, you could prompt for the password on application start-up, but that makes it difficult to use handy restart tools such as Monit. There are also commercial solutions (we'll leave the googling to you) that rely on user certificates to provide a truly secure way of storing individual keys instead of a single master key.

Flip On SSL

You need a declarative way of specifying that certain actions should be allowed to run only under SSL. If those actions are accessed with an http URL, they should be redirected to an https-equivalent URL.

• David Heinemeier Hansson's ssl_requirement plug-in:

```
$ script/plugin install ssl_requirement
```

The solution is easier than you might imagine, but it involves two deft steps: configuring our web server and marking up our controllers. Let's get the web server out of the way first and save the dessert for last.

Suppose we have our trusty web server listening on port 443 and along comes an SSL request. If it's a dynamic request, the web server simply forwards the request to our Rails app. However, Rails needs to know whether the original request came in via https. It's the web server's job to send along this piece of information to our Rails app, and the HTTP way to do that is by setting an HTTP header.

As it turns out, Rails is already waiting for an HTTP header called X_FORWARDED_PROTO. So, in our Apache httpd.conf file, we'll just set the X_FORWARDED_PROTO header to https in the virtual host for port 443. You'll have more stuff in your file, but here are the relevant parts we need to set:

```
<VirtualHost *:443>
  SSLEngine on
  RequestHeader set X_FORWARDED_PROTO "https"
</VirtualHost>
```

If we are using the Nginx web server, we'll set the header slightly differently:

```
server {
  listen 443;
  location / {
    proxy_set_header X_FORWARDED_PROTO https;
  }
}
```

OK, that takes care of the web server. (See, that wasn't so bad.) Our Rails app now automatically knows when an SSL request comes in. We can explicitly check for it using the request.ssl? method.

Next, we need to do something with the information Rails picks up from the HTTP header. Specifically, we want to be able to declare that certain actions must be run under SSL and let Rails "flip" to https when appropriate. That's exactly what the ssl_requirement plug-in does. We'll start by including it in our ApplicationController:

SSL/app/controllers/application.rb

```
include SslRequirement
```

This adds two methods to all our controllers: ssl_required and ssl_allowed. It also adds a before_filter that checks the request.ssl? method. If SSL is required for an action but request.ssl? is false, then we'll get redirected to the https URL for the action. The reverse is also true—running an action under SSL that doesn't require it will redirect to the http protocol.

Now, we don't want any of this to happen when we're issuing requests against our local development (or test) app. So, while we're in the ApplicationController file, let's override the ssl_required? method. In our version we'll check to see whether we're dealing with a local or test request and then run the default checks in the plug-in by calling super:

SSL/app/controllers/application.rb

```
def ssl_required?
  return false if local_request? || RAILS_ENV == 'test'
  super
end
```

At this point we've added all the plumbing we need, so it's payback time.

Over in our controllers, we can now use the ssl_required and ssl_allowed methods, like so:

```ruby
class AccountsController < ApplicationController

  ssl_required :create, :change_password
  ssl_allowed :show

  def create
    # Non-SSL access will be redirected to SSL
  end

  def change_password
    # Non-SSL access will be redirected to SSL
  end

  def show
    # Works either with or without SSL
  end

  def index
    # SSL access will be redirected to non-SSL
  end

end
```

Here's what's going on. Creating accounts and changing passwords involves passing sensitive information around, so we ensure SSL is required for those actions using ssl_required. If the incoming request for those actions isn't using the https protocol, then the request will be redirected to https. On the other hand, showing an account doesn't display any sensitive information, but SSL *can* be used. So, we use ssl_allowed for the show action. That is, the request won't redirect to http if it comes in using the https protocol. Finally, in this case, the index request should always be on an http connection, so we don't have to declare anything for it.

Before we go, we need to check one important setting. By default, Rails will look for static assets (images, JavaScript files, and so on) in the public directory. But suppose we've configured our production environment to link these assets from a dedicated asset server, like so:

```ruby
config.action_controller.asset_host = "http://my-assets.com"
```

Since we've hard-coded the protocol, actions run under SSL will have assets linked via http. Some browsers pop up a security warning when this happens, and consequently users get a little freaked. So to make sure all the assets are automatically linked using the same protocol as the incoming request, we need to remove the explicit protocol:

```
config.action_controller.asset_host = "my-assets.com"
```

Our web server and Rails application are now both on the same page, so to speak.

Discussion

The SslRequirement module adds the before_filter at the point at which it's included. If you want to run other filters before that, you must declare them ahead of including this module.

There are other valid reasons for overwriting the ssl_required? method. For example, you could inspect an @account variable and always flip to SSL if it's a premium account. In other words, you don't always have to rely solely on the declarative style.

Part XIII

Deployment and Capistrano Recipes

Upload Custom Maintenance Pages

Problem

Bad things sometimes happen to good applications. When you need to put out a fire (or do maintenance chores), you want to quickly put up a maintenance page and then get right to work. And you want the temporary page to include your familiar logo, award-winning web design, and a little message that shows you care. Then when you have everything under control, you want to put the application back online just as quickly as you took it down.

Ingredients

- The capistrano gem:

  ```
  $ gem install capistrano
  ```

Solution

If you've had the pleasure of using Capistrano,[1] then you know it lives to serve you. Need to put up a maintenance page in a hurry? Capistrano has your back. Rush over to your keyboard and type this:

```
$ cap deploy:web:disable
```

And when the klaxons stop blaring and the birds start chirping again, taking down the maintenance page is equally satisfying:

```
$ cap deploy:web:enable
```

Great, now for the customization. The standard maintenance page that comes with Capistrano works in a pinch, but it's easy to create a custom maintenance page that sets our app apart from the crowd.

Now, we're certainly no famous web designer, but the guy down the hall is. All we need is a Rails template file that shows our logo, some excuse for the site being down, and an indication when it might return.

---

1. http://www.capify.org/

So, he humors us by whipping up this one:

`capistrano/app/views/admin/maintenance.html.erb`

```
<html xmlns="http://www.w3.org/1999/xhtml"
      version="-//W3C//DTD XHTML 1.1//EN" xml:lang="en">

<head>
  <title>Custom Maintenance Page</title>
  <meta http-equiv="Content-type" content="text/html; charset=utf-8" />
  <link href="/stylesheets/maintenance.css" rel="stylesheet" type="text/css" />
</head>

<body>
  <div id="content">
    <img src="http://railsrecipes.com/images/fr_arr.jpg"
         alt="Recipes" />
    <h1>
      We're currently offline for <%= reason ? reason : "maintenance" %>
      as of <%= Time.now.strftime("%I:%M %p %Z") %>.
    </h1>
    <p>
      Sorry for the inconvenience.  We'll be back
      <%= deadline ? "by #{deadline}" : "shortly" %>.
      Please <a href="mailto:info@railsrecipes.com">e-mail us</a>
      if you need to get in touch.
    </p>
  </div>
</body>
</html>
```

There's nothing extraordinary about this template, but notice the two variables reason and deadline. That's our dynamic content: why the site is down and when it'll return. To fill in those variables, we need to run our handcrafted template through the ERb templating system to get a static HTML file. Then we need to upload it to our web servers.

It turns out that's exactly what Capistrano does with its stock template when we run the deploy:web:disable task. We'll just override this task in our config/deploy.rb recipe file:

`capistrano/config/deploy.rb`

```
namespace :deploy do
  namespace :web do

    desc "Serve up a custom maintenance page."
    task :disable, :roles => :web do
      require 'erb'
      on_rollback { run "rm #{shared_path}/system/maintenance.html" }

      reason    = ENV['REASON']
      deadline  = ENV['UNTIL']
```

```
        template = File.read("app/views/admin/maintenance.html.erb")
        page = ERB.new(template).result(binding)

        put page, "#{shared_path}/system/maintenance.html",
                :mode => 0644
      end
    end
end
```

Did you know you could use ERb directly like that? It's easy: just read in a template file and let ERb render it into a variable. There's a neat trick here, too. The local variables reason and deadline are set based on environment variables. To make them accessible to our template, we hand ERb the current binding.

Now we have the maintenance page template all filled out and in memory. To upload it into a maintenance.html file on all the production web servers, we use Capistrano's put command.

Even if we were to run the deploy:web:disable task right now, it wouldn't disable access to our application. We would end up with a system/maintenance.html file in our Rails app's public directory, but you'd see it only if you typed the filename into the browser. Instead, we need it to be shown whenever *any* dynamic request is made to our application.

The Apache web server has an extremely powerful URL-rewriting engine called mod_rewrite.[2] It works perfectly for what we're trying to do and takes just four lines of web server configuration:

```
RewriteCond %{DOCUMENT_ROOT}/system/maintenance.html -f
RewriteCond %{REQUEST_URI} !\.(css|jpg|gif|png)$
RewriteCond %{SCRIPT_FILENAME} !maintenance.html
RewriteRule ^.*$ %{DOCUMENT_ROOT}/system/maintenance.html [L]
```

Basically this says to redirect all incoming requests (except those for our external CSS file and images) to the static system/maintenance.html file if it exists.

We can do the same thing with the Nginx web server:

```
if ($request_filename ~* \.(css|jpg|gif|png)$) {
  break;
}
if (-f $document_root/system/maintenance.html) {
  rewrite  ^(.*)$  /system/maintenance.html last;
  break;
}
```

---

2. http://httpd.apache.org/docs/1.3/mod/mod_rewrite.html

Now let's say we've been building up to a new version of our app, and it's so much better that we need to take the application offline to do a bunch of system stuff. It'll take about thirty minutes. Here's where those environment variables (and the guy down the hall) pay off.

To put up our custom maintenance page, we use this:

```
$ REASON="an upgrade to the coolest version ever" ↩
  UNTIL="01:43 PM MST" ↩
  cap deploy:web:disable
```

Hitting any Rails action shows our custom maintenance page:

We're currently offline for an upgrade to the coolest version ever as of 01:43 PM MST.

Sorry for the inconvenience. We'll be back by 2:15 PM MST. Please e-mail us if you need to get in touch.

Discussion

You might be inclined to try using Rails helper methods, such as time_ago_in_words, in your maintenance page template. Sorry, but this won't work because Capistrano doesn't load the Rails framework when you call tasks. Then again, if you need helpers in your maintenance page, perhaps it's doing too much.

Generate Custom Error (404 and 500) Pages

By Giles Bowkett and John Dewey (http://gilesbowkett.blogspot.com,http://dewey.cx)

Giles is a programmer, actor, screenwriter, DJ, musician, artist, blogger, and dharma bum. Originally from Chicago, he now lives in Hollywood, Silicon Valley, the northern New Mexico wilderness, and Black Rock City. John is a Ruby developer for the *Los Angeles Times* and better at tetherball than you (unless there's ropies).

Problem

You want a consistent design across your error pages, and you want to be able to maintain this design easily in the face of change. The standard Rails approach to template reuse—partials and layouts—is great, but you can't use them in the dynamic way because you can't write error pages for Rails that depend on Rails working in the first place.

Ingredients

- The capistrano gem:[1]

  ```
  $ gem install capistrano
  ```

Solution

In Recipe 69, *Upload Custom Maintenance Pages*, on page 373, we learned how to use Capistrano and ERb to deploy custom maintenance pages. Using the same combination of power tools, we can cook up a quick and light implementation of partials and layouts for our error pages.

First, we'll write a layout file. We can use ERb syntax but without Rails' helper methods, so things such as link_to and the JavaScript helpers are off-limits.

---

1. http://www.capify.org/

We'll just create a skeleton HTML document and add standard ERb-quoted code (we'll fill in these variables later):

```
capistrano/config/deploy/errors/error.html.erb
<!DOCTYPE html PUBLIC "-//W3C//DTD HTML 4.01//EN"
  "http://www.w3.org/TR/html4/strict.dtd">

<html lang="en">
  <head>
    <title>
      <%= title %>
    </title>
    <style type="text/css">
      <%= File.read(stylesheet) %>
    </style>
  </head>
  <body>
    <div>
      <h1>
        <%= heading %>
      </h1>
    </div>
    <div>
      <%= body %>
    </div>
  </body>
</html>
```

We'll put this error.html.erb file, and our errors.css style sheet file, in the config/deploy/errors directory. You'll want to base the errors.css file on the general CSS for your application but use only a subset necessary for the design of your error pages. You want your CSS cleanly separated from the CSS within Rails. Even if you're not using dynamic options like Sass[2] or CSS in ERb, in some error states your system will redirect every request to the error page, including requests for CSS files.

Next, we'll create a partial template for each error condition: 404 and 500, specifically. These will just include the error-specific HTML we want to include in the page. Here are a few examples:

```
capistrano/config/deploy/errors/_404.html.erb
<p>
  We're terribly sorry, but we couldn't find that page.
</p>
```

---

2. http://haml.hamptoncatlin.com/docs/sass

capistrano/config/deploy/errors/_500.html.erb

```
<p>
  Something failed spectacularly.  Of course, it's all our fault!
  The klaxons are blaring and we'll fix it promptly.
</p>
```

We'll put these files in the config/deploy/errors directory, as well.

Then we need some way to render these error templates. We don't have Rails to do it for us, so we'll just create a simple ERb template engine in a method living in our Capistrano recipe file:

capistrano/config/deploy.rb

```
def template_engine(template, partial=nil, stylesheet=nil, opts={})
  require 'erb'
  unless opts.empty?
    set :title, opts[:title]
    set :heading, opts[:heading]
    set :body, ERB.new(File.read(partial)).result(binding)
  end
  ERB.new(File.read(template)).result(binding)
end
```

This method first takes a hash of options and turns each entry into a recipe variable. To set the value of the :body variable, it passes the error-specific partial to ERb. It then also uses ERb to render the surrounding template, which in this case is our layout file.

By passing ERb the current binding (calling the binding method), we give ERb access to the variables we define here. That way, we can use these same variables in our layout file and our error partials. For example, we use the title, heading, and body variables in our layout file.

Finally, we want to automate the entire process of generating the error page and uploading it to our production server. To do that, we'll write a create_error_pages task in our recipe file:

capistrano/config/deploy.rb

```
def error_template_path(filename)
  ["config", "deploy", "errors", filename].join("/")
end

task :create_error_pages, :roles => [:web, :app] do
  errors = {
    "404" => { "title"   => "Page Not Found",
               "heading" => "Page Not Found" },
    "422" => { "title"   => "Oops!",
               "heading" => "The data you submitted was invalid." },
```

```
        "500" => { "title"   => "Oops!",
                   "heading" => "Kaboom!" }
    }
    errors.each_key do |error|
      template   = error_template_path("error.html.erb")
      partial    = error_template_path("_#{error}.html.erb")
      stylesheet = error_template_path("error.css")
      put template_engine(template, partial, stylesheet,
                    :title => errors[error]["title"],
                    :heading => errors[error]["heading"]
                ), "#{current_path}/public/#{error}.html",
                    :mode => 0644
    end
end
```

In the create_error_pages task—which runs for machines in both the :web and :app roles—we first specify a nested hash of error codes, titles, and headings.[3] We send that to our template engine method, along with the filenames expanded into error template paths by the error_template_path helper method. Finally, the put command uploads the error page contents into their respective files in the public directory on our production servers.

Now when we want to update the error page files living on our servers, we just run the following task:

```
$ cap create_error_pages
```

Discussion

You could extend this example just a little bit to get a full-fledged system for deploying static websites. Before you do that, however, look into StaticMatic[4]—it's a nice, compact system that incorporates the concise, powerful, and popular Haml and Sass metamarkup languages to generate static sites.

---

3. The 422 HTTP code, which stands for "Unprocessable Entity," gets an error page in Rails by default as part of the REST support in Rails.
4. http://staticmatic.rubyforge.org/

Write Config Files on the Fly

By Jamie Orchard-Hays (http://dangosaur.us)
Jamie has developed web applications since the late 1990s. He has worked in ASP, ColdFusion, JSPs, Tapestry, and Ruby on Rails. He created the Elemental plug-in for Rails and contributed the Hpricot Mapper to Solr-Ruby. Currently, he resides in beautiful Charlottesville, Virginia.

You need to set up your deployment servers with various and sundry configuration files: Mongrel, Apache, Nginx, and so on. Since these files often share bits of information, such as the name of your app, keeping them in sync is tedious and prone to error. Wouldn't it be nice to make this all part of a repeatable deployment step?

Capistrano[1] to the rescue again! Let's take the case where we want to create a Mongrel cluster configuration file and drop it into our remote server directory. We don't need a local file to do that. Instead, we'll generate the configuration bits directly in a task within our deploy.rb recipe file and upload the contents into a file on the server:

capistrano/config/deploy.rb

```
namespace :deploy do

  task :upload_cluster_configuration, :roles => :app do
    cluster_config = <<-CMD
      port: 8000
      servers: 4
      address: 127.0.0.1
      cwd: #{deploy_to}/current
      pid_file: tmp/pids/#{application}-mongrel.pid
      user: capistrano
      group: capistrano
      environment: production
    CMD
    put cluster_config, "#{release_path}/config/mongrel_cluster.yml"
  end

  after "deploy:update_code", "deploy:upload_cluster_configuration"
end
```

One benefit of assembling the configuration on the fly like this is being able to reference existing variables such as application and deploy_to in our recipe to keep things DRY.

---

1. http://www.capify.org/

The secret ingredient in this recipe is the put command. It effectively uploads the data (our configuration information) to the given file location. Finally, this task is hooked so it runs after the deploy:update_code task.

Now every time we run cap deploy, we *know* our Mongrels will restart with a consistent configuration. Imagine how easy setting up a new deployment box might be if we had all our configuration files generated this way.

Create New Environments

You need to run in various modes that have environment-specific settings, and the default Rails environments aren't enough.

There's nothing special about the default runtime environments—development, test, and production—except that most projects need those at a minimum. That doesn't stop us from adding new environments.

For example, let's say we have special requirements for our Rails app when it's running on the staging servers. No problem, we'll just create a new staging environment by adding a staging.rb file to the config/environments directory:

Environments/config/environments/staging.rb

```
config.cache_classes = true
config.action_controller.consider_all_requests_local = false
config.action_controller.perform_caching              = true
config.action_view.cache_template_loading             = false

GATEWAY_URL='https://test.authorize.net/gateway/transact.dll'
```

For the most part it's the same as the production-level configuration, but there's a twist. In production, this particular application charges credit cards via an external payment gateway. We don't want to be charging *real* credit cards in the staging environment, so we've set the GATEWAY_URL variable to point to a test server. In production.rb, it points to the honest-to-goodness live server.

Before going any further, we also need to configure a database for the staging environment to use. That's as easy: we'll add a staging stanza to our config/database.yml file:

Environments/config/database.yml

```
staging:
  adapter: mysql
  database: staging_database
  username: stage
  password: fright
```

That's all there is to creating a new environment. When we run with staging as the current environment, Rails will load the staging.rb environment file and use the staging database configuration. Let's try it first in the console:

```
$ ruby script/console staging
Loading staging environment
>> RAILS_ENV
=> "staging"
>> GATEWAY_URL
=> "https://test.authorize.net/gateway/transact.dll"
```

That's a good sanity check that our staging.rb is getting picked up. Now let's fire up the app with its staging face on:

```
$ ruby script/server -e staging
** Starting Rails with staging environment...
```

We set the staging environment differently depending on how we start the application. If we're using the mongrel_cluster gem to run a pack of Rails apps, for example, we'd need to set the environment in the cluster configuration file. Basically, wherever we used production before will change to staging.

Remember that some of the built-in Rake tasks rely on the RAILS_ENV environment variable to know which database to use. (The default is development.) So if we're running migrations in the staging environment, we need to call it out:

```
$ RAILS_ENV=staging rake db:migrate
```

Let's simplify that a bit by writing a couple custom Rake tasks:

Environments/lib/tasks/environments.rake

```
desc "Sets the environment variable RAILS_ENV='staging'."
task :staging do
  ENV['RAILS_ENV'] = RAILS_ENV = 'staging'
  Rake::Task[:environment].invoke
end

desc "Sets the environment variable RAILS_ENV='production'."
task :production do
  ENV['RAILS_ENV'] = RAILS_ENV = 'production'
  Rake::Task[:environment].invoke
end
```

These tasks set RAILS_ENV for us and invoke the :environment task to load Rails in the proper environment. This spares us a few keystrokes every time we run a Rake task that needs the environment name. For example, we can now use this:

```
$ rake staging db:migrate
```

Discussion

You can take this as far as necessary with multiple environments and special configuration values for each.

Also See

If you want to deploy to different machines depending on the Rails environment, see Recipe 73, *Run Multistage Deployments*, on page 387.

Run Multistage Deployments

By Jamis Buck (http://weblog.jamisbuck.org/)

Thanks to Jamis, the creator of Capistrano, for the idea and technical bits for this recipe.

Problem

You're using Capistrano to deploy your application into production, and now you need to deploy the same application to different environments: staging, testing, bobs_mac, favorite_clients_box, and so on.

Ingredients

- The capistrano gem:

  ```
  $ gem install capistrano
  ```

- The capistrano-ext gem:

  ```
  $ gem install capistrano-ext
  ```

Solution

The solution is fairly trivial, but it gives insight into the flexibility of Capistrano recipe files and how they run. When we're done, you may well find other ways to improve your deployment recipes.

Usually when we're deploying into just one environment, we define a single stanza of roles like this:

`capistrano/config/deploy.rb`

```
role :web, 'railsrecipes.com'
role :app, 'railsrecipes.com'
role :db,  'railsrecipes.com', :primary => true
```

But that won't work if we have multiple environments because the roles will always be set to our production machines. Instead, we need to define the roles on a per-environment basis.

An easy way to do that is using a task definition.

So for two roles—staging and production—we'll add two tasks to our recipe file:

```
task :staging do
  role :web, 'staging.railsrecipes.com'
  role :app, 'staging.railsrecipes.com'
  role :db,  'staging.railsrecipes.com', :primary => true
  set  :stage, :staging
end

task :production do
  role :web, 'railsrecipes.com'
  role :app, 'railsrecipes.com'
  role :db,  'railsrecipes.com', :primary => true
  set  :stage, :production
end
```

Then, to set up the roles for a specific environment, we'll call the corresponding environment task before the task that does the real work:

```
$ cap staging deploy
```

```
$ cap production deploy
```

Now let's say we want to change the deployment directory based on the environment. That is, we need to change the following line to include the environment name in the path:

```
set :deploy_to, "/path/to/#{application}"
```

We might be tempted just to use the stage variable in the string, but there's a subtle reason this won't work. The deploy_to variable is evaluated when our recipe is loaded, and we need to defer the evaluation until after we've set the environment up.

Typing a couple extra characters to create a proc is all it takes to cause the variable to be evaluated lazily:

```
set(:deploy_to) { "/path/to/#{application}/#{stage}" }
```

As a do-it-yourself approach, all this works great. In fact, this idiom became so common that Jamis Buck packaged it up in the capistrano-ext gem. Now that you know how it works, let's give it a whirl!

With the capistrano-ext gem installed, we'll start by adding this to the top of our recipe file:

capistrano/config/deploy.rb

```
set :stages, %w(staging testing production bobs_mac)
set :default_stage, 'staging'
require 'capistrano/ext/multistage'
```

Then we can clean up some code. We'll put code that's specific to the testing stage, for example, in the config/deploy/testing.rb file:

capistrano/config/deploy/testing.rb

```
role :web, 'testing.railsrecipes.com'
role :app, 'testing.railsrecipes.com'
role :db,  'testing.railsrecipes.com', :primary => true

set :deploy_to, "/path/to/#{application}/testing"
```

Notice here we do not need to lazily evaluate the deploy_to variable because of the order in which the files are loaded. This works as long as the :application variable is set *before* the capistrano/ext/multistage recipe is loaded. (In general, it's probably good practice to put all such require statements at the end of your deploy.rb file anyway.)

Finally, to deploy to the testing environment, we run this:

```
$ cap testing deploy
```

If we don't specify an environment, we'll end up deploying to the staging environment by default. If you don't set :default_stage, you'll get an error if you try to do anything without explicitly specifying a stage. Some people prefer this to having a default stage. If you do set a default stage, it's always a good idea to pick a default other than production. That way you won't accidentally push new code out into the wild, wooly Web. I knew a guy who did that once....

Safeguard the Launch Codes

You really don't want *the* production database password rattling around on your development machine—you know, the laptop you take with you to software conferences and the local Hackers Anonymous meetings. But how do you deploy without the launch codes?

Well, let's start by putting the real database.yml file, the one with all the secrets, in one place: our production box. Then we can restrict access to it using accounts, permissions, and all that good operating system stuff. We won't check this file in to our regular project—the project will use a database.yml file that simply gives access to the development and testing databases.

Then, when it comes time to push the deploy button, we'll let Capistrano[1] copy the real database.yml file into place for us. All we need is a hook that automatically gets triggered after the latest version of our code has been checked out to the release_path directory. We'll add it to the deploy namespace of our deploy.rb file, like so:

`capistrano/config/deploy.rb`

```ruby
namespace :deploy do

  task :copy_database_configuration do
    production_db_config = "/path/to/production.database.yml"
    run "cp #{production_db_config} #{release_path}/config/database.yml"
  end

  after "deploy:update_code", "deploy:copy_database_configuration"
end
```

Remember: run executes the given command on the *remote* machine. So, our database.yml file gets slipped into place just before the application is restarted, and our hands are clean.

---

1. http://www.capify.org/

Automate Periodic Tasks

By David Bock (http://www.davebock.com)
David is a principal consultant at CodeSherpas, a small company in Northern Virginia providing Java, Ruby, and process improvement consulting services to both commercial and government clients. David is also a frequent speaker for the No Fluff, Just Stuff conference series, the president of the Northern Virginia Java Users Group, and the editor for O'Reilly's OnJava.com.

Problem

Your application needs to have recurring tasks run at periodic intervals: pulling messages off a queue every minute, rotating the log files every night, creating weekly reports, and so on. You want an automated, repeatable way to schedule chores on your production server.

Ingredients

- The capistrano gem:
  ```
  $ gem install capistrano
  ```

Solution

It really doesn't matter what kind of work we're doing. It just needs doin'. So, let's jump right in by encapsulating all the work for the periodic chores in a set of Rake tasks:

`AutomatePeriodicTasks/lib/tasks/chores.rake`

```ruby
namespace :chores do

  task :hourly => :environment do
    chore("Hourly") do
      # Your Code Here
    end
  end

  task :daily => :environment do
    chore("Daily") do
      # Your Code Here
    end
  end

  task :weekly => :environment do
    chore("Weekly") do
      # Your Code Here
    end
  end
```

```
    def chore(name)
      puts "#{name} Task Invoked: #{Time.now}"
      yield
      puts "#{name} Task Finished: #{Time.now}"
    end
  end
```

The task names denote how often they run, and the work they do is totally arbitrary. Feel free to define your own tasks, such as weekday_morning, fiscal_quarter, and so on.

Note a couple of important things here. First, each task depends on the :environment task, which bootstraps the Rails environment so that the task can access our models and such. Second, we're using puts rather than the Rails logger so that we can redirect the output later.

Next, we need to put these tasks on a schedule so they get run at the appropriate time. To do that, we'll use the cron command-line utility for scheduling the execution of periodic tasks.[1] The cron utility reads a file (called a *crontab*) to determine what to do and when.

Rather than creating the real crontab file now, instead we'll create a config/cron.erb template file and have Capistrano fill it in later. Here's what the template looks like:

```
00 * * * * RAILS_ENV=production rake -f <%= current_path %>/Rakefile ↩
  chores:hourly >> <%= deploy_to %>/shared/log/cron/hourly.txt

01 0 * * * RAILS_ENV=production rake -f <%= current_path %>/Rakefile ↩
  chores:daily >> <%= deploy_to %>/shared/log/cron/daily.txt

02 0 * * 1 RAILS_ENV=production rake -f <%= current_path %>/Rakefile ↩
  chores:weekly >> <%= deploy_to %>/shared/log/cron/weekly.txt
```

This looks a bit cryptic, but don't let it throw you. The numbers at the beginning of each line are cron-speak denoting on which day and at what time the command will run. For example, the line 00 * * * * means "run at the top of the hour, every hour, every day." The line 01 0 * * * is somewhat similar, saying "run at the first minute after midnight, every day." The last line can be read "run on the first day of the week."

Associated with each schedule is a command to run. In this case, we're setting our Rails environment to production and running the appropriate Rake task. The command needs some pathing information: where

---

1. The cron utility is typically available in Unix and Linux systems, and with help from tools like Cygwin, it's also available under Windows.

to find the Rakefile and where to redirect the command output. Rather than hard-code absolute directory paths now, we've used ERb syntax to substitute in the values of the current_path and deploy_to variables.

Next, we'll use Capistrano to fill in the variables in our config/cron.erb file, use the results to upload the real crontab file to our production server, and tell cron to start using it.

We need to run the periodic tasks on only one of our production servers. So in our config/deploy.rb recipe file, we'll mark just one of the machines in the app role as the cron machine:

```
role :app, "railsrecipes-1.com", :cron => true
role :app, "railsrecipes-2.com"
```

Then we'll add two Capistrano tasks to our recipe file. The first task starts cron on the cron machine only:

AutomatePeriodicTasks/config/deploy.rb

```
namespace :cron do

  task :start, :roles => :app, :only => {:cron => true} do
    cron_tab = "#{shared_path}/cron.tab"
    run "mkdir -p #{shared_path}/log/cron"

    require 'erb'
    template = File.read("config/cron.erb")
    file = ERB.new(template).result(binding)
    put file, cron_tab, :mode => 0644

    # merge with the current crontab
    # fails with an empty crontab, which is acceptable
    run "crontab -l >> #{cron_tab}" rescue nil

    # install the new crontab
    run "crontab #{cron_tab}"
  end
end
```

The start task begins by using ERb to read our config/cron.erb template file and turn it into a valid crontab file. We hand ERb the current binding so that the current_path and deploy_to variables in the Capistrano recipe are available in the config/cron.erb template file. Then the task uploads the crontab file and runs the crontab command on our production server (railsrecipes-1.com, in this case) to merge the current crontab file with our new one. Finally, the resulting crontab file is installed into the cron utility running on the production server.

The second Capistrano task reverses the process:

AutomatePeriodicTasks/config/deploy.rb

```ruby
namespace :cron do

  task :stop, :roles => :app, :only => {:cron => true} do
    cron_tmp = "#{shared_path}/cron.old"
    cron_tab = "#{shared_path}/cron.tab"

    begin
      # dump the current cron entries
      run "crontab -l > #{cron_tmp}"

      # remove any lines that contain the application name
      run "awk '{if ($0 !~ /#{application}/) print $0}' " +
        "#{cron_tmp} > #{cron_tab}"

      # replace the cron entries
      run "crontab #{cron_tab}"
    rescue
      # fails with an empty crontab, which is acceptable
    end

    # clean up
    run "rm -rf #{cron_tmp}"
  end


end
```

The stop task first does some file munging to remove the entries related to our application from the crontab file (using awk). Then it reinstalls the original cron entries so that we're right back where we started before running the start task.

Finally, we'll hook the cron:start and cron:stop tasks into the standard Capistrano deployment tasks:

AutomatePeriodicTasks/config/deploy.rb

```ruby
before "deploy:stop",  "cron:stop"
after  "deploy:start", "cron:start"
```

This arranges things so that cron is updated on the production server every time we deploy a new version of our application. And if we want to update cron on demand, we just run this:

```
$ cap cron:stop
$ cap cron:start
```

Now we have an automated, repeatable process for scheduling periodic tasks in production. We can manage versions of our config/cron.erb file in version control and set up a production server to run recurring tasks with a single command. And, without any sysadmin work, we can quickly drop in new scheduled tasks when we need them.

Discussion

This recipe makes one assumption that you might want to revisit in your own environment. It assumes that the user account deploying the web application is the same user account that will run the automated tasks. If this is not the case, you'll need to modify the Capistrano tasks to update the appropriate user's cron and make sure the file permissions are correct for accessing the log files and executing the tasks.

If you don't mind removing all the user's cron entries when the cron:stop task is run, you can simply run crontab -r in the task to remove all the entries.

Finally, there's nothing in this recipe that would prevent a developer from updating cron while periodic tasks are running. This could create strange situations where, for example, a long-running periodic task could be executing while a deployment to the production environment takes place. However, I haven't found this to be an issue in practice.

Preserve Files Between Deployments

One of the obvious joys of using Capistrano[1] is the deploy task. It puts the current version of your app in a new directory on the server and then restarts everything from there. But if your app stores user-uploaded pictures, search engine indexes, and other artifacts in the current deployment directory, you lose them when you redeploy.

The solution? When you run the deploy:setup Capistrano task prior to your first deployment, it creates a directory structure on the production server to house your application. One of the directories it creates is called shared. Simply put files you need to preserve across deployments in the shared directory rather than RAILS_ROOT. Then, during the deployment process, have Capistrano link the shared assets into your current deployment directory. Here are two example tasks that do just that:

`capistrano/config/deploy.rb`

```ruby
namespace :assets do

  task :symlink, :roles => :app do
    assets.create_dirs
    run <<-CMD
      rm -rf  #{release_path}/index &&
      rm -rf  #{release_path}/public/images/pictures &&
      ln -nfs #{shared_path}/index #{release_path}/index &&
      ln -nfs #{shared_path}/pictures #{release_path}/public/images/pictures
    CMD
  end

  task :create_dirs, :roles => :app do
    %w(index pictures).each do |name|
      run "mkdir -p #{shared_path}/#{name}"
    end
  end
end

after "deploy:update_code", "assets:symlink"
```

---

1. http://www.capify.org/

Notice that we can chain tasks together: the symlink task first invokes the create_dirs task to make sure the shared directories exist. Then we use symbolic links to point our current release to the shared search indexes and pictures. The after hook makes sure every deployment has all the previously created goodies.

Segregate Page Cache Storage with Nginx

By Josh Susser (http://hasmanythrough.com)
Josh is a full-time Rails developer, a senior engineer at Pivotal Labs in San Francisco, and a frequent contributor to the Ruby on Rails open source project. If you've ever built a model that used a self-referential has_many :through association, you've probably read his blog.

Problem

You want to store your cached pages in a separate directory, keeping them apart from your regular static files to keep things tidy and to preserve cached pages across deployments.

Solution

By default, Rails stores cached pages in the public directory, right alongside all the other application's static files.

Let's start by telling Rails we're in charge and we want cached pages stored in the public/cache directory. Because this is a production-only thing, we'll add this configuration in the production.rb environment file:

`capistrano/config/environments/production.rb`

```
config.action_controller.page_cache_directory =
  File.join(RAILS_ROOT, 'public', 'cache')
```

Next, we need to configure our web server to directly serve the cached pages, if they exist. Because this configuration is just bulky enough to be hard to explain all at once, we're going to take it in steps. Here's the basic location section that we'll add stuff to as we go:[1]

```
location / {
  index  index.html index.htm;
  # needed to forward user's IP address to Rails
  proxy_set_header  X-Real-IP  $remote_addr;
  proxy_set_header  X-Forwarded-For $proxy_add_x_forwarded_for;
  proxy_set_header Host $http_host;
  proxy_redirect off;
  proxy_max_temp_file_size 0;

  # add stuff here as we go
}
```

---

1. This is based on the Nginx configuration for my EngineYard (http://engineyard.com/) account.

First, we'll tell the server to look in the RAILS_ROOT/public directory for regular static files:

```
if (-f $request_filename) {
  break;
}
```

Next, the server should look in the public/cache directory for an exact URL match:

```
if (-f /cache$request_filename) {
  rewrite (.*) /cache$1 break;
  break;
}
```

We'll also add a rule to look in the public/cache directory for the URL with .html appended. That way, we can cache pages for regular URLs with no .html extension as well as URLs with extensions:

```
if (-f /cache$request_filename.html) {
  rewrite (.*) /cache$1.html break;
  break;
}
```

Next, we'll add a rewrite rule to handle the standard Rails page-cached files: it adds .html to the end of the URL and checks the public directory for that file. If it exists, the URL is rewritten to have an explicit .html extension and sent to the final rule.

```
if (-f $request_filename.html) {
  rewrite (.*) $1.html break;
}
```

Last, but by no means least, if no static or cached file exists, the final rule sets all the necessary HTTP headers and proxies the request to the Mongrels:

```
if (!-f $request_filename) {
  proxy_pass http://mongrel;
  break;
}
```

With all these rules in place, we can keep our cached content separate from the regular stuff. Nginx will serve any cached content on demand, and for pages not in the cache, it will seamlessly call into Rails. But we're not quite done....

Our Capistrano recipe needs to do a couple extra things. First, when the deployment environment is set up for the first time by running the deploy:setup task, we'll create a shared/cache directory:

capistrano/config/deploy.rb
```
after "deploy:setup", "create_page_cache"
task :create_page_cache, :roles => :app do
  run "umask 02 && mkdir -p #{shared_path}/cache"
end
```

Then, when a new release is deployed, we'll create a symlink from the RAILS_ROOT/public/cache directory to the shared/cache directory:

capistrano/config/deploy.rb
```
after "deploy:update_code","symlink_cache_dir"
task :symlink_cache_dir, :roles => :app do
  run <<-CMD
    cd #{release_path} &&
    ln -nfs #{shared_path}/cache #{release_path}/public/cache
  CMD
end
```

Finally, we'll hook into the deploy:cleanup task to flush the cached pages by default:

capistrano/config/deploy.rb
```
# default behavior is to flush page cache on deploy
set :flush_cache, true

desc "Retain the page cache"
task :keep_page_cache do
  set :flush_cache, false
end

after "deploy:cleanup", "flush_page_cache"
task :flush_page_cache, :roles => :app do
  if flush_cache
    run <<-CMD
      rm -rf #{shared_path}/cache/*
    CMD
  end
end
```

Now imagine we're deploying a new release and we know the changes don't invalidate the existing cached pages. We can deploy and retain the cache using this:

```
$ cap keep_page_cache deploy
```

Discussion

As an optimization, you might consider adding the following to your Nginx configuration to tell it not to stat the filesystem for images, style sheets, or JavaScript files every time.

```
location ~ ^/(images|javascripts|stylesheets)/ {
  expires 10y;
}
```

We used Nginx in this recipe, but the same technique is possible with Apache as well.

Load Balance Around Your Mongrels' Health

By Josep M. Blanquer (http://rightscale.com)
Josep is a senior software engineer at RightScale, a start-up that provides deployment and management services for cloud computing environments such as Amazon's EC2. Originally from Barcelona, he now lives in Santa Barbara. He gets his kicks from working with scalable and fault-tolerant systems, with which he has about a decade of experience in both academia and industry. Before RightScale, he enjoyed leading the distributed architecture efforts of Citrix' GotoMeeting product. While coming mostly from the Java world, he's fired up about Ruby on Rails and its integration with cloud computing.

Problem

You have a cluster of Mongrels deployed to handle several dynamic Rails requests at the same time. To increase the overall availability of your site, you need an automated way to monitor the health of each Mongrel process and stop forwarding requests to any Mongrels that have gone sour.

Ingredients

- The mongrel gem:

  ```
  $ gem install mongrel
  ```

- The mongrel_cluster gem:

  ```
  $ gem install mongrel_cluster
  ```

- A load balancer that supports periodic health checks such as HAproxy, Varnish, Squid, Pound, NetScaler, or F5 BigIP

Solution

To give the appearance of a unified site, we ultimately need some sort of load-balancing facility fronting our cluster of Mongrels. Most load balancers let you configure a URI that they can use to check the status of a web server before sending it a request. The installation and configuration of the load balancer widely depends on the chosen software or hardware. But don't worry about that for now. We'll set up a health check URI that you can plug right into your load balancer when you're ready.

Now, we could start by writing a Rails controller to serve as our health checker, but that would present two important problems. First, and most important, health-check responses might be severely delayed by a long-running Rails request that has the Mongrel process tied up. If health checks are delayed long enough (typically just a few seconds), the load balancer will perceive it as the Mongrel being down and temporarily stop sending requests to it. Second, a health check built within a controller would be continually acquiring the Rails lock, which could delay other Rails requests from being serviced promptly. If that doesn't scare you away, consider that Rails uses a fair amount of resources for every request.

Mongrel handlers, on the other hand, let us bypass Rails completely so we can perform health checks very often *and* avoid interfering with our site.

Let's start by writing the simplest possible Mongrel handler. We'll put it in the lib/simple_health_check_handler.rb file:

HealthCheck/lib/simple_health_check_handler.rb

```
class SimpleHealthCheckHandler < Mongrel::HttpHandler
  def process(request,response)
    response.start(200) do |head,out|
      head["Content-Type"] = "text/html"
      out.write "Feeling good..."
    end
  end
end

uri "/simple-health-check", :handler => SimpleHealthCheckHandler.new,
                            :in_front => true
```

A Mongrel handler is just a subclass of Mongrel::HttpHandler that implements a process method. This one simply returns an HTTP 200 response when invoked and some cheery text in the response body.

The last line attaches our Mongrel handler to serve a particular URI, in this case /simple-health-check. It also puts this handler in front so that the URI match has priority over other registered handlers. There's just one caveat: the uri method has to be called within the context of the Mongrel's Configurator class, which is instantiated only when Mongrel is starting up.

Fortunately, the mongrel_cluster gem provides a convenient way to execute custom code within Mongrel's Configurator class. We'll go ahead and create the config/mongrel_cluster.yml configuration file for local testing and then switch it to production mode later:

```
cwd: /path/to/rails_app
port: 3000
environment: development
address: 127.0.0.1
pid_file: /path/to/rails_app/log/mongrel.pid
log_file: /path/to/rails_app/log/mongrel.log
servers: 1
config_script: lib/simple_health_check_handler.rb
```

Most of this is standard mongrel_cluster configuration. The important part is the config_script directive. It loads and executes our Mongrel handler within the Configurator context when Mongrel starts up.

Let's give it a whirl. First, we'll start the Mongrel cluster using this:

```
$ mongrel_rails cluster::start
```

Then, to check the health, we hit the registered URL. We'll use the curl command so we can see both the HTTP headers and body of the response:

```
$ curl -D - 'http://localhost:3000/simple-health-check'
HTTP/1.1 200 OK
Connection: close
Date: Fri, 22 Feb 2008 20:16:23 GMT
Content-Type: text/html
Content-Length: 15

Feeling good...
```

So far, so good. We have a lightweight health-check mechanism that doesn't interfere with our Rails application.

Now let's take it up a notch (you knew that was coming). The current handler doesn't provide very deep application checks—it basically just checks that the Mongrel process (and not Rails) is responding. For example, our handler would continue reporting good health even when the Rails database has gone for a long vacation.

Instead, we want our health check to include testing the database connectivity. This involves entering into Rails territory, which brings us up against the same contention problems as using a Rails controller. But it's possible to carefully combine both lightweight checks (using Mongrel handlers) and deeper application checks (using Rails code) in such a way that contention is limited. It's a balancing act.

To do that, next we will write a Mongrel handler that performs only database checks (through Active Record) at specific time intervals. That way the load balancer can check on the health of the Mongrel process every second but check the database connectivity only every thirty seconds, for example. Here's the handler:

`HealthCheck/lib/health_check_handler.rb`

```ruby
class HealthCheckHandler < Mongrel::HttpHandler

  def initialize
    @db_ok_at  = Time.at(0)
    @freshness = 30
    @error     = ''
  end

  def process(request,response)
    check_db if db_stale?

    if ActiveRecord::Base.connected?
      code = db_stale? ? 500 : 200
    else
      code = 200
    end

    response.start(code) do |head,out|
      head["Content-Type"] = "text/html"

      t = Time.now
      out.write "Now: #{t}, DB OK #{t - @db_ok_at}s ago\n"
      out.write "ERROR: #{@error}" if @error != ""
    end
  end

  def db_stale?
    (Time.now - @db_ok_at).to_i > @freshness
  end

  def check_db
    if ActiveRecord::Base.connected?
      begin
        ActiveRecord::Base.connection.verify!(0)
        ActiveRecord::Base.connection.select_value("SELECT NOW()")
        @db_ok_at = Time.now
        @error = ''
      rescue Exception => e
        # Do your logging/error handling here
        @error = e.inspect
      end
    end
  end
end
```

```
uri "/health-check", :handler => HealthCheckHandler.new,
                     :in_front => true
```

Here's what's going on: we're expecting this handler to get invoked every second. There's no need to check the database every time. So instead, the handler returns a 200 response code if it sees that the last database check was successful and it's still within the staleness time limit (thirty seconds). When the staleness period has expired, a new database check will be triggered. If there's a database error, every subsequent health check will cause an access to the database, and subsequent errors will be reported to indicate that the application is not healthy. Then, as soon as the database recovers, OK responses will start being returned again.

This code has a few subtle, but important, details. We skip any database checks if ActiveRecord::Base.connected? returns false. It will return true only after the first Rails request is received and the first Active Record operation is performed. For this reason, we have to make sure we don't report bad health before that first request arrives; otherwise, there would be no way for that first Active Record operation to ever happen! Once a base connection object has been created, we use it to verify and reconnect it to the database. In this example, we use a simple database query to check the database, but you can imagine using an application-specific query, maintaining a health-check table in the database, or even using an existing Active Record model to test the database.

Finally, we'll need to make sure to add this new handler to our mongrel_cluster.yml file. Here's an example of what it might look like for a production configuration:

```
cwd: /path/to/rails_app
port: 8000
environment: production
address: 10.1.1.1
pid_file: /path/to/rails_app/log/mongrel.pid
log_file: /path/to/rails_app/log/mongrel.log
servers: 5
config_script: lib/health_check_handler.rb
```

Once you have that in production, you'll need to configure your load balancer to hit the /health-check URI on a regular interval. Using just the HTTP code to decide whether a server is up or down is a simple but common solution employed by current load balancers.

If everything is up and running, the load balancer will receive an HTTP 200 response. Generally, this is enough for the load balancer to consider the Mongrel process being alive and well.

If the Mongrel is not running or the database has croaked, the load balancer will receive an HTTP 500 response. Consequently, it will mark that Mongrel as not being available and stop forwarding requests to it until it's back up.

Discussion

This monitoring technique is useful not only for detecting Mongrels gone sour but also when managing or reconfiguring the size of your cluster: increasing or decreasing the number of Mongrels, performing rolling upgrades, and cycling machines in and out of the cluster for maintenance reasons.

Instead of waiting for the first Rails request to set up the Active Record connection, we could change the handler to make the connection itself. That way, we'd be reporting on the full application path from the first health-check request and catch database failures and/or misconfigurations even before the first client request arrives.

Finally, the health-check handler could be greatly expanded to return more information: the current load of the machine, service times, and so on. Some more advanced load balancers allow you to perform other validity checks in the response headers and/or body, beyond just the returned HTTP code. The trick is balancing how deep you go while still sending a response to the load balancer in a timely manner. You definitely don't want to slow down your site because of excessive health checking.

Respond to Remote Capistrano Prompts

By Jamis Buck (http://weblog.jamisbuck.org/)
Thanks to Jamis, the creator of Capistrano, for the idea and technical bits for this recipe.

Sometimes the remote machines you're controlling with Capistrano talk back and even go so far as to ask a question! When that happens, how do you answer via your local terminal?

The answer lies in a special use of the venerable run method. You generally use it to fire off a command to all the servers in a given role. However, you can also hang a block off the run call, and it'll get invoked when the remote process responds. You get three block parameters:

- channel is the SSH channel on which you can send data back to the remote process.

- stream identifies the response stream as :err or :out.

- output is (you guessed it) the data that was output from the remote process.

The run method gets us close to a solution, but when a question comes in, we need to prompt for the answer in our local console. That requires one more ingredient: Capistrano uses the HighLine[1] library to process local console input and output. Thankfully, we can get to it simply by accessing the underlying ui object.

Knowing all that, we can write a generic method that takes the name of the command we want to run and the question we expect it to ask us:

```ruby
def run_with_prompt(command, expected_question)
  run command, :once => true do |channel, stream, output|
    if output =~ /#{expected_question}/
      answer = Capistrano::CLI.ui.ask(expected_question)
      channel.send_data(answer + "\n")
    else
      # allow the default callback to be processed
      Capistrano::Configuration.default_io_proc.call(channel, stream, output)
    end
  end
end
```

---

1. http://rubyforge.org/projects/highline/

Note here that the ui.ask method starts the interactive prompt if we get the question we expect. Also, we used the :once => true option on the run method so that it runs only on a single remote host. You'll want to cache the response and reuse it for similar prompts if you're running in a multimachine environment.

Then we can reuse the method inside any task. For example, if we are updating packages using apt-get, we can respond to its specific question:

```
task :app_get_update, :roles => :app do
  run_with_prompt("apt-get update", "Are you sure?")
end
```

As one more interesting use of the run method with a stream (thanks to Chris Wanstrath[2]), this task starts up script/console on a remote server:

capistrano/config/deploy.rb

```
desc "Open script/console on the remote machine"
task :console, :roles => :app do
  input = ''
  cmd = "cd #{current_path} && ./script/console #{ENV['RAILS_ENV']}"
  run cmd, :once => true do |channel, stream, data|
    next if data.chomp == input.chomp || data.chomp == ''
    print data
    channel.send_data(input = $stdin.gets) if data =~ /^(>|\?)>/
  end
end
```

---

2. http://errtheblog.com/posts/19-streaming-capistrano

Monitor (and Repair) Processes with Monit

Your application relies on external processes, and you need to make sure that all the moving parts continue to, er, move in a well-oiled fashion. Of course, you don't want to constantly baby-sit processes, so you need a way to train the computer to do it for you.

You'll need the Monit[1] utility. Many Linux distributions include Monit, and you can use MacPorts to get it for Mac OS X. If all else fails, it's trivial to build from source:

```
$ tar zxvf monit-x.y.z.tar.gz
$ cd monit-x.y.z
$ ./configure
$ make && make install
```

Monit makes it easy to automate the monitoring and mending of processes. For example, in Recipe 43, *Off-Load Long-Running Tasks to BackgrounDRb*, on page 237, we fired up a BackgrounDRb server process and then walked away. In production, however, we are wise to employ Monit to periodically check that the process is running and restart it if something has gone awry.

First, we need to write a simple control file to tell Monit what to monitor and how to react to certain conditions. Monit looks for the control file first in ~/.monitrc, then in /etc/monitrc, and finally in ./monitrc. Pick your favorite spot.

---

1. http://tildeslash.com/monit/download/

The control file starts out with a few global settings:

```
set daemon 30
set logfile /path/to/monit.log
set mailserver smtp.example.com
set alert sys-admin@example.com
set httpd port 9111
    allow localhost
```

In this case, Monit will wake up every thirty seconds and check each process (we'll get there) and log status and error messages to our log file. Any unexpected events will be e-mailed to our sysadmin via the SMTP server. The last line starts Monit's built-in HTTP server on port 9111 and makes it accessible only via the localhost, which is useful for checking the status of processes.

Next, we'll define the services we want Monit to keep an eye on. In this case, we're interested in just the BackgrounDRb server process, so we have only one service entry. The syntax is quite readable:

```
check process backgroundrb_11006
    with pidfile "/path/to/deploy/current/log/backgroundrb.pid"
    start = "/path/to/deploy/current/script/backgroundrb start"
    stop = "/path/to/deploy/current/script/backgroundrb stop"
    if cpu > 90% for 2 cycles then restart
    if totalmem > 256 MB for 2 cycles then restart
    if 4 restarts within 4 cycles then timeout
    group backgroundrb
```

When the BackgrounDRb server starts up, it drops a process ID (PID) file. This is handy because Monit can peek inside the file to determine which process to monitor. If the process has died for some reason, the *start* directive tells Monit how to fire it back up again. The *stop* directive is used if we manually stop or restart the process from the command line (more on that later).

OK, so if the process dies, it gets restarted. But other undesirable things can happen too, such as the process going rogue and chewing up precious resources. So, Monit gives us a way to test process conditions and take appropriate action early. In this case, if our process exceeds 90% CPU or 256MB of memory for a duration of two Monit check cycles (sixty seconds total), then the process will be restarted. And if Monit ends up restarting the process four times in a row, then Monit throws up its hands and calls in the humans.

With the configuration file in place, let's run a quick syntax check and then start Monit from the command line:[2]

```
$ monit -t
$ monit
```

At this point it's a good idea to kill the BackgroundDRb server process manually and watch the Monit log file to make sure it gets started back up on the next cycle.

And that's really all there is to it! We have a fully automated baby-sitter. No news is good news.

To check the status of our BackgrounDRb server and all things being monitored, we just use the status command:

```
$ monit status
The monit daemon 4.9 uptime: 25m

Process 'backgroundrb_11006'
  status                        running
  monitoring status             monitored
  pid                           -1
  parent pid                    -1
  uptime                        32m
  data collected                Thu Dec 27 12:50:25 2007
```

In addition to monitoring processes, you can also use Monit to start, stop, and restart processes. For example, to restart the BackgroundDRb server process by its name, use this:

```
$ monit restart backgroundrb_11006
```

If you have multiple BackgrounDRb server processes together in the backgroundrb group, you can restart them all using the group name:

```
$ monit restart all -g backgroundrb
```

Finally, if you change your control file, you'll need to restart Monit so that it loads the latest configuration:

```
$ monit restart
```

This barely scratches the surface of what Monit can do, but it's all you need to start monitoring the extra processes started by many of the recipes in this book. The next time you're faced with keeping an eye on a resource, let Monit do it for you.

---

2. You may want to start Monit automatically after a reboot using init, and if the Monit daemon itself dies, init will restart it.

Part XIV

Big-Picture Recipes

Manage Plug-in Versions

You've built your application with the help of some Rails plug-ins. Going forward, you want to keep those plug-ins up-to-date, but on your own terms. And the last time you used svn:externals to link in a plug-in, the remote Subversion repository you linked to went for a long vacation, just as you were trying to deploy your app.

You need to take control of the plug-in code and still be able to update to new revisions when you're ready.

- The piston gem:

```
$ gem install piston
```

Piston[1] lets us import plug-ins into our local Subversion repository and sync them up with their master copy whenever we want. Yes, Piston is awesome. So, let's pistonize a plug-in already.

Say our app needs some super-duper pagination and we reach for the will_paginate plug-in. First, we'll import it straightaway into our Subversion repository:

```
$ cd vendor/plugins
$ piston import svn://errtheblog.com/svn/plugins/will_paginate
```

That exports the plug-in from its home on the Web to our vendor/plugins/will_paginate directory. To finish the import, we'll commit the new files:

```
$ svn commit -m 'Importing local copy' vendor/plugins/will_paginate
```

Now we have our own private copy of the plug-in in our local repository. We can even modify the plug-in code, check in our changes, and manage the plug-in just like our application code. So far, so good.

---

1. http://piston.rubyforge.org/

Usually taking a copy of code like this means we couldn't easily sync up with future revisions of the plug-in. But Piston keeps a little secret for us: it remembers where the code came from.

Suppose, for example, that one day the good folks who created the will_paginate plug-in release a tasty new version. It happens to be a slow day around the office and we're itchin' to try something new, so we'll get the latest revision:

```
$ piston update vendor/plugins/will_paginate
Processing 'vendor/plugins/will_paginate'...
  Fetching remote repository's latest revision and UUID
  ...
  Updated to r413 (2 changes)
```

This merges any of our local changes with the latest revision on the remote repository. (If for some reason there's a conflict, Piston doesn't detect it, but Subversion will reject the next commit.) In other words, our changes are preserved when we take new updates. After running the tests, we'll check the updates back into our local repository:

```
$ svn commit -m 'Updated to latest version' vendor/plugins/will_paginate
```

Then let's say we remember that a new version of our application is getting rolled out at the end of the week. It would be a serious bummer if another new version of the will_paginate plug-in was released and the new guy on our project mistakenly merged it into our version right before the deployment. We'll prevent that from happening by locking the version we tested:

```
$ piston lock vendor/plugins/will_paginate
```

Pistonizing plug-ins is so easy that before the deployment we go ahead and pistonize all the plug-ins on which our app depends. That way it won't matter if Bob's Basement Plug-Inns™ repository decides to curl up and die while we're trying to deploy.

Then, later when we want to sync back up with the latest plug-in revision on its remote repository, we'll unlock our copy and update it:

```
$ piston unlock vendor/plugins/will_paginate
$ piston update vendor/plugins/will_paginate
$ svn commit -m 'Updated again' vendor/plugins/will_paginate
```

We can also run piston update in our top-level plugins directory if we want to update all piston-managed plug-ins.

Piston makes light work of plug-in dependency management. Just type a couple of commands, and you're on to other tasks. And once you've pistonized a plug-in, folks on your project who don't have the Piston gem installed can happily check out and update the plug-in via your local Subversion repository.

Discussion

If you're currently using svn:externals to manage your plug-ins, you can use piston convert to convert them to Piston-managed folders.

One important caveat: Piston doesn't preserve change history from the remote repository. Piston just takes the latest revision, or differences between what you currently have and the latest revision, and merges those changes into your checked-out copy. However, you can examine the changes before committing them to your local repository.

You could also use Piston to manage the version of Rails in your vendor/rails directory. However, the update process that Piston uses is known to be slow. This usually isn't a big deal with plug-ins because they tend to be relatively small chunks of code that don't change all that often. However, updating and storing local copies of Rails in each application you write feels a tad heavy-handed. I usually just keep versions of Rails checked out on the production servers and symlink the application's vendor/rails directory to a specific version after deployment using a Capistrano hook.

Fail Early

By Mike Naberezny (http://maintainable.com)

Mike is the founder of Maintainable Software (http://maintainable.com), a software development company in the San Francisco Bay Area. He is also the coauthor of *Rails for PHP Developers* (ND08), published by the Pragmatic Programmers.

You've no doubt had this experience: you run your application against the wrong migration version, and it either blows up in spectacular ways or, worse yet, introduces subtle behavioral changes. It's one thing when this happens on your development box. But when it happens in production, the results can range from embarrassing to downright disastrous. Thankfully, problems like this are easy to catch before they snowball.

Rails 2.0.2 introduced a new feature to address the problem of pending migrations. Since that version, running rake test will abort if there are any pending migrations. Combine this with another new Rails feature: Ruby files in the config/initializers directory are automatically run on start-up for all environments. Mix these features together, and it is trivial to prevent your application from starting with the wrong migration.

Here's a check_pending_migrations.rb initializer file that checks that the migration version in your database is the same version as the biggest numbered migration file in your db/migrate directory. If it's not, you may be in for trouble. So, this little canary in a coal mine fails early with a message to get your attention.

FailEarly/config/initializers/check_pending_migrations.rb

```ruby
unless defined?(Rake) # skip when run from tasks like rake db:migrate

  migrator = ActiveRecord::Migrator.new(:up, 'db/migrate')
  pending_migrations = migrator.pending_migrations

  if pending_migrations.any?
    abort "Database has #{pending_migrations.size} pending migrations"
  end

end
```

Now let's suppose you bumble into the office in the morning and check out all the latest code, but you get interrupted and forget to run rake db:migrate.

No worries. When you fire up the application, you're already on top of the problem:

```
$ script/server   ...
** Starting Rails with development environment...
Database has 2 pending migrations
Exiting
```

This technique works equally well for other application-level invariants. For example, if your app depends on specific MySQL database encodings, adding this initializer file gives you an early-warning system:

FailEarly/config/initializers/check_database_encodings.rb

```ruby
unless defined?(Rake) # skip when run from tasks like rake db:create
  DATABASE_ENCODING = "utf8" unless defined? DATABASE_ENCODING

  variables = %w(character_set_database
                 character_set_client
                 character_set_connection)

  variables.each do |v|
    ActiveRecord::Base.connection.
      execute("SHOW VARIABLES LIKE '#{v}'").each do |r|
      unless r[1] == DATABASE_ENCODING
        abort "Please set your #{r[0]} variable to '#{DATABASE_ENCODING}'."
      end
    end
  end
end
```

Things can and do go wrong. It's better to be safe than sorry, *especially* when dealing with production environments.

Give Users Their Own Subdomain

By Mike Mangino (http://www.elevatedrails.com)
Mike is the founder of Elevated Rails. He lives in Chicago with his wife, Jen, and their two Samoyeds.

Problem

All the cool sites seem to allow you to have your name or organization in your account URL: mike.famousprogrammers.com, acme.jobpostings.com, and so on. It's the vanity plate of the Web. How do you give *your* users their own URL?

Solution

Let's assume we already have an Account model and all of its supporting code in our application. We just want to be able to access an account with its own special subdomain URL.

First, we'll add a subdomain attribute to our Account model. Here's the migration snippet to add the column to our accounts table:

```
add_column :accounts, :subdomain, :string
```

Then, just for convenience, we'll add a for class method to our Account model to fetch the account for a given list of subdomains:

```ruby
class Account < ActiveRecord::Base
  def self.for(subdomains)
    find_by_subdomain(subdomains.first) unless subdomains.blank?
  end
end
```

When users access our site by typing in their unique URL, we need to load up their account. We'll use a before_filter in the AccountsController to do that:

`Subdomains/app/controllers/accounts_controller.rb`

```ruby
class AccountsController < ApplicationController

  before_filter :require_account

  def index
    render :text => "<h1>Welcome to your site!</h1>"
  end
end
```

In the require_account method, we'll use the subdomains of the incoming URL to attempt to find an account. If an account can't be found, we'll just redirect to the main host (more on that later). The require_account method goes in the ApplicationController:

```
class ApplicationController < ActionController::Base
  def require_account
    @account = Account.for(request.subdomains)
    if @account.nil?
      redirect_to welcome_url(:host => MAIN_HOST, :port => request.port)
    end
  end
end
```

To test this, we'll need some example domain names that point to our development server. We'll just add entries to our /etc/hosts file.[1] We'll need to define at least a few different hostnames: one for testing subdomains, one for our main host, and one to test a subdomain with no account.

```
127.0.0.1  mike.example.com www.example.com fake.example.com
```

In a production environment, you will of course want to set up your DNS server. You should create an A record for your www.example.com domain. Then create a CNAME record for *.example.com that points to www.example.com.

Once we've configured our domain names, we'll define the MAIN_HOST constant in our development.rb environment file:

Subdomains/config/environments/development.rb

```
MAIN_HOST = "www.example.com"
```

You'll need to set the appropriate URL in your other environment files, as well. For example, you'll use a different MAIN_HOST in development than in production.

Now when we go to http://mike.example.com:3000, we see the welcome URL because we don't have an account. So, let's create an account:

```
$ ruby script/console
>> Account.create(:subdomain => "mike")
```

If we now go to http://mike.example.com:3000, we should see the welcome message for that custom URL. That is, the before_filter found our account and let us into the AccountsController.

---

1. On Windows, the hosts file is in the C:\Windows\System32\Drivers\etc directory.

So far, so good. Now let's say we don't want to require our users to log in on their own subdomain. Instead, we'll let them log in at www. example.com and then redirect them to their subdomain, such as mike. example.com. To do that, we need to make sure all the cookies will use the example.com domain. That's easy enough—we'll just add this to the production.rb environment file:

Subdomains/config/environments/production.rb
```
ActionController::Base.session_options[:session_domain] = '.example.com'
```

This code forces all cookies to use the example.com domain, and things will work.[2]

Let's do one better: we'll allow our users to set up a CNAME so that their site can be accessed by a custom domain. For example, they can have their registered customdomain.com domain point to their mydomain. example.com subdomain on our application.

To make this work, we first need to add a domain column to our Account model. Then we'll change the Account.for method to first try to find the account by the domain name. Here's the final version of our model:

Subdomains/app/models/account.rb
```
class Account < ActiveRecord::Base

  def self.for(domain, subdomains)
    account = find_by_domain(domain)
    unless subdomains.blank?
      account ||= find_by_subdomain(subdomains.first)
    end
    account
  end

end
```

We also need to change the before_filter to shuttle the domain parameter through to the Account.for method:

```
def require_account
  @account = Account.for(request.host, request.subdomains)
  unless @account
    redirect_to welcome_url(:host => MAIN_HOST, :port => request.port)
  end
end
```

---

2. It won't work, however, if you set :session_domain to anything related to localhost.

Custom domains make for nice branding. Unfortunately, it confuses our sessions because all our cookies are set up for .example.com. At first blush, it may seem we could just change the cookie domain in our require_account before filter, such as this:

```
ActionController::Base.session_options[:session_domain] = '.customdomain.com'
```

Sadly, this won't work. By the time our require_account before filter is executed, the outbound session cookies have already been created. Instead, we'll have to poke around in the CGI library and change the domain of each cookie after the fact.

Subdomains/app/controllers/application.rb

```
def set_cookie_domain(domain)
  cookies = session.instance_eval("@dbprot")
  unless cookies.blank?
    cookies.each do |cookie|
      options = cookie.instance_eval("@cookie_options")
      options["domain"] = domain unless options.blank?
    end
  end
end
```

Yes, it's ugly and brittle but necessary to support custom domains as well as subdomains. When using both subdomains *and* custom domains, you should configure the session options like you would for subdomains and call set_cookie domain only when a custom domain is used.

Now that we have a way to set the cookie domain, we'll change our require_account method again to use it:

Subdomains/app/controllers/application.rb

```
def require_account
  @account = Account.for(request.host, request.subdomains)
  if @account
    if request.host == @account.domain
      set_cookie_domain(@account.domain)
    end
  else
    redirect_to welcome_url(:host => MAIN_HOST, :port => request.port)
  end
end
```

Now our users can have vanity URLs for their accounts. Adding support for subdomains was fairly straightforward. Things got a bit trickier when we went all out with custom domains. In the end, though, it's all possible with very few changes to our application.

Discussion

You'll want to exclude people from registering www as a subdomain, as well as pop, pop3, smtp, mail, ftp, and friends, too. Also, be careful when allowing users to register a subdomain under your main domain name. If a user picks the name of an existing host, they may not be able to use your application. For example, suppose your app domain is example.com and somebody picks dev.example.com as their subdomain. It may well be that dev.example.com is a machine that hosts a completely different application, so requests won't go where you think they will.

If your application uses SSL, you'll need a wildcard SSL certificate for the subdomains. However, custom domains (for example, mike.otherurl.com) and SSL don't work well together.

Customize and Analyze Log Files

By Geoffrey Grosenbach (http://nubyonrails.com)
Geoffrey is the host of the Ruby on Rails Podcast (http://podcast.rubyonrails.org) and producer of PeepCode Screencasts (http://peepcode.com).

Problem

You want to extract information from your log files for improved analysis. Unfortunately, the standard Rails log format does not contain enough data for your needs.

Solution

A vanilla Rails production log file might look like this:

```
Processing PeopleController#index (for 74.6.24.207 at 2007-11-05 09:30:44) [GET]
  Session ID: BAh7BzoMY3NyZ19pZCI1NmIxMTY3NDA5YmN1OGIyYzk3ZD
  Parameters: {"action"=>"index", "controller"=>"people"}
Rendering template within layouts/people
Rendering people/index
Completed in 0.03973 (25 reqs/sec) | Rendering: 0.03875 (97%) |
  DB: 0.00027 (0%) | 200 OK [http://yourdomain.com/people]
```

There's enough information there to do rudimentary analysis, but what if we wanted to do performance analysis or look at what happens at particular times? There's no consistent time-stamping of log entries. We need to do some customizing.

First, we need to use a logger that supports customization. Unfortunately, the logger that comes with Rails 2.0 doesn't. So, we'll change our environment to force Rails to use the more flexible Logger class:

```
config.logger = RAILS_DEFAULT_LOGGER = Logger.new(config.log_path)
```

Now, we could open the Logger class and redefine how log entries are formatted. But the Logger class offers us a way to avoid poking around in its internals. By assigning a custom formatter using the formatter= method, we leave the Logger to its business of logging messages. We'll write our RecipesLogFormatter class shortly—for now, let's just assign it to the logger:

```
config.logger.formatter = RecipesLogFormatter.new
```

And that's pretty much it. We'll probably want to change the default log level, so the whole stanza might look like this in our production.rb environment file:

LogFiles/config/environments/production.rb

```
require 'recipes_log_formatter'
config.logger = RAILS_DEFAULT_LOGGER = Logger.new(config.log_path)
config.logger.formatter = RecipesLogFormatter.new
config.logger.level = Logger::INFO
```

(Having to set RAILS_DEFAULT_LOGGER as well as config.logger is unfortunate but is required nonetheless. Without it, script/server won't use our logger, for example.)

Next, we'll define our RecipesLogFormatter class with a call method:

LogFiles/lib/recipes_log_formatter.rb

```
class RecipesLogFormatter
  def call(severity, time, program_name, message)
    datetime = time.strftime("%b %d %H:%M:%S")
    message        = (String === message ? message : msg.inspect)
    "#{datetime} -- #{message}\n"
  end
end
```

When it comes time to format a log entry, the Logger will invoke the call method. It receives four parameters: the log entry's severity, when it occurred, the name of the program it occurred in, and the message to be logged. Our formatter uses only the time and the message, ignoring the other parameters. The message parameter can be any object, so remember to convert it to a string if it's not already a string (we just used inspect).

Now when we run our application in production, we'll see a time stamp for each log entry in the production.log file:

```
2007-11-05 09:42:46 -- Processing PeopleController#index...
2007-11-05 09:42:46 -- Session ID: BAh7BzoMY3...
2007-11-05 09:42:46 -- Parameters: {"action"=>"index", "controller"=>"people"}
2007-11-05 09:42:46 -- Person Load (0.000286)   SELECT * FROM `people`
2007-11-05 09:42:46 -- Rendering template within layouts/people
2007-11-05 09:42:46 -- Rendering people/index
2007-11-05 09:42:46 -- Completed in 0.04700 (21 reqs/sec) |
  Rendering: 0.04554 (96%) | DB: 0.00029 (0%) | 200 OK
```

Things get more exciting when you consider that we can easily modify the call method to format log entries so that they conform to formats recognized by existing log file analyzers.

Rails 2.0 Has a New Logger

Back in the old days (prior to Rails 2.0), Rails used Ruby's Logger class for the default Rails logger. Nowadays Rails uses a custom BufferedLogger as the default logger. It's tailored to be as fast as possible. Unfortunately, that means it doesn't support custom log entry formats. Consequently, we need to assign the (old) Logger using config.logger= in this recipe.

Say, for example, we want to generate log files in the syslog format.[1] Here's an example syslog-compliant log entry:

```
Nov 5 09:14:05 topfunky rails[1234]: Is this thing on?
```

In addition to the time stamp and message, we now also need the hostname (topfunky is my hostname), the process name (rails), and the process ID (1234).

To format log entries in the syslog format, we'll modify our custom formatter slightly. Here's the revised call method:

`LogFiles/lib/recipes_log_formatter.rb`

```ruby
def call(severity, time, program_name, message)
  datetime = time.strftime("%b %d %H:%M:%S")
  process  = "rails[#{$PID}]"
  hostname = Socket.gethostname.split('.')[0]
  message  = (String === message ?
               message : message.inspect).gsub(/\n/, '').strip
  "#{datetime} #{hostname} #{process}: #{message}\n"
end
```

We ignore the program_name parameter and instead use the process name rails to keep things consistent. Also, because the syslog format is picky about whitespace, we tidy up the message. This call method is a tad more involved, and you might want to experiment with it in script/console, for example:

```
$ ruby script/console production
>> RAILS_DEFAULT_LOGGER.error 'Is this thing on?'
```

---

1. To learn more about syslog, use man syslog.

You'll need to check the production.log file to see whether the output is in the correct format. Then, when you run your app in production, you should see something like this in the production.log file:

```
Nov 05 09:45:16 topfunky rails[1234]: Processing PeopleController#index...
Nov 05 09:45:16 topfunky rails[1234]: Session ID: BAh7BzoMY3...
Nov 05 09:45:16 topfunky rails[1234]: Parameters: {"action"=>"index"...
Nov 05 09:45:16 topfunky rails[1234]: Person Load (0.000277)   SELECT * FROM...
Nov 05 09:45:16 topfunky rails[1234]: Rendering template within layouts/people
Nov 05 09:45:16 topfunky rails[1234]: Rendering people/index
Nov 05 09:45:16 topfunky rails[1234]: Completed in 0.04401 (22 reqs/sec) |
    Rendering: 0.00141 (3%) | DB: 0.00028 (0%) | 200 OK
```

Now that we have log entries in the syslog format, what can we do? Basically, we can now run our production log files through any log file analyzer that expects the syslog format. For example, we could install the ProductionLogAnalyzer gem:

```
$ gem install production_log_analyzer --include-dependencies
```

Then, to identify potential performance bottlenecks in our application, we'd use the pl_analyze command against our production log file to generate a report:

```
$ pl_analyze log/production.log
Request Times Summary:    Count   Avg     Std Dev Min     Max
ALL REQUESTS:             8       0.011   0.014   0.002   0.045

PeopleController#index:   2       0.013   0.010   0.003   0.023
PeopleController#show:     2       0.002   0.000   0.002   0.003
PeopleController#create:  1       0.005   0.000   0.005   0.005
PeopleController#new:     1       0.045   0.000   0.045   0.045
PeopleController#edit:     1       0.004   0.000   0.004   0.004
PeopleController#update:  1       0.005   0.000   0.005   0.005

Slowest Request Times:
  PeopleController#new took 0.045s
  PeopleController#index took 0.023s
  PeopleController#update took 0.005s
  PeopleController#create took 0.005s
  PeopleController#edit took 0.004s
  PeopleController#index took 0.003s
  PeopleController#show took 0.003s
  PeopleController#show took 0.002s

# DB times and Render times follow
```

To get a performance report on a recurring basis, we could run the pl_analyze command in a cron job and use the -e option to send the results to an e-mail address. Or we could generate a performance report on demand using the following Capistrano task:

```
desc "Analyze Rails Log remotely"
task :analyze, :roles => :app do
  run "pl_analyze #{shared_path}/log/#{rails_env}.log" do |ch, st, data|
    print data
  end
end
```

It really doesn't take much to change the log files to suit your needs. Once you have them in a recognizable format, you can use external analysis tools to get the most out of your logs.

Also See

The Rails Analyzer Tools[2] include other handy tools for analyzing Rails log files. For example, the rails_stat command shows a real-time report of application performance by analyzing log files in the syslog format.

---

2. http://rubyforge.org/projects/rails-analyzer

Bibliography

[Fau06]   Cody Fauser. *RJS Templates for Rails (PDF book)*. O'Reilly & Associates, Inc, Sebastopol, CA, 2006.

[Fow06]   Chad Fowler. *Rails Recipes*. The Pragmatic Programmers, LLC, Raleigh, NC, and Dallas, TX, 2006.

[FS03]   Niels Ferguson and Bruce Schneier. *Practical Cryptography*. John Wiley & Sons, New York, 2003.

[GH04]   Otis Gospodnetic and Erik Hatcher. *Lucene in Action*. Manning Publications Co., Greenwich, CT, 2004.

[HL06]   Christian Hellsten and Jarkko Laine. *Beginning Ruby on Rails E-Commerce: From Novice to Professional*. Apress, 2006.

[ND08]   Mike Naberezny and Derek DeVries. *Rails for PHP Developers*. The Pragmatic Programmers, LLC, Raleigh, NC, and Dallas, TX, 2008.

[TH05]   David Thomas and David Heinemeier Hansson. *Agile Web Development with Rails*. The Pragmatic Programmers, LLC, Raleigh, NC, and Dallas, TX, 2005.

[ZT08]   Ezra Zygmuntowicz and Bruce Tate. *Deploying Rails Applications: A Step-by-Step Guide*. The Pragmatic Programmers, LLC, Raleigh, NC, and Dallas, TX, 2008.

Index

It All Starts Here

If you're programming in Ruby, you need the PickAxe Book: the definitive reference to the Ruby Programming language, now in the revised 3rd Edition for Ruby 1.9.

Programming Ruby (The Pickaxe)

The Pickaxe book, named for the tool on the cover, is the definitive reference to this highly-regarded language. • Up-to-date and expanded for Ruby version 1.9 • Complete documentation of all the built-in classes, modules, and methods • Complete descriptions of all standard libraries • Learn more about Ruby's web tools, unit testing, and programming philosophy

Programming Ruby: The Pragmatic Programmer's Guide, 3rd Edition
Dave Thomas with Chad Fowler and Andy Hunt
(900 pages) ISBN: 978-1-9343560-8-1. $49.95
http://pragprog.com/titles/ruby3

Agile Web Development with Rails

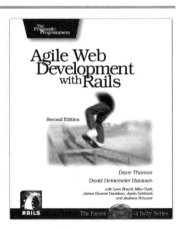

Rails is a full-stack, open-source web framework, with integrated support for unit, functional, and integration testing. It enforces good design principles, consistency of code across your team (and across your organization), and proper release management. This is the newly updated Second Edition, which goes beyond the Jolt-award winning first edition with new material on:

• Migrations • RJS templates • Respond_to
• Integration Tests • Additional ActiveRecord features • Another year's worth of Rails best practices

Agile Web Development with Rails: Second Edition
Dave Thomas and David Heinemeier Hansson with Leon Breedt, Mike Clark, James Duncan Davidson, Justin Gehtland, and Andreas Schwarz
(750 pages) ISBN: 0-9776166-3-0. $39.95
http://pragprog.com/titles/rails2

Web 2.0 is here

Get up-to-date on the well-formed web, and take the pain out of Ajax.

The Accessible Web

The 2000 U.S. Census revealed that 12% of the population is severely disabled. Sometime in the next two decades, one in five Americans will be older than 65. Section 508 of the Americans with Disabilities Act requires your website to provide *equivalent access* to all potential users. But beyond the law, it is both good manners and good business to make your site accessible to everyone. This book shows you how to design sites that excel for all audiences.

The Accessible Web
Jeremy Sydik
(304 pages) ISBN: 1-934356-02-6. $34.95
http://pragprog.com/titles/jsaccess

Prototype and script.aculo.us

Tired of getting swamped in the nitty-gritty of cross-browser, Web 2.0–grade JavaScript? Get back in the game with Prototype and script.aculo.us, two extremely popular JavaScript libraries that make it a walk in the park. Be it Ajax, drag and drop, autocompletion, advanced visual effects, or many other great features, all you need is write one or two lines of script that look so good they could almost pass for Ruby code!

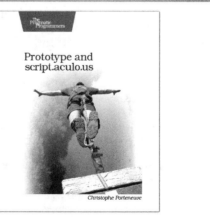

Prototype and script.aculo.us: You never knew JavaScript could do this!
Christophe Porteneuve
(330 pages) ISBN: 1-934356-01-8. $34.95
http://pragprog.com/titles/cppsu

More Rails and Ruby

Deploy your Rails applications the right way, and learn how to integrate Ruby with enterprise technologies.

Deploying Rails Applications

Until now, the information you needed to deploy a Ruby on Rails application in a production environment has been fragmented and contradictory. This book changes all of that by providing a consistent, level-headed book containing advice you can trust. You'll get the inside angle from those that have built, deployed, and maintained some of the largest Rails apps in production, anywhere.

Deploying Rails Applications: A Step-by-Step Guide
Ezra Zygmuntowicz, Bruce Tate, and Clinton Begin
(284 pages) ISBN: 978-0-9787392-0-1. $34.95
http://pragprog.com/titles/fr_deploy

Enterprise Integration with Ruby

See how to use the power of Ruby to integrate all the applications in your environment. Learn how to
• use relational databases directly and via mapping layers such as ActiveRecord • harness the power of directory services • create, validate, and read XML documents for easy information interchange • use both high- and low-level protocols to knit applications together

Enterprise Integration with Ruby
Maik Schmidt
(360 pages) ISBN: 0-9766940-6-9. $32.95
http://pragprog.com/titles/fr_eir

Even More Ruby

Use Ruby for cross-platform GUIs, and see how to use Ruby for day-to-day chores to help you be more productive.

FXRuby

Get started developing GUI applications using FXRuby. With a combination of tutorial exercises and focused, technical information, this book goes beyond the basics to equip you with proven, practical knowledge and techniques for developing real-world FXRuby applications. Learn directly from the lead developer of FXRuby, and you'll be writing powerful and sophisticated GUIs in your favorite programming language.

FXRuby Create Lean and Mean GUIs with Ruby
Lyle Johnson
(240 pages) ISBN: 978-1-9343560-7-4. $36.95
http://pragprog.com/titles/fxruby

Everyday Scripting with Ruby

Don't waste that computer on your desk. Offload your daily drudgery to where it belongs, and free yourself to do what you should be doing: thinking. All you need is a scripting language (free!), this book (cheap!), and the dedication to work through the examples and exercises. Learn the basics of the Ruby scripting language and see how to create scripts in a steady, controlled way using test-driven design.

Everyday Scripting with Ruby: For Teams, Testers, and You
Brian Marick
(320 pages) ISBN: 0-9776166-1-4. $29.95
http://pragprog.com/titles/bmsft

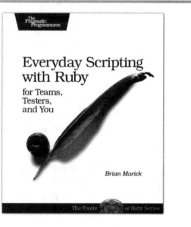

Real World Tools

Learn real-world design and architecture for your project, and a very pragmatic editor for Mac OS X.

Release It!

Whether it's in Java, .NET, or Ruby on Rails, getting your application ready to ship is only half the battle. Did you design your system to survive a sudden rush of visitors from Digg or Slashdot? Or an influx of real-world customers from 100 different countries? Are you ready for a world filled with flaky networks, tangled databases, and impatient users?

If you're a developer and don't want to be on call at 3 a.m. for the rest of your life, this book will help.

Design and Deploy Production-Ready Software
Michael T. Nygard
(368 pages) ISBN: 0-9787392-1-3. $34.95
http://pragprog.com/titles/mnee

TextMate

If you're coding Ruby or Rails on a Mac, then you owe it to yourself to get the TextMate editor. And, once you're using TextMate, you owe it to yourself to pick up this book. It's packed with information that will help you automate all your editing tasks, saving you time to concentrate on the important stuff. Use snippets to insert boilerplate code and refactorings to move stuff around. Learn how to write your own extensions to customize it to the way you work.

TextMate: Power Editing for the Mac
James Edward Gray II
(200 pages) ISBN: 0-9787392-3-X. $29.95
http://pragprog.com/titles/textmate

Getting Groovy

Expand your horizons and see what Groovy has to offer.

Programming Groovy

Programming Groovy will help you learn the necessary fundamentals of programming in Groovy. You'll see how to use Groovy to do advanced programming techniques, including meta programming, builders, unit testing with mock objects, processing XML, working with databases and creating your own domain-specific languages (DSLs).

Programming Groovy Dynamic Productivity for the Java Developer
Venkat Subramaniam
(320 pages) ISBN: 978-1-9343560-9-8. $34.95
http://pragprog.com/titles/vslg

Groovy Recipes

See how to speed up nearly every aspect of the development process using *Groovy Recipes*. Groovy makes mundane file management tasks like copying and renaming files trivial. Reading and writing XML has never been easier with XmlParsers and XmlBuilders. Breathe new life into arrays, maps, and lists with a number of convenience methods. Learn all about Grails, and go beyond HTML into the world of Web Services: REST, JSON, Atom, Podcasting, and much much more.

Groovy Recipes: Greasing the Wheels of Java
Scott Davis
(264 pages) ISBN: 978-0-9787392-9-4. $34.95
http://pragprog.com/titles/sdgrvr

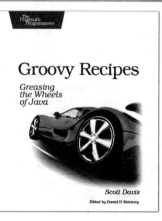

Leading Your Team

See how to be a pragmatic project manager and use agile, iterative project retrospectives on your project.

Manage It!

Manage It! is a risk-based guide to making good decisions about how to plan and guide your projects. Author Johanna Rothman shows you how to beg, borrow, and steal from the best methodologies to fit your particular project. You'll find what works best for *you*.

• Learn all about different project lifecycles • See how to organize a project • Compare sample project dashboards • See how to staff a project • Know when you're done—and what that means.

Your Guide to Modern, Pragmatic Project Management
Johanna Rothman
(360 pages) ISBN: 0-9787392-4-8. $34.95
http://pragprog.com/titles/jrpm

Agile Retrospectives

Mine the experience of your software development team continually throughout the life of the project. Rather than waiting until the end of the project—as with a traditional retrospective, when it's too late to help—agile retrospectives help you adjust to change *today*.

The tools and recipes in this book will help you uncover and solve hidden (and not-so-hidden) problems with your technology, your methodology, and those difficult "people issues" on your team.

Agile Retrospectives: Making Good Teams Great
Esther Derby and Diana Larsen
(170 pages) ISBN: 0-9776166-4-9. $29.95
http://pragprog.com/titles/dlret

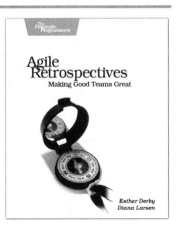

Getting It Done

Start with the habits of an agile developer and use the team practices of successful agile teams, and your project will fly over the finish line.

Practices of an Agile Developer

Agility is all about using feedback to respond to change. Learn how to apply the principles of agility throughout the software development process • establish and maintain an agile working environment • deliver what users really want • use personal agile techniques for better coding and debugging • use effective collaborative techniques for better teamwork • move to an agile approach

Practices of an Agile Developer: Working in the Real World
Venkat Subramaniam and Andy Hunt
(189 pages) ISBN: 0-9745140-8-X. $29.95
http://pragprog.com/titles/pad

Ship It!

Page after page of solid advice, all tried and tested in the real world. This book offers a collection of tips that show you what tools a successful team has to use, and how to use them well. You'll get quick, easy-to-follow advice on modern techniques and when they should be applied. **You need this book if:** • You're frustrated at lack of progress on your project. • You want to make yourself and your team more valuable. • You've looked at methodologies such as Extreme Programming (XP) and felt they were too, well, extreme. • You've looked at the Rational Unified Process (RUP) or CMM/I methods and cringed at the learning curve and costs. • **You need to get software out the door without excuses**

Ship It! A Practical Guide to Successful Software Projects
Jared Richardson and Will Gwaltney
(200 pages) ISBN: 0-9745140-4-7. $29.95
http://pragprog.com/titles/prj

The Pragmatic Bookshelf

The Pragmatic Bookshelf features books written by developers for developers. The titles continue the well-known Pragmatic Programmer style and continue to garner awards and rave reviews. As development gets more and more difficult, the Pragmatic Programmers will be there with more titles and products to help you stay on top of your game.

Visit Us Online

Advanced Rails Recipes
http://pragprog.com/titles/fr_arr
Source code from this book, errata, and other resources. Come give us feedback, too!

Register for Updates
http://pragprog.com/updates
Be notified when updates and new books become available.

Join the Community
http://pragprog.com/community
Read our weblogs, join our online discussions, participate in our mailing list, interact with our wiki, and benefit from the experience of other Pragmatic Programmers.

New and Noteworthy
http://pragprog.com/news
Check out the latest pragmatic developments in the news.

Save on the PDF

Save on the PDF version of this book. Owning the paper version of this book entitles you to purchase the PDF version at a terrific discount. The PDF is great for carrying around on your laptop. It's hyperlinked, has color, and is fully searchable.

Buy it now at pragprog.com/coupon.

Contact Us

Phone Orders:	1-800-699-PROG (+1 919 847 3884)
Online Orders:	www.pragprog.com/catalog
Customer Service:	orders@pragprog.com
Non-English Versions:	translations@pragprog.com
Pragmatic Teaching:	academic@pragprog.com
Author Proposals:	proposals@pragprog.com